PUBLICATIONS
OF THE
ARMY RECORDS SOCIETY
VOL. 26

MAJOR-GENERAL OLIVER NUGENT AND THE ULSTER DIVISION 1915–1918

The Army Records Society was founded in 1984 in order to publish original records describing the development, organisation, administration and activities of the British Army from early times.

Any person wishing to become a member of the Society is requested to apply to the Hon. Secretary, c/o the National Army Museum, Royal Hospital Road, London, SW3 4HT. The annual subscription entitles the member to receive a copy of each volume issued by the Society in that year, and to purchase back volumes at reduced prices. Current subscription details, whether for individuals living within the British Isles, for individuals living overseas, or for institutions, will be furnished on request.

The Council of the Army Records Society wish it to be clearly understood that they are not answerable for opinions or observations that may appear in the Society's publications. For these the responsibility rests entirely with the Editors of the several works.

The Society's website can be found at
www.armyrecordssociety.org.uk

Portrait of Major General Sir Oliver Nugent, by William Conor.
(Reproduced by kind permission of Belfast City Council)

MAJOR-GENERAL OLIVER NUGENT AND THE ULSTER DIVISION 1915–1918

Edited by
NICHOLAS PERRY

Published by
SUTTON PUBLISHING LIMITED
for the
ARMY RECORDS SOCIETY
2007

First published in the United Kingdom in 2007 by
Sutton Publishing, an imprint of NPI Media Group Limited
Cirencester Road · Chalford · Stroud · Gloucestershire · GL6 8PE

British Library Cataloguing in Publication Data
A catalogue record for this book is available from the British Library.

ISBN 978-0-7509-4880-7

Typeset in Ehrhardt.
Typesetting and origination by
NPI Media Group Limited.
Printed and bound in England.

Contents

Preface	xiii
Abbreviations	xvii
Introduction	1
Prelude: Hooge, July to August 1915	9
1 The Somme, September 1915 to July 1916	17
2 Messines and Third Ypres, August 1916 to August 1917	96
3 Cambrai and St Quentin, September 1917 to June 1918	170
Postscript: India and Ireland, July 1918 to June 1926	235
Appendix 1: Biographical Notes	242
Appendix 2: 36th Division Order of Battle	247
Notes	249
Bibliography	274
Index	279

Preface

Major-General (later Sir) Oliver Nugent commanded the 36th (Ulster) Division from September 1915 to May 1918, a period covering 31 of the 37 months it spent on operational service during the First World War. He led it in five major battles – the Somme in 1916, Messines, Third Ypres and Cambrai in 1917, and the Kaiserschlacht in 1918 – in which it earned its reputation as one of the best New Army divisions. The assault on the Schwaben Redoubt on 1 July 1916 was not only a fine, if ultimately unsuccessful, feat of arms: it was also one of the defining experiences of the Ulster Protestant/Unionist tradition in the twentieth century.

There is a certain irony, therefore, in the fact that the attack was planned and directed by a man who sometimes felt an outsider in a formation that was tightly bonded by political and religious belief, and who was not always in sympathy with the feelings which inspired many of his fervently loyalist soldiers. Nugent's relations during the war with politicians at home, superiors at the front and, on occasion, his own subordinates were to be strained by the tension that existed between the professional military standards he sought to apply and the political connections of the formation he commanded. The military problems he had to address (quite apart from fighting the Germans) – such as securing suitable officers, imposing discipline on his troops, keeping the Division up to strength and cooperating with other Irish units – touched on matters like national and regional identity and commitment to the war effort which were politically highly sensitive and which reflected the complexities of Ireland's involvement in the Great War.

Nugent's Western Front correspondence, which illustrates these themes, forms part of a larger family archive, known as the Farren Connell collection after the Nugent family's Co. Cavan estate, stretching back to the fifteenth century and now in the Public Record Office of Northern Ireland (PRONI) in Belfast. In total the archive contains some 80 volumes and 10,000 documents and represents a remarkably complete record of an Irish gentry family over a period of 500 years. Nugent's own papers were acquired by PRONI in 1993 and are described fully in

PRONI's 1992–3 Annual Report. They cover his military career from 1882 onwards but of most interest are those relating to his service in the First World War, when he commanded successively the Hull defences (1914–15), the 41st Infantry Brigade (1915), the Ulster Division (1915–18) and the Meerut Division (1918–20). Their core, and the section of the archive on which this book is primarily based, is a series of over 600 letters written to his wife Kitty from the Western Front between April 1915 and April 1918. Produced at an average of four a week in flowing longhand with scarcely a correction or deletion, they represent in effect a diary as Nugent recorded his activities, thoughts and, on occasion, frustrations. In the same letter he might cover the Division's operations, the progress of the war more generally, Irish politics, the activities of his family and the running of the estate. Limitations of space mean that his domestic interests, which for him represented an escape from his immediate preoccupations at the front, and his comments on wider political and military developments are included only occasionally in the documents reproduced here: but it is important to remember that his range of interests went much further than simply command of his division. The Farren Connell collection also includes a relatively small but important section of official and semi-official correspondence, several items from which are included here, between Nugent, Sir Edward Carson, the War Office and others, mainly relating to the question of Irish recruitment. There are also a large number of official military documents – plans, intelligence reports, official narratives, maps – which are available in the Divisional war diaries at The National Archives at Kew and which have not therefore been reproduced here.

The Farren Connell correspondence in this volume has been supplemented, particularly for the period 1915–16, by a number of documents from related collections which cast additional light on aspects of Nugent's command. These include, from PRONI, letters by Sir Edward Carson and Captain W. B. (later Sir Wilfrid) Spender; and from the Royal Archives, the Imperial War Museum and the British Library, examples of Nugent's correspondence with George V and Generals Maxse and Hutton.

Acknowledgements

In editing these papers for publication I owe particular gratitude to General Nugent's family: to his daughter, Alison Hirschberg, who though in her 92nd year when we first met recalled her father very vividly for me and explained many references in the correspondence which would otherwise have been obscure; and to his grandson Myles Stoney and his wife Susan, who made me very welcome at Farren Connell and were a mine of information also, and who have encouraged this project from the outset.

I have also incurred a debt to a great many others. The Deputy Keeper of the Records of Northern Ireland, Dr Gerry Slater, his predecessor Dr Anthony Malcomson and their colleagues, notably Ian Montgomery, have been outstandingly helpful, friendly and professional throughout; so too have the staff of the Imperial War Museum reading room and their counterparts in the National Archives, National Army Museum and National Library of Ireland.

For permission to examine and reproduce papers and documents in their possession and/or copyright, and for other assistance, I am grateful, in addition to PRONI and General Nugent's family, to the trustees of the Imperial War Museum, the National Army Museum, the National Library of Ireland, the British Library Board, the Royal Ulster Rifles Museum and the Liddell Hart Centre for Military Archives, King's College London; the editor of *The Belfast Newsletter*; Mrs Rose Hunt; Mr Tony Maxse; Lt Col Ian McCausland (Royal Green Jackets); Mr D. McElwaine; Mr Alisdair Murray; Mrs Rowena Vining and Mr Tony Whitfeld. Material from the Royal Archives appears by permission of Her Majesty Queen Elizabeth II. Crown copyright material in the National Archives is reproduced by permission of the Controller of Her Majesty's Stationery Office.

Without the support of the Army Records Society, and in particular Professor Ian Beckett and Drs William Philpott and Jim Beach, this book would not have seen the light of day.

Amongst the Irish scholars and friends from whom I have learned much about the broader context of Ireland's involvement in the Great War are Professors Keith Jeffery, Paul Bew and David Fitzpatrick; Jane Leonard; Martin Staunton; Margaret Baguley; and Drs Tim Bowman and Terence Denman (the last an honorary Irishman for these purposes). I have also benefited greatly from the erudition of my fellow members of the Military History Society of Ireland, a model of what such a society should be.

I also owe an enormous amount to my colleagues in the British Commission for Military History, whose gatherings are always an education, in more ways than one, and from whom I have learned a great deal about military history in general and the First World War in particular: in addition to those already mentioned they include, especially, Chris McCarthy, Kate Mazur, Brian Bond, Gordon Corrigan, Tony Cowan, Christopher Duffy, Bryn Hammond, Paul Harris, Mike Hibberd, Richard Holmes, Simon Jones, John Lee, Michael Orr, Pete Robinson, Gary Sheffield, Peter Simkins, Andy Simpson, Keith Simpson and Hew Strachan.

I am especially grateful to Keith Jeffery, Chris McCarthy, Tim Bowman and Annie Jackson for reading the entire manuscript in draft, and suggesting many useful improvements.

It goes without saying that none of those mentioned bears any responsibility for any errors in this volume.

Finally, like all those who have worked on the Ulster Division, I owe a considerable debt to one of its former officers and its first historian, Cyril Falls. In rereading his history of the Division when researching this volume I have been struck yet again not only by its elegant but economic style, but also by its accuracy, balance and understatement, qualities which are particularly impressive given the time (1922) it was published. The notes in this volume are evidence of the extent to which I have relied on him.

Editorial Method

In selecting the documents included here I have concentrated on items that illustrate Nugent's operational concerns and political pre-occupations, and the interplay between them. In editing the papers I have omitted salutations; ellipses have been employed where text has been excluded from within a document but not where opening or closing material has been removed. The source of each document is given at the end of each extract. Very little editing of grammar or spelling has been required (Nugent shared the same English master at Harrow as Winston Churchill); where such editing has taken place it is indicated by the use of square brackets.

The locations from where Nugent's letters were sent (he gave his address, quite properly, only as 'Headquarters 36th Division') have been derived from the Divisional history and war diaries, and are shown in square brackets.

Abbreviations

Military

AA&QMG	Assistant Adjutant and Quartermaster General
ADC	Aide-de-Camp
AG	Adjutant-General
BGGS	Brigadier-General General Staff
CIGS	Chief of the Imperial General Staff
C-in-C	Commander-in-Chief
CO	Commanding Officer
CRA	Commander Royal Artillery
DCIGS	Deputy Chief of the Imperial General Staff
DSO	Distinguished Service Order
GSO	General Staff Officer
KOYLI	King's Own Yorkshire Light Infantry
KRRC	King's Royal Rifle Corps
KSLI	King's Shropshire Light Infantry
MC	Military Cross
RIC	Royal Irish Constabulary
UUC	Ulster Unionist Council
UVF	Ulster Volunteer Force

Archives and Publications

BL	British Library
FC	Farren Connell papers
IWM	Imperial War Museum
LHCMA	Liddell Hart Centre for Military Archives
NA	National Archives
NAM	National Army Museum
NLI	National Library of Ireland
OH	*Official History*
PRONI	Public Record Office of Northern Ireland
RA	Royal Archives
SP	Spender papers

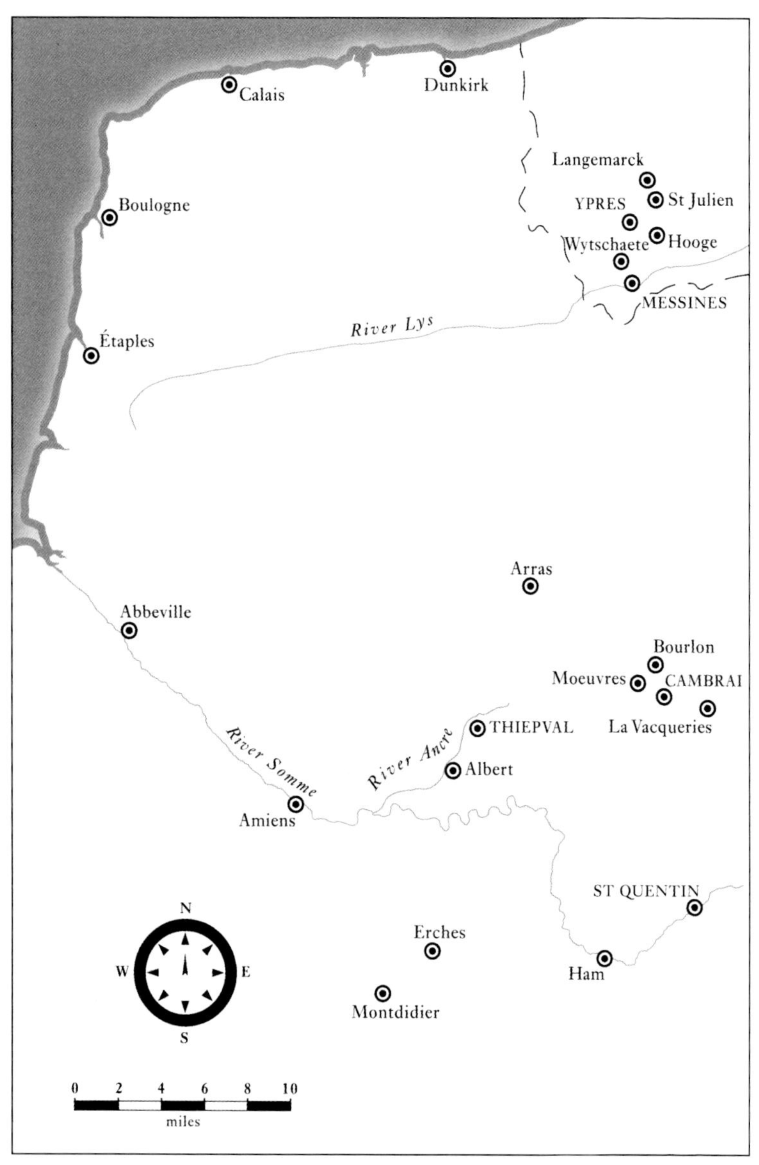

Oliver Nugent and the Ulster Division on the Western Front, 1915–18.

Introduction

Oliver Stewart Wood Nugent was born on 9 November 1860 in Aldershot where his father was serving as a staff officer. The Nugents were an important Irish county family whose Hiberno-Norman origins went back to the late twelfth century, when Hugh de Nugent arrived in Ireland and carved out significant landholdings in the Irish midlands. Oliver's branch of the family were descended from the medieval Lords Delvin, subsequently Earls of Westmeath, and had lived on the Farren Connell estate in south Cavan since the seventeenth century. They had managed, in the wake of the Williamite Wars and in contrast to many of their Nugent relations, to retain their lands by converting to Protestantism, and by the second half of the eighteenth century were fully integrated into the Protestant Irish ascendancy. But though a Unionist and a committed member of the Anglican Church of Ireland, Oliver Nugent always had a strong sense of his Irish roots, which in turn coloured his political views.

His father, St George (1825–84), was a regular soldier who as an ensign in the 29th Regiment had fought in the First Sikh War and been seriously wounded at Sobraon; he subsequently held staff appointments in Aldershot, Nova Scotia, Ireland and Malta before retiring as a Major-General in 1880. He was a rather severe figure and he and his son were not especially close. He had married in 1856 Emily Litton from Co. Tyrone, whose father Edward had been one of Ireland's senior judges and Conservative MP for Coleraine. Oliver was the only one of their four sons to survive (two brothers died in infancy, and another in his twenties). He was educated at Harrow and in 1882 followed his father into the Army.

That he did so was in one sense not surprising. The military tradition was a central strand of the Irish gentry's sense of identity (the term here being taken to encompass the peerage also): indeed, they have been described as the closest thing the British Army has had to the Prussian Junker class.[1] The number of senior British commanders Ireland produced in the second half of the nineteenth and first half of the twentieth centuries is certainly evidence of their influence. Fifteen of the

40 operational Field Marshals created between 1894 and 1956 were Irish or of Irish origin (including nine of the 16 CIGSs appointed between 1912 and 1956), as were 10 of 46 non-royal Admirals of the Fleet appointed in the same period.[2] The records of prominent Irish 'military' families – such as the Brookes in Fermanagh, the Goughs in Waterford and the Pakenhams in Westmeath – displayed levels of commitment to service in arms comparable to the von Kleists and von Richthofens of Prussia. Thirty-nine of the 55 male Vandeleurs of Kilrush, Co. Clare, to survive to adulthood between 1750 and 1950 served in the Army, 19 reaching the rank of Lieutenant-Colonel or higher and seven dying on active service; 53 Brookes of Colebrooke and their cadet branches served in the two World Wars, 12 being killed; three generations of the Adair family of Loughanmore, Co. Antrim, produced between 1780 and 1920 four Royal Marine generals, two admirals, an Army brigadier and a Marine captain killed on HMS *Victory* at Trafalgar.[3]

The Irish gentry's readiness to pursue military careers is usually attributed to a combination of historical and economic factors. As a landed elite, it is argued, many of whose forebears had acquired their estates largely by force and who, at least outside the north-east, generally differed from the rest of the population in terms of politics and religion, they had inherited a tradition of bearing arms both as protection against rebellion at home and in the service of the state, on whose support their position in Ireland ultimately depended. This inclination was reinforced by the fact that many Irish estates were too impoverished, and alternative careers for gentlemen in Ireland too limited, to provide suitable employment for many younger sons other than the armed forces.[4]

However, quantifying more systematically the extent of the gentry's involvement and how this compared with their counterparts elsewhere in the United Kingdom is more difficult. An analysis by Edward Spiers of the regional background of senior Army officers suggests that the proportion of Irish officers fluctuated in the late nineteenth and early twentieth centuries: the survey found that 11 of 95 colonels in 1854 were Irish (12 per cent), 21 of 107 in 1899 (20 per cent), and six of 87 in 1914 (7 per cent); and, amongst the generals, 19 out of 121 in 1854 (16 per cent), 15 of 91 in 1899 (16 per cent), and 12 of 91 in 1914 (13 per cent). (The equivalent percentages for Scotland were 12 per cent, 12 per cent and 8 per cent for colonels, and 20 per cent, 12 per cent and 17 per cent for generals.)[5] Although the sample sizes are relatively small, the overall trend appears to indicate a gradual decline, at least numerically, in Irish representation in the Army's officer corps.

There are, though, few signs that service in the armed forces was losing its appeal for the Irish gentry during this period. It is true that as the nineteenth century drew on their political and economic position eroded steadily (though their social prominence in their localities survived longer). At the level of national politics they felt increasingly threatened by the growth of the Home Rule movement and the widening electoral franchise; local government reforms reduced their influence in the counties; and land reform over half a century from 1870 onwards culminating in the compulsory purchase and redistribution to their tenants of the bulk of their estates dismantled the basis of their historic economic dominance. Most of these measures were driven through by successive British governments in recognition of changing political realities in Ireland. Yet far from reducing the willingness of the gentry to serve the state, in many cases their enthusiasm for military service seems actually to have increased, both as a means of escape from their declining pre-eminence at home and as a demonstration of loyalty to ideals, in monarchy and empire, that transcended the 'sordidness' of domestic politics. The tendency was reinforced by the increasing numbers of Irish landed families who, from the middle of the nineteenth century, sent their sons to public schools in Britain, with their strong imperial and militarist ethos.[6]

An analysis of the network of landowning families, of which the Nugents formed part, in Cavan and three adjoining counties (Fermanagh, Longford and Monaghan) illustrates the continuing strength of the military connection over this period. These counties contained 73 landed families which, before compulsory purchase, had owned estates of 1,000 acres or more and which still had significant landholdings at the outbreak of the Great War. Forty per cent of the male heads of these families in August 1914 had seen regular service; another 19 per cent who had not had held commissions in the militia. (This compares with the 43 per cent of their fathers who had been either regular or militia officers.) Similarly, around 40 per cent of their brothers were or had been regular soldiers: these, unsurprisingly, were more likely to have made the Army their career.[7]

It was in this sense that it was slightly unusual that Oliver chose a military career. His father, as a younger son, had had limited options since Farren Connell had been inherited by his older brother, but when Oliver was 21 he was bequeathed (though did not immediately inherit) the estate. At around 1,800 acres, and with a rateable value in the 1870s of just under £1,400, Farren Connell was of moderate size, but many

Irish landowners successfully maintained themselves on smaller and poorer estates. Although Oliver had military antecedents on both sides, neither the Nugents nor the Littons had especially strong traditions of military service. But, while passionately devoted to Farren Connell, he found that soldiering agreed with him and on succeeding some years later to the estate he stayed in the Army, leaving its day-to-day running to a succession of stewards.

He followed a route into the Army used by many contemporaries (including John French, Henry Wilson and Bryan Mahon), first securing a commission in the militia and then transferring into the regular Army. In July 1882 he joined the Royal Munster Fusiliers but in April 1883 transferred to the 60th Rifles (the King's Royal Rifle Corps). It was no accident that he did so. At this period members of well-off Irish families did not generally join Irish line infantry regiments or, for that matter, the Indian Army, instead going for more socially exclusive regiments such as the Household Brigade, the cavalry, and rifle and Highland regiments. The Nugents, though not rich, could just afford to send their son to a prestigious regiment, but concerns over money were never far from his thoughts throughout his military service.

He joined the 1st KRRC in Dublin where, as a brother officer put it, 'during his first few years' service in Ireland – although he soon made a reputation as an all-round sportsman and good man to hounds – no one recognised in the rather feckless Irishman the keen and able soldier and forceful character into which he was soon to develop'.[8] In 1886 he joined the 4th Battalion in India, a formative experience, and when, in 1891, as a captain, he returned to the 1st Battalion, now on the North-West Frontier, to those who had known him before he 'was a surprise and a revelation. He had left them an undeveloped boy, with no more serious interest in life than sport. He returned a keen and level-headed soldier and a strong character, and was soon recognized as a coming leader of men'.[9]

In 1891 he took part in the Hazara and Miranzai expeditions (in the second serving as orderly to the British commander, Sir William Lockhart), and in 1892 fought against the Isazai: while relatively minor affairs they provided operational experience. By the time of the Chitral campaign in 1895 'he was undoubtedly the outstanding personality of the Battalion'.[10] The 1st KRRC formed part of the 15,000-strong column under Sir Robert Low despatched to relieve the besieged fort at Chitral, and on 3 April 1895 took part in the assault on the Malakand Pass, held by some 12,000 tribesmen. British technological superiority carried the day – one account described, apparently without irony, how 'The Maxims playing from right and left of the gorge created an ideal picture of a civilised attack on a savage enemy'[11] – but the engagement was not without danger for the attackers. A newspaper reported how Nugent, attempting with a party of riflemen to silence an enemy position, occupied a sangar only to find 'that one of his men was lying wounded outside and exposed to the enemy's fire, when he at once sprang out together with [a corporal] and brought the wounded man to safety'.[12] The campaign was concluded successfully a short time later; Nugent was awarded the DSO for his services.

In 1897–8 he attended the Staff College at Camberley, obtaining his place through nomination by the CinC India, now Lockhart.[13] Amongst his fellow students were some of the most important British military leaders of the Great War: future field marshals and generals in his own year included William Robertson, Archibald Murray, George Barrow and Colin Mackenzie; in the year ahead Douglas Haig, Edmund Allenby, George Macdonagh, Richard Haking, Thomas Capper and William Furse (as well as James Edmonds and Reginald Dyer, who for different reasons became famous as brigadiers); and in the year behind Aylmer Hunter-Weston, John Fowler, Arthur Lynden-Bell and Walter Braithwaite.[14] There he established contrasting relationships with two fellow students which, typically of the personalised internal politics of the late Victorian/Edwardian Army,[15] had an important effect on his future career: his friendship with Archie Murray, who was DCIGS at the time of his appointment to command the Ulster Division, and the mutual antipathy that developed, for reasons which are obscure, with his future commander-in-chief Douglas Haig.

In 1899 Nugent married Catherine (Kitty), daughter of Evan Lees, a wealthy Cheshire cotton magnate turned Dorset landowner. She was intelligent, attractive and vivacious, and Nugent was absolutely devoted both to her and, in due course, to their son and two daughters.[16] With his family, indeed, he displayed a sentimental and affectionate side of his nature which would have astonished his military colleagues had they known of it. A few months after the wedding he embarked with the 1st KRRC for South Africa.

There he took part in the first major engagement of the Boer War. His battalion formed part of a force occupying Dundee in northern Natal when, as dawn broke on 20 October 1899, they discovered that Boer commandos had siezed several hills overlooking the town. Penn Symons, the British commander, launched an attack to dislodge the Boers from one of the most prominent, Talana Hill. The Rifles and the 2nd Dublin Fusiliers led the advance up the steep slope, with the 1st Irish Fusiliers in support. Initially the attack went well, despite heavy Boer fire, but eventually the British were pinned down. Nugent led his men in a further charge, and was almost immediately hit three times, in the knee, hip and back. He crawled to the crest, as did a number of his soldiers, at which point the supporting British artillery shelled them by mistake, causing numerous casualties. Nugent wrote later: 'I felt rather beat then. It seemed so hard, after escaping the Boers, to be killed by our own people.'[17] Eventually the error was realised, but not before Nugent's CO had been killed while signalling to the guns to cease fire. As the British reached the top the Boers escaped down the other side. British losses were over 250, with officer casualties being particularly high (including Symons, fatally wounded). The British force, which included Nugent's friend Archie Murray, withdrew to Ladysmith but Nugent, too badly injured to be moved, was left behind.[18] He spent several months as a prisoner before being invalided home following Lord Roberts's capture of Pretoria in June 1900.

From 1901 to 1906 he held staff and regimental appointments in Ireland, England and Bermuda, recovering slowly from his wounds. At one stage he feared he might have to sell Farren Connell following a series of economically difficult years, but Kitty's private income and the compulsory purchase of over half the estate under the 1903 Wyndham Act prevented this. From 1906 to 1910 he commanded the 4th KRRC in the UK and India and from 1911 to 1914, as a colonel, the territorial Hampshire Infantry Brigade. Then, in 1914, he went on half-pay and returned to Ireland and the deepening Home Rule crisis.

There he threw in his lot with the Ulster Unionists and was soon involved in raising and training the Cavan UVF (CVF), supervising their manoeuvres on the estate of his neighbour and friend, Lord Farnham. Although opposed to Home Rule his primary motive appears to have been a desire to provide leadership to an isolated Protestant community at the periphery of the main Ulster resistance movement. In contrast to the militancy of some UVF units elsewhere, the posture of the CVF under Nugent was defensive. His instructions for it stated:

> It must not be forgotten that the CVF is formed for defence and not for aggression and that that is the principal reason why its organization has a civil and not a military basis. The CVF is formed for mutual support and for defence against unprovoked attack. It is

> not intended that it should be used against any of the Armed Forces of the Crown, but on the contrary, to assist them, should occasion arise, in the maintenance of peace and security in the County.[19]

As a serving officer, albeit currently unemployed, he was a relatively unusual figure in the UVF, but sympathy for Ulster's resistance was widely shared within the Army's officer corps. One estimate suggests that over 60 per cent of the UVF's senior leadership comprised former Army officers, not all of them Irish, while the stance taken by Gough's 3rd Cavalry Brigade at the Curragh received widespread support in garrisons across Ireland and beyond.[20] Nevertheless, Nugent was not in retrospect comfortable about his UVF involvement, writing later that he had 'disagreed all along on the policy which created the UVF' and that 'the physical force movement was a mistake' [32, 62]. His unease over this episode deepened his instinctive distrust of all politicians, Unionist as well as Nationalist, and contributed to the difficult relationship he was to have with them during the Great War.

The immediate crisis in Ireland was averted by the outbreak of hostilities in August 1914. The extraordinary flowering of Irish military talent in the Second World War – Alanbrooke, Alexander, Auchinleck, Dill, Gort, Montgomery, to name only the field marshals – has tended to obscure the fact that Ireland produced some of the most important British leaders of the Great War also: a Secretary of State for War (Lord Kitchener, born in Kerry albeit of English parents); a First Lord of the Admiralty (Sir Edward Carson); a CIGS (Sir Henry Wilson); military commanders-in-chief in France, Salonika and Mesopotamia (respectively French, Mahon and Maude); naval commanders-in-chief of the Grand Fleet and in the eastern Mediterranean (Beatty and de Robeck); and an Army commander in France (Gough). There were also a considerable number of corps, divisional and other commanders at various levels, as well as officers serving on the staff, including Kiggell and Harington. Nugent went to war, therefore, with brother officers whom he had known, not just from his previous military service but in many cases from home also. The Irish gentry responded to the war effort with an enthusiasm unmatched by any other social group in Ireland. In the landed families of Cavan and the adjoining counties already referred to, 59 of 112 males (53 per cent) aged 50 or under in 1914 saw military service, about four times the Irish national average – the figure for those aged under 30 was closer to two-thirds; and of these one in four was killed, more than double the rate for Irish servicemen as a whole, reflecting their exposed position by and large as officers.[21] For Nugent's class the war was a devastating experience, one subsequently obscured by the trauma of the post-war Troubles.

His dalliance with the UVF notwithstanding he was quickly given the task of organising the Hull defences against invasion, but officers of his experience were too valuable to be left in such posts and on 6 May 1915 he took command of an infantry brigade (the 41st) in a New Army formation, the 14th (Light) Division. Twelve days later he was in Flanders.

Prelude
Hooge, July to August 1915

Introduction

Most of Nugent's four months with the 14th Division were spent in the Ypres Salient, an area he came to hate.

After a short spell in the line with the 28th Division to gain experience, 41 Brigade in mid-June took over a sector of the front on the Menin Road, east of Ypres. Here occurred, on 30 July 1915, one of the most traumatic events Nugent experienced during the war. His brigade, comprising the 7th and 8th KRRC and 7th and 8th Rifle Brigade, had just taken over a newly captured sector at Hooge (the Crater) when the Germans launched a dawn attack using flamethrowers, the first time these weapons had been used against the British, supported by a hurricane bombardment. The two battalions in the forward trenches (7th KRRC and 8th Rifle Brigade) were forced to retreat with heavy loss and Nugent spent a frantic few hours in the front line stabilising the defence. The Corps commander, Sir John Keir, then insisted on an immediate counter-attack to regain the lost trenches, and overruled Nugent's urgent protests that insufficient artillery was available to support it. The assault that afternoon was a disastrous failure, the British (mainly the other two battalions of 41 Brigade) being mown down as they emerged from Zouave and Sanctuary Woods, until Nugent halted the attack on his own initiative. In all his brigade lost 55 officers and 1,181 other ranks on 30/31 July, without doing any appreciable harm to the Germans. The position was retaken a week later by the 6th Division, in a properly prepared attack with adequate artillery support, at the cost of only 100 casualties, but could not be held in the face of intense shelling.[1]

Nugent was extremely bitter about the 30 July attack, blaming Keir squarely for the massacre [1, 2]. He was also, however, anxious that he would be made the scapegoat for the defeat and took some comfort in Keir's invitation to dinner two nights later, concluding that 'I think

Sir J Keir meant it to show that he realised I could not be blamed for the attack having been a failure'.[2]

Nugent's concern was shared by the Colonel Commandant of the KRRC, Lieutenant-General Sir Edward Hutton, who forwarded Nugent's account of the battle [3] to Lord Stamfordham, the King's private secretary, suggesting that he show it to the King. In his covering letter Hutton described Nugent as 'one of the best comdg officers that the Regiment has had for many years and a strong forceful leader', and added

> There are sure to be unkind things said of the Brigadier General and his command upon the occasion of a reverse such as this sad business, but in such cases I always think there are two sides to a question. In this I am convinced that Nugent and his Riflemen are not to blame.[3]

Others clearly agreed, since Nugent shortly received welcome news of promotion. Keir was eventually dismissed in the summer of 1916.

1
Nugent to his wife

[Holograph] [Ypres]
1 August 1915

I have written the story of the 41st Brigade.[1] The bitter grief it is to me to write it. I feel one can have no confidence in leaders who send men callously or ignorantly to certain death against the opinion of the man who might know, being on the spot. If they had accepted my opinion before instead of after, more than 1500 good men would have been alive today.

FC, D/3835/E/2/4

2
Nugent to his wife

[Holograph] [Ypres]
5 August 1915

Dearest, I am so glad you don't seem to have realised that it would be my brigade which was fighting at Hooge. I daresay you were quite surprised to get my telegram 'untouched' if you did get it. I sent it from a Belgian PO in Poperinghe . . .

I am very low-spirited and sad. I can't get over that terrible day and hour after hour I think of all those gallant officers and men sent to their deaths by a man who had never seen the ground and who would not listen to me who had. I am also coming to the conclusion after questioning various people and putting their stories together that the battalion which met the brunt of the attack and the liquid fire lost their heads and didn't make as strong a resistance as they could have done. New troops and inexperienced officers, though the officers were splendid all through.

FC, D/3835/E/2/4

3
Nugent to Lt Gen Sir Edward Hutton

[Typescript] [Ypres]
12 August 1915

I was so glad to hear from you and thank you so much for your generous sympathy and good wishes to my poor brigade.[2]

I cannot forget and I shall never forget or forgive the order that sent my brigade into the inferno of a counter attack against an impossible position without Artillery preparation, in broad daylight and after two days of strenuous work without food or water. The Brigade did all it could, no troops could have done better, but it was an impossible task and I went up and stopped any further attacks when I saw that the lines of men were simply being mown down in swathes as they came out of the woods.

We had been holding the trenches in the Salient for over 6 weeks with the 14th Division, losing heavily every day from shell fire, when the 5th Corps blew up a mine in the German trenches at Hooge and occupied about 100 yards of German trenches on either side of the Crater. They then cleared out and my brigade was ordered to take over this sector in the very apex of the salient.

From the instant I saw the position created by occupying the strip of German 1st line trench, I knew and told Couper (commanding 14th Division) we should have trouble. We were hemmed in by German trenches all round us and we held a point overlooking their line from behind. It was a pivot but not an end in itself and we were too much of a thorn in the side of the Germans to allow them to consent to our remaining there.

The waste began from the day we took it over which was two days after the mine had been exploded. From then onwards the Germans began to systematically destroy the trenches by minenwerfer and shellfire.

Day by day and night by night, they shelled the fire trenches, the support trenches, and the communication trenches. Gradually they blew them down faster than we could repair them; whole sections of men at a time were blown to pieces and there was no place to withdraw the men to. We were shelled from the flank, from the front, and from the rear. At the end of the 1st week there were hardly any trenches left and the two Battalions in front were getting shaky. On the night of the 29th/30th July, I relieved them by the other two battalions.

The same night at 3.20 am the Germans opened a burning gas attack along the front of the trenches we had captured from them 10 days before, at the same time a terrific shell and minenwerfer fire was opened on the trenches.

What actually was the effect of the flame attack we don't know. None ever came back to tell. The German trenches were not more than 20 yards off at that point. The only evidence is an Officer's servant, who was in the trench at the time, but just clear of the gas. He said that after the flame had died down and after the bombardment he saw the Germans come out of their trench (the bombardment on this front only lasted two or three minutes, all minenwerfers, which are appalling in the devastation they create). When he saw the Germans he ran down the trench to find a way out, and says there was not a man living; all whom he saw who were not buried by the shells were lying dead. He got away and that was his story.

Meanwhile the Germans lifted their fire on to the woods where the reserve companies were and assaulted in three separate columns. We beat them off on two sides, but when they had gassed the front trench they poured in and took the rest of my sector in reverse . . .

The news reached me in my Hdqrs in the ramparts at Ypres about 1½ miles back at 3.30 am that the Germans were attacking. I called up the Artillery and sent out to stop the two battalions coming out and sent them back to the wood. Meanwhile the Germans had got into the support trenches . . . and were digging themselves in, and had rushed up a number of machine guns . . .

I got up to Zouave Wood as soon as I could and found the situation unchanged. Our bombers were holding the communication trenches leading to Zouave Wood and were fighting hard there and just south of the Menin road.

As soon as I saw the situation, I judged it would take a Division to get the Germans out and at least 12 hours bombardment with heavy guns. I accordingly reported and was told I must counter attack at once.

I replied that I wanted two brigades, one to attack the German flank from the west to enable my brigade to get out of the woods, and also insisted on the necessity of destroying the German trenches and redoubt on my right before I attempted an advance. The ground from the woods to the Menin road is a sheer glacis without a stick of cover.

I was then given one battalion of 43rd Bde (Duke of Cornwall's Lt Inf) as reserve and the 9th 60th who were not placed under my orders, but ordered to co-operate by an attack along the Menin road.

I was also told the Corps Artillery would bombard the position for ¾ hour. I fixed 2 pm for the bombardment and 2.45 for the assault, but it was with a very heavy heart I gave my orders to attack in successive lines from Zouave and Sanctuary woods in a depth of 2 battalions in each and kept the D.C.L.I. belonging to the 43rd Bde in reserve.

The bombardment was ineffective, so much so that the Germans opened a heavy M.G. fire . . . at 2.30 in the Woods and from the edge of the Woods we could see the Germans standing up in the trenches.

Precisely at 2.45 the attack moved forward. The men behaved very well and the Officers with a gallantry no words can adequately describe.

As they came out of the woods the German machine gun and shell fire met them and literally swept them away. Line after line the men struggled forward only to fall in heaps along the edge of the woods.

First Maitland 7th R.B. (Lt Colonel Heriot-Maitland Rifle Brigade) sent me word that he had only one Company left and immediately afterwards Green (Lt Colonel Green – cmdg 7th Battn The King's Royal Rifle Corps) sent up to say the men could not get forward.

I sent an order to all C.O.s to incur no further avoidable losses and to hold the edge of the Woods till dark.

As soon as I could I collected reports and sent for the C.Os.; their first reports were absolutely staggering; out of the whole brigade, I could only lay hands on 720 men. Meanwhile orders came from the Corps that I was to attack again which I answered by saying that it was impossible – two more battalions were sent up to reinforce me during the evening and I withdrew the remnants of the Brigade after dark into reserve and replaced them by the fresh battalions with orders to drag [*sic* – dig] themselves in along the edge of the woods and to send out officers' patrols to find out what they could. During the night I heard . . . an unfinished communication trench, was unoccupied above the barrier, so I moved a company into it to flank the Germans if they tried to attack.

At 2.20 a.m. the Germans made an attack on Zouave Wood preceded by liquid flame. I was standing just behind Zouave Wood so I saw the flame which appeared more like incandescent smoke than jets of fire, but that was probably because I was in front of it. This attack was very soon stopped and then the Germans opened the most terrific rifle fire I ever heard in my life all along their front and commenced a very heavy shelling of Zouave Wood. They kept this up without ceasing till daylight. At first I thought it was an attack, but as they kept lights going continually, I came to the conclusion that they thought we were going to attack.

We held on all day to the Woods losing men continually and finally in the afternoon the 41st Bde. were withdrawn after 10 days of as severe a trial as any troops could have. We lost 53 officers and 1400 men in the fighting on the 30th and during the whole period over 2000 men.

The 6th Division were then ordered to retake the trenches we had lost. I told Congreve (x) that he might retake them but that he would never hold them.

They bombarded the German trenches off and on for a week and then on the morning of the 9th August culminated in an intense bombardment by the major part of the Artillery of the 2nd Army assisted by the French Artillery. The 6th Division walked into the trenches we had lost and even into some German trenches west of our former line which we had not held, they had hardly any losses. The Germans had either retired or had been blown to pieces, but as soon as they were in the trenches the Germans turned their Artillery and minenwerfers onto them and literally blew them out of the trenches with a loss of 1600 men.

That is the actual truth of the situation at the present moment.

Congreve has reported that the position is untenable; he has already lost over 2000 men.

The 6th Division jeered our men when they passed each other a week ago as rotten fellows who couldn't hold a trench. I fancy they wouldn't jeer them now.

There was a conference this morning with the C.in C. I have not heard what decision has been come to.

The curse of the Salient has been heavy on the 14th Division; we have lost over 4000 men in it already. It nearly broke my heart to see my brigade come back. Officers of a class we shall never be able to replace, the pick of English or British public school and Varsity life. Heroes in battle, they led their men with the most sublime courage, knowing as I am certain they did that they were going to certain death. The splendour of it, and the utter waste! 8th R.B. have 3 officers left, other battns. 6 or 7 and the best all gone.

Of course we are going to win . . . George Cockburn (Brig. Gen. Cockburn D.S.O. Comdg. 43rd Inf. Bde) has gone home, too old. Markham (Brig. Gen. Markham comdg. 42nd Inf. Bde.) is now sick and likely to be invalided . . .

To all whom you meet, believe me there is nothing in the conduct of these young battalions of the 60th and the R.B. that you cannot relate with satisfaction and pride. They have had a fiery trial prolonged over nearly 6 weeks, culminating in the events of the 30th and 31st July and they have acquitted themselves like Britons.

Chaplin (Colonel Chaplin comdg. 9th Battn. The King's Royal Rifle Corps) was killed, most gallantly leading his battalion the 9th 60th, 42nd Brigade and his men did even better than mine, because they came up on the flank and did recover some of the trenches on our left which we had to evacuate when they were left in the air by the centre going.

(x) Col. and local Major Gen. Congreve.

RA, PS/Q824/1–3

I
The Somme, September 1915 to July 1916

Introduction

Nugent heard of his appointment to command the Ulster Division – which he attributed to Sir Archibald Murray, now DCIGS [35] – in his dugout on the outskirts of Ypres on 6 September; he formally took over command at Bramshott, near Aldershot, eight days later.[1] (His predecessor, General Powell,[2] had expected to take the Division to France, but it was generally recognised that he was too elderly and militarily outdated for the task.)

The Division was due to leave for France in early October, and the intensive preparations for both embarkation and the review by the King on 30 September meant that Nugent had time to gain only an initial impression of his new command before arriving in France on 3 October. Once the Division had concentrated a few days later at Flesselles, near Amiens, he began a more searching appraisal.

The Ulster Division was one of the most distinctive New Army formations. Formed largely from the UVF it embodied Ulster Unionism's commitment to the war effort. Including the pioneers, five of its 13 battalions were recruited in Belfast, two each in Cos Antrim and Down and four in the rest of the province (see Appendix 2). Its political supporters hoped that its service would provide a contrast to Nationalist lack of support for the war, exerting pressure on the Government for a favourable post-war Irish settlement. The Unionist press in Ireland followed the Division's progress closely while many of its officers corresponded regularly with politically connected friends or family at home, with the result that opinions and incidents in the Division soon became topics of conversation in drawing-rooms in Belfast and London or appeared in the newspapers. In the period 1915–16 in particular, when the Division's senior ranks included several Ulster MPs and peers who travelled home regularly on political business, it represented something of a military outpost of the Ulster Unionist Council (UUC). The Division's political character was not, however, unique: the 16th (Irish) Division performed a similar role for Redmondite Nationalism, though the core of National Volunteers around which that division was formed was rather smaller than the UVF component of the Ulster Division; while, in a different context, the 38th (Welsh) Division owed its existence to Lloyd George's wish to create a Welsh Army Corps, and to the Liberal Party's machinery in Wales.[3]

Recent research has modified the view that the 36th Division was composed entirely of pre-war UVF members.[4] Many Army reservists in the UVF had been recalled to their regiments at the outbreak of war and other UVF personnel had enlisted in other formations before the creation of the Division was finally agreed; relatively high proportions of some UVF units, particularly in rural areas, did not volunteer for overseas service; and several country units had never in any event had enough members to form complete battalions without external reinforcement. Nevertheless, more than 30,000 UVF members enlisted during the war and the organisation provided over 80 per cent of Protestant enlistments in Ulster in 1914; there is no doubt that the great majority of soldiers in the Division's Belfast battalions and a large proportion in the others were UVF personnel, representing a critical mass more than sufficient to shape the Division's ethos. Its overwhelmingly local character is demonstrated by the fact that ten of its 13 battalions in July 1916 were composed of over 90 per cent Ulstermen, and two of the other three over 80 per cent.[5]

Its senior posts in October 1915 were dominated by UVF or other Unionist figures. Of the three infantry brigadiers, Couchman (107 Brigade) had commanded the Belfast UVF, Hacket Pain (108) had been the organisation's chief of staff and Hickman (109), an English MP, had been its inspector-general. James Craig, the Ulster Unionist leader, had been invalided from the Divisional staff some months previously but Captain Wilfrid Spender, an ex-regular officer who had resigned his commission to play a leading role in organising the UVF, remained as GSO2. Other MPs serving with the Division included Charles Craig, brother of James (11th Irish Rifles); Peter Kerr-Smiley (14th Rifles); Hugh McCalmont (12th Rifles); and Hugh O'Neill (Divisional staff). Other members of the UUC included Lord Leitrim and Lord Farnham (whom Nugent appointed as his ADC). Seven of the 12 infantry battalions were commanded by former UVF officers.[6]

Nugent's overriding concern was not the background of his officers, however, but their competence. The decisiveness with which he acted to address the shortcomings he found reflected both operational necessity and his uncompromising personality. A tough-minded professional soldier, he could be ruthless and, occasionally, unjust. His temper was notoriously uncertain, especially early in the day. Cyril Falls, who served on the Division's staff from 1916 to 1918, wrote later 'I have nothing to say against any of the divisional commanders whom I served, except that the first [Nugent] had a shocking temper'.[7] This was due in part to the injuries he had sustained in South Africa from which he never fully recovered: prolonged spells in the saddle or long walks over difficult ground caused him pain. One officer commented after Nugent's death that he had 'an unbending will, was self-confident in his judgments and had not the happy knack, which a few strong characters have, of subordinating his own judgment when it clashed with that of authority'.[8] Neither military superiors nor political acquaintances went unscathed, which helps explain why he did not get the promotion his abilities deserved. Frank Crozier later wrote that Nugent 'did his own shooting so well (in the front line with weapons, on paper with such an acid pen, and in the conference room with such a cutting tongue and subtle wit) that he was sent to India at a critical period when he should have been promoted to an army corps', while Spender observed of him in April 1916 'but for his temper he would have done better as there are elements of greatness in him'.[9]

But though demanding he was always intensely concerned for his soldiers' welfare. Before the Division left for France he told his officers and NCOs 'you must work on the principle that there is nothing too small to worry over if it tends to the comfort, health or fighting efficiency of your men. You must never think of your own needs until you have satisfied yourself that the men are all right. It is what you are in the position of an officer or NCO to do.'[10] He made a point of visiting his units five or six days a week when possible.[11] He also had a well-developed sense of humour, and an awareness of his own failings. His reputation preceded him: word in the 10th Inniskillings was that their new general was 'very soldierly but the devil of a straffer'.[12]

Nugent immediately began weeding out those he felt were not up to the job. Couchman was removed within days of the Division arriving in France; Hacket Pain, who was physically unfit as well as militarily unsound, went home in December; and Hickman, at his own request, returned to the House of Commons, to Nugent's relief, in the spring of 1916 [8, 18, 52]. The Division's chief administrative officer, Lt Col

Meynell, had gone by the end of October 1915; Lt Col Russell, the charming but ineffective GSO1, lasted only until April 1916 [9, 13, 38, 44]. By January 1916 six battalion commanders (three successively in the 14th Rifles) had been replaced on the grounds of inefficiency or ill-health.[13]

Nugent's ruthlessness was consistent with practice throughout the BEF, as officers who had trained the New Armies at home but were unsuited to front-line service were replaced. Significantly Spender, whose relationship with Nugent was often tense, regarded none of the changes as unwarranted. But in removing these officers Nugent antagonised an Ulster political establishment already suspicious of him and made enemies ready to speak out against him at home.[14] Nevertheless, from his perspective the changes worked. By early 1916 he had assembled a group of key subordinates who remained with him for most of his period in command. His artillery brigadier (Brock), two of his three infantry brigadiers (Griffith and Withycombe) and both his senior staff officers (Comyn and Place) stayed with him for the next two years, which by Great War standards represented remarkable stability.[15]

Nugent turned with equal energy to the task of training the Division. In mid-October 1915 he held a divisional exercise [10] after which he delivered a brutally frank debrief. The second in command of the 10th Inniskillings recalled:

> few of the officers who were privileged to listen to his pow-wow after the performance will forget it. Very gravely, he opened his remarks by saying how glad he was to have at last seen the famous Ulster Division going through an attack practice, but (still more gravely) how much more glad he was to know that it was only a practice attack, for had it been a pukker attack on the German lines he very much feared that he would not have had the pleasure of speaking to any of the participating officers again in this world! The general went on to congratulate the officers on the excellence of their North of Ireland eyesight – he had observed that although they all were equipped with field glasses, none of them had ever found it necessary to use them, even during the initial stages of the attack! As a lecture it was superb, and did a lot of good, even though the officers did feel a little bit small, and more than a little bit aggrieved, at the nature of their commander's witticisms. Field glasses, compasses and other implements of the trade were used most assiduously – almost aggressively indeed – in General Nugent's presence on future occasions of the kind.[16]

An officer of the 12th Rifles recalled that the 'remarks of our General on the day's performance were, to say the least of them, hardly as complimentary as we should have wished. They left an impression on the minds of those who heard them that will never fade'; while a platoon commander in the 11th Inniskillings wrote that Nugent 'told us quietly and firmly what he thought of us . . . we had a good name as a division but he did not know how we got it. Every rudimentary mistake that could be made had been made by officers that day . . . He did not know what sort of training we had had in Ireland, but it was very poor.'[17] The pace of training accelerated, and each brigade did a spell in the trenches under the tutelage of a more experienced division.

But it was not just the Division's tactics which Nugent sought to improve. The quality of the Division's units was uneven, and he was particularly concerned about poor discipline in the five Belfast battalions – the 8th, 9th, 10th and 15th Royal Irish Rifles in 107 Brigade and the 14th Rifles in 109 Brigade. His assessment was shared by others: an officer of the 4th Division told Spender that while the 12th Rifles was a first-class battalion, the 14th 'had no officers worth anything and very few NCOs'; Crozier believed that, while the 9th and 10th Rifles were competent units, the 8th and 15th were not.[18] Nugent blamed weak leadership [12] and summoned the officers of 107 Brigade to tell them so. Crozier recalled:

> General Nugent . . . assembles all the officers of our brigade in a village schoolroom and delivers a strafe, not wholly deserved but very good for us, which I shall always treasure in my mind as the complete example of what can be said by the powerful to the powerless in the shortest space of time possible, consistent with the regulation of words for breathing, in the most offensive, sarcastic and uncompromising manner possible.[19]

A short-lived experiment, under which a New Army brigade was exchanged for a regular one in each Kitchener division, led to 107 Brigade being sent to the 4th Division in early November, where it remained until February 1916 [11, 14]. Nugent and Withycombe had already replaced a number of COs and other officers in the brigade, but there were more drastic measures also. Only four men of the Ulster Division were executed during the First World War, but it is no coincidence that three of them, all from 107 Brigade, were shot in early 1916, all for desertion [38]. When the brigade returned to the Division the combination of the executions, command changes and front-line experience had brought about a marked improvement.[20]

Nugent imposed pre-war regular standards of cleanliness and discipline with singlemindedness and occasionally ferocity. His insistence on spotless billets led his men to joke that the Division was 'sweeping onward through village after village in the North of France'.[21] No aspect escaped his notice, including disputes between his chaplains [15, 58]. This experience of occasionally uncomfortable adjustment to operational conditions was common to all New Army divisions (Tim Bowman's work indicates that overall the Ulster Division's disciplinary record during the war was broadly similar to that of other New Army formations).[22] But there was an additional dimension to Nugent's attempts to impose himself which was as much political and cultural as military.

Nugent ultimately was an Irish rather than an Ulster Unionist, and had little in common with the largely Belfast-based leadership of Ulster Unionism. Socially, as a landowner with long-established roots in the Irish midlands and family and social connections extending predominantly southwards, he had relatively few personal contacts in the north-east [34, 162]. Professionally, he was sensitive to the suspicions that existed within and outside the Army towards so political a formation, and was determined not to allow external 'interference' in his command. Personally, he found the more extreme manifestations of Ulster loyalism uncongenial, and while no supporter of Home Rule, nor an especial admirer of Irish Catholicism, he tried hard to discourage overt displays of party political affiliation and sectarianism in the Division (he issued instructions, for example, that Catholic churches were to be treated with respect, which to his amusement earned him a papal medal) [27, 30]. Politically, he had a fundamentally different perception to many Ulster Unionists of what the war experience meant for Ireland. For Nugent, as for others – including, for different reasons, both southern Unionists and Redmondite Nationalists – the war was a potentially unifying experience, an opportunity to submerge domestic political differences and create a basis for future cooperation. He believed, however unrealistically, that if Irishmen were forced to participate and 'real government' imposed on Ireland, then opposition to the war effort would evaporate [57, 100]. Over time he came increasingly to the view that a compromise settlement should be accepted by Ulster Unionism in exchange for full Nationalist support for the war effort, including conscription [102, 115, 129].

Unionists like Spender had, inevitably, a different outlook. The war for them was an opportunity to differentiate loyal Ulster from Nationalist Ireland. Common cause with their political opponents was not what they sought. The point is illustrated by the contrasting reactions to a speech by Redmond in November 1915, following a visit to the front, in which he called for Nationalists and Unionists to fight side by side. Nugent thought the speech a good one, and felt that Carson should respond in kind; Spender was alarmed and indignant, and saw the suggestion as a trap to lure Ulster into a Home Rule settlement [18, 21]. (He reacted similarly to a rumour in late 1915 that the 16th and 36th Divisions were to be brigaded together [23].) Spender was suspicious of Nugent's politics, which he reported back to Carson and Craig through his wife [19]. Nugent was aware of this, and was even more guarded and prickly with Spender as a result.[23]

Three episodes in the first half of 1916 illustrate Nugent's political views. The first was a dispute between two Ulster Unionist ladies' committees – the Ulster Women's Unionist Council Gift Fund in Belfast, run by the formidable Lady Richardson, and its offshoot in London, headed by the Duchess of Abercorn, of which both Kitty and Mrs Spender were members, and the Irish Women's Association, avowedly non-political but led by the Catholic Lady MacDonnell and with John Redmond's wife as an active member – over which should provide support to Ulster Division prisoners-of-war. Nugent and Spender, anxious to prevent a row between the Division and the committee members (and their politician husbands), issued a stream of advice to their wives [36, 37, 40, 43, 58] and a compromise was eventually reached: but Nugent was left deeply irritated by the episode.

The second, more serious, event was the Easter Rising. Nugent was in England on leave during the fighting in Dublin and his immediate reactions are not reflected in the correspondence; however he, like many Irish Unionists, while supporting severe measures against the insurrection's leaders, regarded the rebellion as merely the work of a lunatic fringe and an argument for firm measures rather than concessions [51, 53, 56, 61].

The third issue affected Nugent more directly. In May and June 1916 Lloyd George led efforts, in the aftermath of the Rising, to secure a political settlement in Ireland based on the introduction of Home Rule in 26 counties and the exclusion of the six north-eastern counties (the timing of implementation of Home Rule, and the duration of Ulster's exclusion, being left vague for the purposes of negotiation). The MPs and peers in the Ulster Division were summoned home for consultations and in early June 1916, despite the opposition of Farnham and others, the UUC agreed that Cavan, Monaghan and Donegal should not form part of the excluded area. Nugent, Farnham and Spender were united in their sense of betrayal [60, 64–7]. Although the Lloyd George initiative collapsed in July, Nugent's view of the Ulster Unionist leadership was permanently affected (though his regard for Carson did recover to a degree).

Another issue preoccupying Nugent was manning. By late 1915 the lack of depth in the manpower available to Irish units was already clear as recruitment rates in Ireland, proportionately lower than in Britain, began to fall away further and the impact of the 10th (Irish) Division's heavy casualties at Gallipoli was felt. Both Nugent and the Unionist leadership, and the Army high command, were aware of the difficulties the Irish divisions would face once they began to sustain serious casualties [5, 6, 46, 47, 63]. Nugent, like other senior officers, was a supporter of Irish conscription and lobbied Carson and other politicians constantly on the subject. His trenchant criticism of the lack of support he felt he was receiving became another irritant between them. The manpower crisis came to a head in the autumn of 1916, and is discussed more fully in the next chapter.

From the spring of 1916, however, Nugent's energies were bent on preparing his division for the forthcoming offensive. From February 1916 onwards it had held a sector of the Fourth Army front on the Somme and in the first few weeks successfully repelled a number of minor German attacks as well as mounting the first of many raids of its own [45, 50, 62, 66, 69]. Nugent was a highly aggressive commander who did not believe in a 'live and let live' approach. He was determined to dominate his opponents at all times, despite the reservations of those like Spender who wondered whether the benefits outweighed the losses. The Ulster Division quickly earned and retained a reputation for aggression in the front line.

Nugent's approach to operations was set out in a series of talks and papers he prepared for the Division. Before it left England he lectured officers and NCOs on both the traditional military virtues – care for their men, discipline, loyalty to their superiors – and the key features of war on the Western Front, including the importance of artillery, machine-guns, grenades and new weapons like gas and flamethrowers.[24] He was characteristically direct, warning them, for example, of the impact of trench mortars ('I have seen men crying like children after a series of these shells . . . reduced to gibbering idiots'), and also setting out his philosophy of command:

> In all my experience of life as a soldier, I have never seen a regiment which made or maintained a reputation which had not discipline. Discipline is the cement which binds every body of men into a homogenous whole and without which any body of soldiers has little to distinguish it from an ordinary mob . . . It is the spirit of discipline which enables you and the men you have to lead to face losses, to go steadily to your front and to confront difficulties and dangers which would probably have frightened you into a lunatic asylum 8 months ago . . . All men are not equally brave or equally under discipline, some have less control than others over their emotions. Those are the men who in a big fight begin to look behind them, to become siezed with panic and try to get away to the rear. The bad example of one man is contagious and may affect a number in his vicinity. Every officer and NCO has a great responsibility at such times. A rot must always be stopped before it spreads. You would be justified in using every means even to the most decisive to prevent an individual whose nerve has gone from being a cause of infection. You would not only be justified in any step you took to deal with such cases but I shall expect it of you.

He outlined his thoughts on offensive operations in trench warfare in a paper in January 1916 in which he stressed the need for initiative, speed and aggression and for troops to push on to their objectives irrespective of what was happening on their flanks.[25] The importance of junior commanders exercising initiative was a theme he stressed throughout his period in command [28].

Planning for the Somme offensive began at his headquarters in April (a process initially made more cumbersome by the inexperience of the staff of X Corps in which the Division was serving[26]). From the outset the key issue was how to capture the Ulster Division's main objective, the Schwaben Redoubt, while neutralising the village fortress of Thiepval on the Division's right flank. Nugent's original plan proposed a narrow thrust up the Ancre valley to outflank the Redoubt from the north, using the slope of the ground to provide cover from Thiepval's machine guns, but this was overruled when 32nd Division, tasked with assaulting Thiepval, complained it was being left unsupported. So the plan eventually used was adopted instead. On 1 July the Ulster Division would attack south of the Ancre with two brigades up – 109 Brigade on the right passing close to Thiepval, and 108 Brigade advancing beside it but with two detached battalions attacking north of the river to cover the Division's left flank – and with the remaining brigade (107) in support. The leading brigades' objective was the first three lines of German trenches, including the Schwaben Redoubt: 107 Brigade would then pass through to take the forward edge of the German second main position, an advance of almost two miles, and await reinforcements. Nugent recognised from the outset that if the divisions on his flanks failed the Ulster Division would be left badly exposed, but his objections were overruled [80]. Neither he nor Colonel Place, his GSO1, believed that Thiepval could be taken by frontal assault and were concerned that X Corps had no plan to outflank it: while they hoped their assault on either side of the Ancre valley would go well they remained anxious about their right flank.[27]

Nugent did what he could to reduce the threat. He decided to push his leading waves into no-man's-land before zero hour to enable them to rush the German trenches as soon as the barrage lifted, a tactic that proved extremely successful. He arranged for smokescreens to mask the German positions on his flanks, which on the day were only partially effective. He also organised additional bombardments of Thiepval's northern edge in the days before the assault, which did not work. He examined the German lines from an aircraft, the first time he had flown, and encouraged his subordinates and superiors to do the same, and he put his units through an intensive programme of rehearsals over mock ups of the German trenches [55, 57, 59, 80]. Controversially, he refused to allow his battalion commanders to accompany their units into the attack, to preserve them to help rebuild their units after the battle [80]; in this he succeeded but the COs resented the order deeply and senior officers proved to be in short supply once the troops got into the German positions.

The British bombardment began on 24 June. The density of guns proved insufficient to destroy the German defences and along much of the front the German wire remained uncut. Fortunately for the Ulster Division observation for the artillery in its sector was relatively good and south of the Ancre – though not to the north – the German wire was largely destroyed.

Shortly after 7 a.m. on 1 July Nugent's leading waves moved into no man's land. At 7.30 a.m. the bombardment lifted and the leading units went in, overrunning the first two lines of German trenches. The two battalions (9th Irish Fusiliers and 12th Rifles) north of the Ancre were less fortunate, the wire here being less well cut and the enemy forward positions relatively unscathed: attempting to advance in a series of rushes they were virtually annihilated, losing over three-quarters of their men. At 7.40 a.m. the second wave battalions advanced through heavy machine-gun and shell fire, suffering severe casualties, and became embroiled in fighting for the third line of German trenches and the Schwaben Redoubt. By 9 a.m. the Redoubt had been captured [75, 87].

Nugent watched the initial assault from an observation post but haze limited visibility and he soon returned to his forward headquarters. Within an hour it was clear that the flanking divisions had failed and he asked permission of the Corps commander (Morland) to hold back 107 Brigade. The response was that they should be committed. Forty-five minutes later came a second order telling Nugent to hold them back, but it was too late: First World War communications did not permit last-minute alterations of this sort [80]. 107 Brigade got across no man's land with considerable loss. Passing through their comrades, by mid-morning the survivors had captured part of the forward edge of the German second position despite running into their own artillery barrage. By 11 a.m. the Ulster Division had taken five lines of trenches and reached the limit of its advance; German counter-attacks were already beginning.[28]

Nugent knew that this success could still be exploited if he was reinforced quickly. Major-General Perceval, commanding 49th Division, the Corps reserve, had heard of the Ulster Division's advance and, expecting his troops to be committed in support, went to Nugent's HQ for a briefing, sometime after 9 a.m.: 'I saw Nugent and his staff. The impression that I got after talking to them was that there was not a moment to be lost and that it might be too late to do more than secure what had been gained.'[29] Perceval hurried to Morland to urge him to reinforce Nugent. Morland declined. Instead one of Perceval's brigades and part of another were used to assist 32nd Division in further unsuccessful attacks on Thiepval, while the third was deployed behind 32nd Division and remained uncommitted all day. Not until late evening, after much confusion, were two battalions of 49th Division extricated and made available to Nugent, too few and far too late.[30] The mishandling of the X Corps reserves – the lack of advance planning for their deployment, their piecemeal commitment and their use in reinforcing failure rather than success – is a reminder of how much the British Army had still to learn operationally in 1916: such errors would scarcely have occurred in 1918.

By 3 p.m. the surviving attackers had been forced back to the rear of the German first position. Nugent, handicapped by lack of information, did what he could, sending up supplies, arranging for Thiepval to be shelled again (without effect) and appealing for reinforcements. At around 7 p.m. he despatched forward the two Yorkshire battalions already mentioned. But the German attacks continued unabated and by 10 p.m. the Division was left clinging to part of the old German front-line. At 11 p.m. Nugent was offered a brigade of 49th Division to launch a night attack, but accepted the advice of his frontline brigadier, Withycombe, that the proposal was unworkable.[31]

By the following morning it was clear that a further major effort in this sector was impossible. There was nothing more to do but bring in the wounded and reorganise the defences. During the night of 2/3 July 49th Division relieved the Ulster Division. Of 9,000 men in the attack over 5,000 became casualties, including 190 of 300 officers; nearly 2,000 were killed. The Division won four of the nine Victoria Crosses awarded for the 1 July attack [86].[32]

After the battle Nugent was torn between pride for his Division and grief at its losses; he thanked each brigade in person, and was gratified by the flood of congratulations that poured in [72–8]. Grief and pride were also mixed in the reaction at home, with many local communities in Ulster left devastated by the casualty lists. Inevitably, however, the Division's performance began to be exploited for political purposes, to Nugent's increasing frustration [79–80, 84]. He was also deeply angered by an 'anonymous' eyewitness account, in fact taken from a letter written by Spender, which appeared in several newspapers in the days after the battle. Beginning memorably 'I am not an Ulsterman, but yesterday as I followed their amazing attack I felt I would rather be an Ulsterman than anything else in the world', it went on to say that their General 'now knows he has commanded the best troops in the world and confesses it'. Nugent's fury at the implication that he had not previously appreciated the quality of his men was palpable, and relations between the two never recovered. Fortunately for Spender, he left the Division on promotion shortly after [83, 85]. In the battle's aftermath Nugent was briefly hopeful that he himself might be promoted, particularly if the rumours of the shakiness of some existing corps commanders proved true, but he was to be disappointed [81, 85, 90].

In mid-July the Division moved north to Flanders and Plumer's Second Army, where it soon faced a crisis of a different kind.

4
Nugent to his wife

[Holograph] [41 Bde, 14 Div, Ypres]
6 September 1915

I have news which will thrill you but which you must not breathe till it is official.

I have been told I have been given command of a Division and so will be promoted to Major General. The Division is the Ulster Division of all others. It is now I believe at Aldershot and is coming out almost at once but any rate I shall be home for a while and I may be on my way home before you get this even. I'll send you a wire as soon as I get orders and possibly you might think it worthwhile to come over and meet me in London! . . .

Arthur is in the Ulster Division and I hope he will come as my ADC and I have a mind to ask Pip if he would care to come as my 2nd ADC.[1] It would keep him more out of danger than as a 2nd Lieut in a battalion and I dare say Ponto and Evie would be glad if he cared to come, but I expect Pip would think that he ought to stay with his batn.

Sweetheart, I can hardly believe that I may be seeing you all again very soon. It is too good to be true, I keep thinking.

All the same I feel a kind of feeling that I should have liked to have commanded the 41st Bde in a <u>successful</u> fight. Still it looks as if the War Office and the Army authorities out here recognised that it was not through my error that the 30th July was so fateful a day.

Last night the Germans shelled all round my Headquarters here with gas shells and it is really very painful. Everybody was going round with their eyes red and streaming for [*sic*] noses. It is such a futile method of war too, because these particular 'frightfulnesses' are only painful and irritating but don't appear to be dangerous. They will probably do it again this evening as they are very fond of repeating these forms of entertainment.

FC, D/3835/E/2/4

5
Sir Edward Carson to Nugent

[Holograph]

London
23 September 1915

I am leaving town today. I will be returning Tuesday morning. If it is convenient to you I could see you on Wednesday, either here in the morning or at the House of Commons in the afternoon. There is much I would like to say to you on the question of recruiting, about which I recently had an interview with the Adjutant General, and unless drastic changes are made, I am very doubtful whether the supply will be kept up.

However we can discuss it all when I see you. My congratulations and best wishes and good luck on your appointment to our Ulster Division in which I need hardly say I am most deeply interested.

FC, D/3835/E/2/20

6
James Craig to Capt W. B. Spender, 36th Division

[Holograph]

Cornwall
24 September 1915

I do so hope that, throughout, you will confide in me quite frankly and will recognise that my whole heart is constantly with the Division and that you can always thoroughly rely upon my discretion.

Any changes so far have been good ones and the only fear in my mind is the break-up of the Ulster in the event of casualties being heavy. The Reserve Battalions are not filling up as they should and consequently some of your Battns when washed away may be replaced by 'strangers' or, worse again, your Battns may be given away to fill up other Armies! I am genuinely worried about this, as I always like to look ahead . . .

Please explain to General Nugent that any mortal thing I can do will always be his for the asking. 'Help not hinder' must be the motto for us all.

SP, D/1295/3/11

7
Nugent to his wife

[Holograph] [Flesselles]
4 October 1915

I am well known tonight, quite as [*sic*] a Divisional General, in a real Chateau, very fine and large but decidedly draughty.

I am at a place called Flesselles, NW of Amiens, about 5 miles from it.

The first person to receive me with his face wreathed in smiles on my arrival at the Chateau was my dear Beamish,[2] who had squared the French authorities and had got himself transferred to me. I was really delighted to see him and he was to see me . . .

I am so thankful it is not in the mud and slime of Belgium that the Division will have to spend the winter . . .

The account Beamish gave me of the attack at Bellewaarde Ridge and Hooge the other day is rather bad. We captured the trenches. Pip's brigade did this, the 42nd or was his the 43rd? Anyhow the 42nd Bde made the attack and the Germans hardly made any resistance, but as soon as they were in the German trenches, they turned 45 batteries of artillery on to them and behind them so that no reinforcements could reach them and they could not get away and we had only 14 batteries to reply with. The Germans then attacked the 42nd Brigade with an overwhelming number of bombs and in the end they were driven out of the trenches with the loss of 3000 men out of 4000 so Beamish tells me and the same thing happened to the Division on the right which tried to capture the German trenches round Hooge. They got them but were blown out of them again. The truth is never told in an official dispatch. He could tell me nothing of Pip, of course, but I am writing to the 14th Division to ask for some news if they have any.[3]

FC, D/3835/E/2/5

8
Nugent to his wife

[Holograph] [Flesselles]
10 October 1915

I have had to write to one of my Brigadiers and tell him he won't do, so beastly, but quite unavoidable.[4] I might have delayed it, but what good and a good man is badly wanted at once.

I am afraid v possibly 2 of my staff may have to go as well, but we shall see. I will give them a trial. We can't afford to run risks of breakdown through people not knowing their jobs.

FC, D/3835/E/2/5

9
Nugent to his wife

[Holograph] [Flesselles]
12 October 1915

The new armies are not really fit to take care of themselves and require a great deal of supervision.

Entre nous Meynell is, I am afraid a useless staff officer, always making heavy weather of everything and no more initiative than a clerk.[5] I have to think of everything in his branch and he gets on my nerves. I am afraid I shall have to get him removed. It is horrible work and it is so wrong to send staff officers to staff appointments who are no use. Not fair on them or on their General.

I have had to recommend the removal of another CO today.[6]

My Hdqrs Chaplain came to see me today for the first time since I took command.[7] I am afraid rather the neurotic type. He did not impress me . . .

I enclose a note giving my views on the sort of comforts which would be most useful to the men which you can use as my official opinion.

FC, D/3835/E/2/5

10
Nugent to his wife

[Holograph] [Flesselles]
16 October 1915

I have been up to the trenches where one of my Brigades is learning its work. I did not go into them myself as I had too much to do behind them but I took Arthur and Henry my No. 2 ADC[8] and they spent a most happy day in the fire trenches and saw the German trenches and saw our people fire a trench mortar into the German trenches and saw German shells bursting in reply and were sniped and explored dugouts and both returned as pleased as 2 schoolboys.

They were on the point of starting off covered with revolvers, but I told them it wasn't necessary and it would only make a story at our expense. They are quite the 'tenderfeet'.

I had a field day today with thc whole Division except the Brigade in the trenches which was quite interesting and after which I delivered a long criticism. There were too many mistakes and shortcomings I am sorry to say for a Division supposed to be ready for war.[9]

FC, D/3835/E/2/5

11
Nugent to his wife

[Holograph] [Domart, nr Abbeville]
23 October 1915

The Ulster Division is being broken up I am sorry to say. That is to say we are to lose 1 Brigade of Ulstermen and get another Brigade in its place of regulars.[10] This is to happen to all the New Divisions, I understand. I am very sorry and I am afraid it will cause a great feeling of disappointment and will I fear have a bad effect on recruiting in Ulster. I hope it may only be for a while and that later on the 3 Ulster Brigades will be all under one roof again. It is in many ways a good thing no doubt as the new battalions will have a better opportunity of picking up useful knowledge when they have regular battalions alongside them to learn from.

FC, D/3835/E/2/5

12
Nugent to his wife

[Holograph] [Domart]
26 October 1915

I certainly should not venture to let the Ulster Division know that you pray for them in Westminster Cathedral (bless you!). I hope you are not letting Florence influence you![11] Still I don't mind where you pray my Sweetheart, for wherever you were I know I should have your prayers still.

I am not too happy about the Ulster Division for it cannot be denied that some of them have very little discipline. The Belfast Brigade is awful. They have absolutely no discipline and their officers are awful. I am very much disturbed about them.[12]

I don't think they are fit for service and I should be very sorry to have to trust them. Don't breathe one word of this to a living soul please. It is all due to putting a weak man in command of the Brigade to start with and giving commissions to men of the wrong class.

FC, D/3835/E/2/5

13
Nugent to his wife

[Holograph] [Domart]
31 October 1915

Meynell's successor has arrived and I think is going to be a great improvement on Meynell.[13]

Meynell remains on and won't go. It is most uncomfortable for everyone. He has applied for another staff appt and no one will have him. He has the reputation of being the worst staff officer in the Army and a most unpleasant man to live with. It is such a shame to have appointed him and of course he has a grievance against me for having forced him out so soon.

I like Russell but of course he is a regular diplomat with an atmosphere of courts about him.[14]

It of course never occurred to him that Mrs R would write and tell you how much he likes being with me. Besides I am not half so funny as he pretends to find me when I break out into scintillations of wit. His paroxysms of appreciation of my humour would put Fania[15] in the shade. Still we are all human, even a 'distinguished' person like myself and I prefer his diplomacy to poor Meynell's sulky manners . . .

Allenby is here and no one is particularly rejoiced I can assure you . . .[16]

The Ulster Volunteer Force has sent the Ulster Division 20,000 sandbags. Sir F Richardson wrote to say there was a loving thought in every stitch!

I wrote back to say we were much moved and that when they came I would build them into the front line of our trenches if we were in any and that with a stout Ulsterman behind them no Boche would ever find out what was the other side of them. I expect my reply will be printed in the local papers, so you will probably see it.

FC, D/3835/E/2/5

14
Capt W. B. Spender to his wife

[Holograph] [Domart]
2 November 1915

107 Bde are furious with Genl. He was very rude to them yesterday and they have gone off to the new Div to which they are to be attached for 2 months swearing that they don't want to come back and will do their best not to if he commands. It is a great pity but undoubtedly this Brigade required some tail-twisting tho' I think it could have been done differently perhaps.[17]

SP, D/633/1/1/40

15
Nugent to his wife

[Holograph] [Domart]
9 November 1915

I have had to settle such a silly dispute between the Presbyterian and Church of Ireland chaplains of the Division. Really not the Ch of Ireland people as they made no trouble, but the Presbyterians who wanted to resign because they got their orders through the Senior Chaplain who happens to be Ch of Ireland. It is done in every Division and the Senior Chaplain in the whole Army is a Presbyterian but these narrow, intolerant Ulster Presbyterians objected, so to avoid friction I said that orders to them should come from my office direct. Silly idiots.

FC, D/3835/E/2/6

16
Capt W. B. Spender to his wife

[Holograph] [Domart]
23 November 1915

I was out teaching the bombers today and found it necessary to take personal control myself. The GOC appeared when I was in the middle of it. Perhaps it was just as well that I was there or there would certainly have been some strafing. As it is he is holding an inspection with 'live bombs' tomorrow, when the difficulty is not to carry out the drill but to let the GOC see it in safety.

What do you think of Redmond's tour.[18] Perhaps it is well for the papers to make the most of it, as the recruiting in S Ireland is proving such a fiasco, and as there is real danger of trouble there – if it is not dealt with firmly at once. I wish someone would write to the papers to suggest that there should be a new punishment for unpatriotic agitators, to take the form of so many months deportation to the trenches. It would stop it at once as they are all blustering funks, and wouldn't we have some fun in showing them round!

SP, D/1633/1/1/72

17
Nugent to his wife

[Holograph] [Domart]
25 November 1915

What a ghastly thing about Longford.[19] I expect it may well be true as I don't think the Turks rescued any of our people out of the woods and one hears of so many who were left wounded when the brush caught fire . . .

Our artillery just out from England has now been definitely told to join us, so that is settled and you might tell Lady C[arson] so.

One of my Brigades has just come back from the trenches after its fortnight in, they enjoyed themselves immensely and everybody up there was impressed with their keenness and intelligence.

This was General Hackett Pain's brigade, the 108th.

I had a bombing inspection today of one of the brigades, General Hickman's. The brigade bombing officer, one Munn, who is I believe amateur champion at golf in Ireland, had a really first-rate programme, full of incidents of all sorts. Of course it was carried out with live bombs and these Ulstermen love throwing them and the air was full of exploding bombs.

FC, D/3835/E/2/6

18
Capt W. B. Spender to Sir Edward Carson

[Holograph] [Domart]
25 November 1915

I am moved to write about Redmond's latest and not least wicked speech.[20] I will deal only with that part of it in which he refers to the [*sic*] Dublin and the Ulster Division[.] I do not know whether you could take some steps to take the wind out of the Nationalist sails and at the same time inspire our men, by writing to the papers saying that you know the Ulstermen will continue to show the utmost toleration to their Nationalist comrades who have proved themselves worthy sons of the Empire by joining the colours, and that they need not fear that the country will take a false view of their attitude in this respect . . . Genl Hacket Pain is still with us, but expects to leave any day, and I sincerely hope one of our own COs may succeed him, as it is very disheartening for first-class men like Hessey to see a youngster brought in from outside over his head.[21] Unluckily, General Nugent does not think Irishmen are good in command of their own countrymen, but prefers a mixture, I think.

Carson Papers, D/1507/A/14/14

19
Capt W. B. Spender to his wife

[Holograph] [Pont Remy, nr Abbeville]
28 November 1915

I fancy K[err] S[miley] must be like his wife. He was running (?) [*sic*] an outpost scheme of the 14 RIR when the GOC went out and watched. After 5 mins the battalion was ordered to march home! Genl said he was not out to watch children's play . . .

Gen N[ugent] is not at all keen about a separate Ulster and would willingly compromise with the Nationalist party if it meant support by the Govt. There is no fervour about his faith in this respect and he will want watching later after the war. I think Sir E[dward] ought to know this. It is not against him of course but simply that he has quite different convictions to the stalwarts of the Covenant and believes in the possibility of agreement.

SP, D/1633/1/1/80

20
Nugent to his wife

[Holograph] [Pont Remy]
30 November 1915

I hear General Allenby inspected the Pioneer battalion of my Division unexpectedly the other day when they were at work. He was not expected and only the Orderly Officer was there. When he saw Allenby coming he was so frightened that he tried to run away and fell into a barbed wire fence and then was so terrified that he couldn't remember what regiment he belonged to. Then Allenby got into a trench and used such language that the guide climbed out of the trench and did run away. Allenby then slipped and sat down very hard on the point of a brick and his language was such that the men took refuge in dugouts. Finally he stepped on to the roof of a dugout which was unfinished and fell through and ended up his inspection by saying 'So you're the kind of men we have got to expect from the New Armies, are you'. As a matter of fact they are very intelligent men in my Pioneers and more nearly gentlemen many of them than A himself.

FC, D/3835/E/2/6

21
Nugent to his wife

[Holograph] [Pont Remy]
3 December 1915

I think Redmond made a very good speech the other day. I think it is almost time Sir E Carson said something on the same lines. I wonder if he would care to be invited to visit the Ulster Division later on. Perhaps you could sound Lady C. I would not suggest it unless he would like to come.

I am afraid Lord K[itchener] will do no one any good nor help anyone. I hear he never expresses an opinion and is no help to the Cabinet, but the question is what to do with him. The British public think he is indispensable. However the man who more than anyone else ought to be got rid of is Asquith. Will nothing or nobody push him out.

FC, D/3835/E/2/6

22

Capt W. B. Spender to Sir Edward Carson

[Holograph] [Pont Remy]

3 December 1915

I have heard from my wife today that she has mentioned to Lady Carson about the appointment of three RC staff officers. In case this may give a wrong impression, I am writing to say that one has left owing to ill health (Ryan). Both the other two, Comyn and Mayne, are good chaps and Unionist, and though it is not a tactful thing to have done on the part of the authorities, I feel sure they are not themselves intriguers.[22]

The men seem to have quietened down since Redmond's speech, and I hope Xmas will go by without any unfortunate incident, unless he again attempts any 'rousings'.

We expect the Division to be transferred to another Corps very shortly, and I personally shall be glad, as two of the Corps staff were formerly very anti-Ulster. General Greenly, who is an old staff college friend of mine, took a very strong line against us then, and though he is I think too good a fellow, to harbour any feelings now, it is better for many reasons that we should be moved.[23]

Carson Papers, D/1507/A/14/17

23

Capt W. B. Spender to his wife

[Holograph] [Pont Remy]

14 December 1915

The latest report will, if true, very nearly succeed in making me wish to leave the Division. It is that the 16th [Division] is to be put with us in the same corps. There are some well-meaning shortsighted people who will not only not look ahead but even refuse to see the present state of affairs staring them in the face in Ireland, for all the world to see. These let themselves be imposed upon by others who have other motives and so these experiments n political fusions are to be tried. It would be a doubtful experiment in peace but in war it is criminal. Imagine what will happen if one of our units is late in coming up in support through no fault of their own, or vice versa, or if one of their patrols gets fired on by our guns. The mutual suspicion will become certain distrust, and then military cooperation the secret of success would go overboard and the Germans would get in.

Even if the experiment were safe it would still be wicked. What do you suppose is the motive at the bottom of it. Better understandings better feelings? If so for what purpose? To try to make them live peacibly [*sic*] together in future? If this be the reason, then obviously the S Irish ought to be mixed with the English so that their hate of the British may be lessened by better acquaintance. To mix the N and S Irish in this way is presumably to make them willing to agree to set up an independent household together apart from the British, to remove their mutual antagonisms so that they may be content to have Home Rule. In a few days the papers will be rhapsodizing over the reconciliation of the Irish etc etc, and people will begin to think that Home Rule will not be so bad after all and the trickiness of Redmond will begin to work. Later if the Ulstermen should do well you will see in the papers 'grand stand by the Irish'. The 'Irish' corps will probably be so called, because it has one brigade of S Irish and one division of Ulstermen, and the Irish will get the credit.

SP, D/1633/1/1/103

24
Nugent to his wife

[Holograph] [Domart]

11 January 1915 [*sic* – 1916]

We have to move again because the XIVth Corps to which we now belong wants to come here. There is seemingly no rest for us. It really is too bad. That will be the 5th move in a little over 3 months . . .

Sir E Carson told me that Lloyd George's meeting in Glasgow to try and induce the workmen to do better and to allow unskilled labour to be used in the works was a tragic failure. Lloyd George was with the men from 10 pm to 4 am one night and could hardly get a hearing. The men cursed him and shook their fists at him and finally said 'To h—l with you and the war. We know we are going to lose this war and we mean to make all we can out of the war while it lasts'. Fine patriotism isn't it. What unspeakable brutes. He also said that we should never win the war with the present Govt in office and called Asquith a d—n old fool, Balfour an old woman and Bonar Law an honest ass.

I asked him why he didn't turn the Govt out. He said he would do it tomorrow but it would be no use. If there was a general election they would come back and Asquith would never resign until he was hunted out.

FC, D/3835/E/2/8

25
Nugent to his wife

[Holograph] [Domart]
12 January 1915 [*sic* – 1916]

Our new Corps Comdr came today to see me, Cavan by name, seems a good fellow and knows how to begin an acquaintance because he said 'I am so glad to meet you, I have heard so much about you'! He also said he had noticed the smartness of the Ulster boys whom he passed on the road, and that he had heard that the Ulster Division was the best in the New Armies. So I took quite a fancy to him.[24] Tomorrow I am going to have a farewell dinner with Congreve and the HeadQrs staff of XIIIth Corps.

FC, D/3835/E/2/8

26
Nugent to his wife

[Holograph] [Domart]
17 January 1916

I wondered if you would notice my promotion![25] So I said nothing about it in my last 2 letters. I am pleased, of course, though I do cease to be an ADC and lose £200 pa. Still, I get a better pension!

I have been promoted over the heads of about 250 other Colonels. Did you notice the heading to the announcement 'for distinguished service in the field'. I was pleased at that too.

It would have been so very awkward and difficult to explain if the war ended and I had not been promoted and sank to Colonel again!

FC, D/3835/E/2/8

27
Nugent to his wife

[Holograph] [Bernaville]
19 January 1916

I came to my new HQ yesterday, a beast of a day. It rained all day. We are not nearly as well off as before. The Doctor and his wife with whom Arthur, Russell and I are lodging and where my mess is, are most kind and have done all they can for us. We have their dining room which is quite a good-sized room for the mess and sitting room and they have given me their salon for my private room and office. It is one mass of antimacassars but still it is very kind of them and they have retired with their daughter to a sort of living room next to the kitchen. Most of the French of that class use a sort of living room and keep their dining room and drawing room for state occasions, so I think they would not be using the rooms we have in any case . . .

What do you think I got today. My head RC Chaplain is a Jesuit Father and lives in Rome though he is English, Strickland by name. He had an audience with the Pope and showed him an order

I published about treating RC Churches out here with the same respect as a Protestant Church at home, a matter some of the Ulstermen were bad about. The Pope seems to have been much touched and sent me a silver medal and his blessing! Very nice of him.

FC, D/3835/E/2/8

28
Nugent to his wife

[Holograph] [Bernaville]
26 January 1916

I had a field day today and harangued the mob after it. I told the young officers that they must show more initiative, that they would probably be d—d whatever they did but it would certainly be d—d if they did nothing and there was just the off chance that if they did something they might do the right thing. They were much amused and I hope impressed . . .

We hear that the Division will probably take over a part of the trench line permanently very soon, possibly next week. If so I shall again be moving my Hdqrs the 7th time.

FC, D/3835/E/2/8

29
Nugent to his wife

[Holograph] [Bernaville]
27 January 1916

We had a most successful dinner party last night . . . I consulted the Primate[26] as to how we were to settle the question of who was to say Grace, himself or the RC chaplain and he advised me to settle it on the lines that it was settled when he and a RC Bishop dined at Kilkenny to meet King Edward. The King said he recognised one Church so far as he was concerned and that the protestant bishop was to say Grace and then the Primate suggested that he should say it before and the RC after dinner and King E said he did not object but that it was the bishop's suggestion not his. So with this illustrious ruling, I asked the Primate before and the RC Father Strickland after and all was peace. The cook produced an excellent dinner and we had music afterwards. The Primate had been up to the trenches and came back greatly delighted because he had been under shell fire and 1 shell had burst within 25 yards or so and covered him with mud, so he felt he had really been under shellfire as he was.

Cavan is to go to Flanders to take over the 6th Corps and the 6th Corps staff are to come down here and take over the 14th Corps. We are greatly disappointed. We all wanted to have Cavan as Corps Commander and he wanted to stay. The 6th Corps is commanded by Sir John Keir who commanded the 6th Corps when the 14th Division was in it and he was the man who overruled me and forced me to make that disastrous attack on 30th July. He is an artilleryman and has no knowledge of infantry and I think it is a very poor exchange. However I am glad we are not going into Flanders and the Ypres Salient again.

FC, D/3835/E/2/8

30
Nugent to his wife

[Holograph] [Bernaville]
3 February 1916

I have not the least doubt there will be plenty of people in the north of Ireland who will quote the Pope's medal as a proof that I am a traitor and a RC. I don't mind. I have no sympathy with the narrow-minded outlook of the extremists up in the north, any more than I have with the Sinn Feiners. The enclosed from Lord Cavan is very gratifying from a Guardsman.[27] You can show it round and I expect Sir Edward Carson will like it too.

FC, D/3835/E/2/8

31
Nugent to his wife

[Holograph] [Bernaville]
5 February 1916

I went up to the line yesterday and went on to a hill where one gets a good view of the German trenches.[28]

It was a very clear day without a cloud. There was a certain amount of shelling going on, but nothing came our way. I saw a German officer through my glass get out at the back of his trenches and walk up the whole length of a field. Of course he could not be seen from our trenches which were in the lower ground to where I was peering from. He was out of shot any how even if I had a gun.

I'll be able to ride to within safe distance of most of the trenches, which will be a good thing for my health and Acheux is at the top of a hill so there will be fresh air. It is quite a good piece of line and we are not overlooked by the Germans at all points as we used to be in the Ypres Salient . . .

I had a command performance of the cinema for myself last night.[29] It was really very good and I saw the Ulster review, one of the principal episodes depicted is my kissing the King's hand at the end. I come out very well and quite overshadow the King as I am nearest the camera . . .

FC, D/3835/E/2/8

32
Nugent to his wife

[Holograph] [Bernaville]
5 February 1916 [*sic*]

The enclosed from Sir Curley Hutton, refers to a proof of the account of Hooge which he is writing for the Regimtal Chronicle and sent to me for correction. He had put in a reference to my connection with the UVF which I struck out as being out of place. Apparently he thinks I struck it out because I was ashamed of it.

I am going to write and tell him that by unanimous consent there are no references in this Division to politics now and that is why I have struck it out.

He takes a very high view of my acts in the past. I think he refers to my having told him that I joined the UVF not for the purpose of rebellion or civil war because I disagreed all along on the policy which created the UVF but because I thought I should do more good in my own country by organising a force for defence in case of attack and that I would never consent to leading them in an unprovoked attack on anyone and that I said at the time that those were the conditions on which I would take part and on no other. They were not popular outside of Cavan.

Nevertheless Curley Hutton is rather an extremist in his views, hence his high-pitched views on it.

FC, D/3835/E/2/8

33
Nugent to his wife

[Holograph] [Acheux]
14 February 1916

Arthur and I went up to look at our 2nd line today. I found some men walking about outside the communication trench and showing themselves, so I gave them a severe wigging. A little further on we found the mud so bad and so much water that after making quite sure we could not be seen by the men I had wigged, we climbed out and continued our walk in the open ourselves. Today has been quiet but no doubt the Boche is preparing something unpleasant in return for our shelling of yesterday. They blew up a mine in front of my trenches yesterday.

We were mining too and 1 man was buried. I have not heard if he was got out alive but I am afraid it is not likely . . .[30]

We have had a good number of casualties since we came up, partly no doubt because the men are new to the game and partly because the Germans are much more active with their artillery than they were. That also may be because they know we are new. They are always supposed to know every thing that takes place in our lines.

FC, D/3835/E/2/8

34
Nugent to his wife

[Holograph] [Acheux]
18 February 1916

F E Smith[31] was out here the other day and he had the cheek to take the car of General Macready, the Adjutant General, without leave and go off to see W Churchill. General Macready sent a wire on ahead of him and immediately he arrived at his destination he was put under arrest.

I hope he was kept there and in a damp cellar too . . .

I shouldn't be annoyed or disappointed at all at not appearing to interest people on the Committee. After all you are to some extent still a stranger and I suppose most of them are friends and acquaintances of long standing.

You will win your way. You always do, bless you. You see, people in the north of Ireland don't really know anything about me nor of the Nugent family. We are not really a N of Ireland family and as a matter of fact, the Nugents were for James and against William in the days when the North was founding itself. All our family associations lie in the midlands of Ireland and it is merely a geographical accident that we live inside Ulster.

Then I daresay I am still suspect as to my politics. D—n their politics. I wish I had refused to have anything to do with them. I always feel just the same with this Division that they would really rather have someone else. I know they are always writing home about everything I do or say and can't stand anything but praise. They had too much butter given them while at home.

FC, D/3835/E/2/8

35
Nugent to his wife

[Holograph] [Acheux]
19 February 1916

This evening about 5.30 pm the Germans opened a heavy bombardment on my trenches, which is going on now. We are all standing by ready to move up into the various positions where our reinforcements go. Our guns are hammering away at the German trenches and the sky is alight with the flash of our guns and the Germans and the bursting of shells. We don't know what is up yet. The Germans may mean an attack, but it isn't the usual time to begin one with a long dark night in front. However we shall know more later on. It may be only a spasm of hate to try and catch our reliefs moving up and transport which of course goes up to the line at night.[32]

I do not think the Germans are likely to make any big attacks just yet. They have been making a number of local attacks all along the line and in some cases getting into our frontline trenches, but there is no present sign of any great push. The country is too waterlogged for movement on a grand scale.

I see the trenches at Hooge have got it again and the Germans have captured the frontline, so there will be another fight there I suppose. How many 1000s of lives that salient has cost us . . . I did not hear that A Murray was fighting with his Generals in the Mediterranean. It would be so much better to fight Germans, but perhaps it isn't true. I hope it isn't. I owe him my present command I think, so I naturally wish him well, besides we have always been friends more or less since we were at the S[taff] C[ollege] together . . .

The bombardment seems to be dying down and my 2 Brigadiers up in front say they are all right.

FC, D/3835/E/2/8

36
Nugent to Spender

[Typescript copy] [Acheux]
[n.d. but 20 February 1916][33]

I fully sympathise with the desire of the Committee of the 'Ulster Women's Gift Fund' to keep in their own hands the care of the interests of men of the Ulster Division who may become prisoners of war.

I understand from Lady Richardson's letter that another Committee, called the 'Irish Women's Association', is working in the same direction.

I presume that both Committees have the same aims, that is, the amelioration of the lot of prisoners of war.

I gather the Irish Women's Association is desirous of helping <u>all</u> Irish soldiers, whereas the Ulster Women's Gift Fund wishes to confine its work to the Ulster Division.

Lady Richardson asks that Commanding Officers shall appoint the latter Committee as the Official Fund for dealing with prisoners of war of their units.

In a matter of this kind, involving what appears to be a discrimination between two Committees, both presumably activated by the same public spirit and both apparently anxious to help Irish soldiers, it seems desirable to avoid any public action which could offend.

I should be greatly surprised if any C.O. in the Division were to express publicly an opinion on this question without ascertaining my views.

At present I have no views on the subject and have had no communication from any source in reference to the matter.

No decision is therefore possible, but you can assure Lady Richardson that when I am put in possession of the information on which to come to a decision, I shall be ready to decide in accordance with what I consider to be the interests of the Ulster Division after ascertaining the views of Commanding Officers.

SP, D/1633/1/1/177

37
Nugent to his wife

[Holograph] [Acheux]
25 February 1916

I suspected the question of the Committee to look after prisoners of war would come up at your Committee. I heard from Belfast and also from the Duchess of Abercorn asking me to approve of the Ulster Committee or Lady Carson's looking after our prisoners of war and not Lady MacDonnell's Committee.

It would have seemed quite natural, but that at the same [*sic*] I got other letters from Ulster ladies abusing Lady MacDonnell and her Committee and saying what a dreadful thing it would be for her Committee to look after our prisoners of war. I must say that made me thoroughly angry. What does it matter so long as they are doing good whether a Committee is composed of Nationalists or Unionists. Why should we out here be asked to take sides in such a dispute. D—n politics while the war lasts and at all times in the Army. I wrote however very politely and said that as I understood Lady MacDonnell's Committee had already been officially recognised, I thought it would be treading on delicate ground to ask us out here to disavow a Committee formed to help Irish soldiers without distinction. I thought our action would be open to criticism and that I had asked COs to express no opinions until I had consulted with them. I declined of course to express any preference myself but ended with the suggestion that the D of A's Committee should obtain official recognition and I would then gladly leave it to COs to select which of the 2 Committees, if any, they would select to look after their prisoners' interests.

I purposely did not tell you this before so that you could say you knew nothing of my views and that I had not told you. That is how the matter stands at present. It is rather pitiful and I daresay Lady MacDonnell is as much to blame as the other side, but that is no reason why we should have to join in.

FC, D/3835/E/2/8

38
Nugent to his wife

[Holograph] [Acheux]
26 February 1916

The German attack on Verdun seems really a serious affair, but this weather won't help the Germans and will enormously add to their casualties as the wounded left out in the snow and blizzard must die, poor brutes.

I have to shoot a man of this Division tomorrow morning I'm sorry to say.[34] He deserted from the trenches. We don't actually shoot them in presence of their battalion but the battalion is formed up and the crime and sentence read out and then the man is led away behind a house and shot. The battalion hear the shots but don't actually see the shooting . . .

Entre nous, I am rather sorry to see Mrs Russell is on the Comforts Committee, because I do not think he will remain on my Staff. He is not really a soldier, but a courtier, most charming and so forth, but now the time is coming when I must have a really good Staff Officer. It did not matter while we were behind, but it must come I am afraid soon that I shall have to tell him and it will be awkward for her. I want to try and get him a job on the Army or GHQ Staff more suited to him.

He would be excellent as a Liaison Officer with the French army. I am really sorry and hate having to tell him but what can do [*sic*].

FC, D/3835/E/2/8

39
Nugent to his wife

[Holograph] [Acheux]
6 March 1916

I am taking over some fresh trenches on the other side of a river and went to look at them.[35] Very interesting trenches they are. They are for the most part in a wood and run up to the top of a ridge from which one gets a wonderful fine view over the German lines to the North. I could see into the German trenches in some places and even see the Boches working behind the lines, but too far off to shoot at them with a rifle. They will be rather pleasant interesting lines in spring when the leaf is out and we shall be very much better concealed from the German view there than we are now. Some parts of the new line are much exposed all the same and will want a lot of repairing. It has been a good deal shelled and the winter has not helped to repair it.

When we got back to Acheux, I found an unpleasant surprise because the Boches had suddenly taken it into their heads to shell us and we got back to my Chateau with an occasional shell bursting only about 200 yards off. I don't think they were trying to shell the Chateau nor the village, but one of the balloons which has its roosting place in an old quarry beside one of the Chateau woods and which must be quite visible from the air. We have had several German aeroplanes over quite recently and no doubt they spotted it, so if the Germans do this sort of frightfulness again we will be obliged to move the balloon.

FC, D/3835/E/2/9

40
Capt W. B. Spender to his wife

[Holograph] [Acheux]
10 March 1916

I really think Lady R[ichardson]'s committee has made the most appalling mess of things, and yours not much better over the prisoners of war. Why on earth you could not have said that the Ulster W[omen's] G[ift] F[und] had been dealing with prisoners from Ulster since Jan 15 and that Lady M[acdonnell] had come in and got official recognition in Jan [1916] the whole thing would have been as clear as it is now involved. Your 2 committees by not having taken steps to get properly registered have of course made a mess of things, but this would have been made absolutely all right if all the facts had been promptly stated. I wish to goodness you had not written to the Genl but let the Duchess or better still Mrs Nugent carry on . . .

Am just back from the trenches – my peaceful wood of the other day – quite another place today as it was being heavily shelled, and I arrived just after the orderly room dugout had been pretty well riddled with bits of high explosive and the window blown in. All the time I was there loud explosions were constantly occurring and I passed trees cut in half and uprooted. None were near me at all, but it spoilt the effect of the woods.

SP, D/1633/1/1/194

41
Nugent to his wife

[Holograph] [Acheux]
19 March 1916

You really must be very careful how you even breathe that you would rather I commanded a regular Division. The good people of Ulster think it is the highest honour that can befall a human being to command this Division. It was discussed all over Ulster whether I was really fit for the honour, not so much whether I was a soldier but whether I was sound in politics . . .

I saw such a pretty fight in the air today between one of our small scouts and a big German. The German was manoeuvring against another of ours and the scout came up behind and above him and then dived at him. The German did not apparently see him till he was close on him and then threw up his tail and dived for his lines with the scout after him, firing at him, but in the end it was rather like the small dog rushing at a big dog, the small machine seemed to recollect that it had business elsewhere and suddenly turned and went away. There were a tremendous lot of machines up today. A warm spring day. I saw Palm out today and primroses and bees. Think what the smell must be like at Verdun. Nothing like primroses there.

FC, D/3835/E/2/9

42
Nugent to his wife

[Holograph] [Acheux]
23 March 1916

I spent the morning crawling about as near as I could get to the Germans, reconnoitring ground over which we may eventually have to attack and in the afternoon I went to a demonstration of gas and liquid flame by the Chemical experts of the Army. It was interesting to see the very form of attack we had to experience at Hooge. It was most alarming to see the great sheet of flame sweep over the trenches and yet the men in the trench were perfectly safe so long as they sat on the bottom, because the flame cannot descend. If my men in the 41st Bde had only known last July and not tried to bolt from it, a good many lives would have been saved.

FC, D/3835/E/2/9

43
Nugent to his wife

[Holograph] [Acheux]
25 March 1916

I wrote to the D[uchess] of A[bercorn] and told her I had no objection to any battalions which wished to do so, asking her Committee to look after their prisoners of war. I wanted to make sure of my ground before I wrote and so was making inquiries as to the procedure out here. I was not going to be made a catspaw myself nor allow the Division to become one to scratch Lady MacDonnell.

The Belfast Committee wrote and talked of Lady MacD's interference with the Ulster Division, by sending comforts to some of our men who were prisoners of war.

I wrote back quite straight and said I did not regard Lady MacD's act as 'interference' but as a kindly act and that I would welcome any such acts from whatever source they came and I deprecated any suggestion of unworthy motives for any act of kindness done to prisoners of war. I hope they liked it. They are a narrow intolerant lot up there and I don't like them . . .

Funny about Squiffy. I should say his illness was possibly not unconnected with drink. Heavens! Fancy a drunken Prime Minister in wartime, but I believe Pitt used to drink to [*sic*]. I inspected my new Hdqrs this morning so poky and at present unclean to a degree but before we go there, I will send a party to clean the place out thoroughly.

We are getting a lot of new Divisions some from one place and some from another, but not a word of this, so we have to crowd up. I am unlucky as I have not got a village with a single decent house in it.

FC, D/3835/E/2/9

44
Nugent to his wife

[Holograph] [Harponville]
4 April 1916

Russell left today. I was really sorry for him. He felt it so much and said when he left that he was so sorry he had failed me. He promised to go and see you but I daresay he will feel it to be awkward. However he is going home to take up an appointment in the London District and that is all you should know. I would not say 'I'm so sorry you have become ungummed' when you meet him.

The Germans seem to have got some new guns up. They were shelling our front line pretty badly today with larger shells than I have seen or heard since I was at Ypres . . .

My new Staff Officer vice Russell is a man called Place an RE officer.[36] He comes tomorrow. I hope he will be a success.

FC, D/3835/E/2/9

45
Capt W. B. Spender to his wife

[Holograph] [Harponville]
7 April 1916

There was another scoup [*sic*] attack last night, and again our men played up and the enemy failed to get in tho' it was our weakest unit – you can guess which I mean[37] – I believe they did well. For the 4th (?5th) time the huns failed with us but succeeded in the next Division.[38] I'm afraid our men will not be altogether sorry as the next Division treated us with 'marked discourtesy'. They are known as the 'incomparables'. The GOC when they came offered to send up some of our experienced officers to teach them the line they were taking over and which we had held. Their GOC gladly accepted so our officers went up. They arrived at the front line about m.night and were sent straight back with the retort 'I don't think we have anything to learn from a 6 months' division'.

SP, D/1633/1/1/209

46
Nugent to his wife

[Holograph] [Harponville]
18 April 1916

I do hope Sir E Carson will be successful today in forcing the Government to do its duty,[39] but I do not think we shall ever win the war so long as the present govt is in office. No one can have any confidence in them. We are 3 months too late. There are no men coming in and the men enlisted now cannot be ready till next year, so another year has been wasted.

It makes everybody out here simply mad to know how our chances are being frittered away by miserable politicians in England.

I see President Wilson is going to write another note to Germany. He ought to be careful. He will get writer's cramp if he writes so much . . .

I don't think the Germans are likely to move on this front while we have a strong line and while they are pretty fully occupied at Verdun. All the same I think no troops but Germans and no General Staff but the German would have persisted as they have for 2 months against such terrific losses.

At any rate I sincerely hope we shan't be asked to try. I don't think we could do it and it would mean wiping out whole Divisions, as we all hope it has done with the Germans.

FC, D/3835/E/2/9

47
Nugent to his wife

[Holograph] [Harponville]
19 April 1916

I think matters are really critical at home. There are no recruits and unless we get universal service we shan't have them and we must be beaten in the end. Sir W Robertson is a very strong man and if he is backed up by Lord K[itchener], as I am sure he is, even the present cabinet must I hope give way, but they ought then to resign. A government which does not believe in a measure which they bring in, in response to pressure, is sure to make a bad measure of it.

People must be losing confidence in the Government, I should hope. I know we have out here.

I think the present cabinet ought to be driven out. If we only had a strong King. Now would be his time.

I go to my new Hdqrs tomorrow. Shan't be sorry, this is a smelly little place. I am putting one of my Brigadiers into it.

FC, D/3835/E/2/9

48
Nugent to his wife

[Holograph] [Hedauville]
6 May 1916

Here I am back again at the dreary round after such a lovely and peaceful 8 days [leave]. You can't imagine how I loved my time nor how hard it was to return again to this. Everything was perfect, house and family and it was peace. The train from Charing X was packed as it was the Bombay Express as well and full of all sorts of people, but mostly soldiers.

It was a flat calm going over and we were escorted by a destroyer all the way over. I noticed that all ships crossing were escorted now, so I suppose the Admiralty think there may be German submarines about. The car was waiting and I got back to my Hdqrs at 5.30 pm last night. There was a raid by the Division next to us on the German lines and as usually happens we got a lot of shelling and had 9 men killed and about 20 wounded. I do grudge those sort of losses, just sitting in the trenches and doing nothing, but it has to be incurred.

I found rather an atmosphere of friction going on between one of the Brigades and Division headquarters and I had to take a rather decided line in saying that unmannerly letters must not be written to Division Hdqrs.

You never saw a country so changed in 8 days as this. When I left it was early spring, hardly any green and cold and raw. Yesterday the whole country has burst into early summer, hedges and trees all clothed in green and the fields green everywhere. I rode today and it seemed so monstrous to think of men killing each other when all nature is busy in reproducing and the sun shining and the air soft and warm.

FC, D/3835/E/2/9

49
Nugent to his wife

[Holograph] [Hedauville]
8 May 1916

This is a typical May day. It began warm, then rained and got very cold. I had a ride this morning while watching one of my brigades do a tactical exercise. Then after lunch went round the trenches in the wood, a good deal of shelling going on today. The leaf is so thick that some parts of the woods in which my lines are is quite dark. They are useful cover from view if no protection against shells and the Boche is not so apt to fire shells where he can't observe their effect.

One of my battalions, Colonel Ricardo's, is making a raid tonight on the German trenches about midnight. I hope it will be successful. It is not a big affair. It will begin with half an hour's bombardment of the German trenches to which they will of course reply and there will be a serious disturbance and at a certain moment to which everyone's watch will be set, a party which had previously crept out of our trenches and lain down in front of the German trenches will make a rush. We hope the bombardment will have driven the Germans into their dugouts and if our men get in quick they will catch them before they come out again and either make them surrender or bomb them in the dugouts. Then they will come away with any prisoners they get and get back to our lines as quickly as possible before the German artillery can turn on them. If successful it should be done with very little loss. If the Germans are ready and our Artillery does not prepare the way for us effectively it will be a failure and we shall probably lose a number of men.

I shan't go to sleep until I hear the result. I went over this afternoon to wish him good luck. Of course he will not go out himself as it is only a small raid. It has all been very carefully rehearsed and all the plans were settled before I came home the other day but I would not allow it to be carried out in my absence in case of unforeseen contingencies happening.

FC, D/3835/E/2/9

50
Nugent to his wife

[Holograph] [Hedauville]
9 May 1916

We had a truly strenuous night and I am sorry to say a good many casualties. Our raid was extremely successful, but the Germans chose the same night for making a raid themselves in another part of the line held by the Division next door to us and on the part of it which actually touches my line. The Germans were bombarding and we were doing the same.

My raiding party got out first, got into the German trenches just in the nick of time. The Germans had taken cover in their dugouts during their [*sic*] bombardment and when that was lifted to let our raiding party go forward the Germans came out of their dugouts. We met them as the men jumped into the trenches and the occupants of 6 dugouts were promptly attacked and driven back into their dugouts where we kept them while a very brisk fight took place outside in the trench between our men and the Germans. We got the best of this temporarily but as the Germans were evidently on the alert and were bound to outnumber us before long, the officer in command decided to deal with the Germans who were bottled up in the dugouts and then clear out. He summoned them to surrender and come out, but they hesitated and anyhow didn't accept the invitation so he ordered them to be bombed in the dugouts. This was done and shrieks and groans resounded through the midnight. They continued to bomb the Germans until all sounds of life ceased and then withdrew. We believe we bagged between 50 and 60 as there were 8 to 10 men in each dugout.

The raiding party had 1 man killed and 1 wounded in the raid. Then unfortunately instead of clearing off back to our lines at once, they halted in a sunken road to count numbers and before they got away the Germans opened a tremendous bombardment of the road and we had 9 men killed and 22 wounded. Eventually they all got back bringing their dead and wounded with them.[40]

Then the Germans attacked on the other side of the wood and we had to send men up to help the Dorsets who were being hard pressed. The Germans got in there and were driven out again, but the Dorsets lost 25 killed and 35 wounded and we lost 19 killed and 69 wounded, but we killed a good many Germans. I went round this morning, the wood is tremendously battered and big trees are lying about everywhere, trenches flattened out and wire cut to pieces. A good few German dead lying about outside. It was the biggest small affair we have had hitherto and the Division did very well indeed.

What a contrast between such a life and the conditions of only 4 days ago when I was with you.

FC, D/3835/E/2/9

51
Nugent to his wife

[Holograph] [Hedauville]
10 May 1916

I see Redmond has had the audacity to complain in the House that the executions in Dublin are causing dissatisfaction in Ireland which is about the coolest piece of cynical impertinence I have heard for a long time. I suppose however that Asquith will give in and the remainder of the rebel leaders will go unscathed.

Douglas Haig is coming here tomorrow. I invited him to lunch but was told that he never lunched with Divisional commanders. Tut! too small fry, I suppose.

I was round the part of the line which was so heavily strafed the other day. It is in a desperate condition, trees lying over the trenches, smashed to pieces by shell fire and most of my trenches knocked flat, a lot of work to get them in proper trim again . . .

The French paysan is rather wonderful. They have got their fields tilled and cropped right up to our rear trenches, but they are illogical sort of people because they come and complain because we ride over them or march or drive over them as of course we have to do. We pay very heavy compensation so possibly that is why they grow crops where no crops have much chance of coming up.

I do so much wonder if there is any chance of Ireland being made to come into the Compulsory Service Act. I am afraid not and I do not particularly trust the Ulster members in the matter any more than the Nationalists. I am sure there will be no strength of purpose in Squiffy and his following.

FC, D/3835/E/2/9

52
Nugent to his wife

[Holograph] [Hedauville]
11/12 May 1916

Douglas Haig, Com. in Chief came today and spent some time in talking over eventualities. I rode this morning and again this afternoon, no rain and not so cold.

We invited the owner of this house and his wife to dinner tonight. It was terribly boring as I had one on each side and I flapped away in broken winged French and had to choose topics to talk about that I knew the French for.

It wasn't a very good dinner. Our French-Brazilian cook has left and the Wilson Line ship's cook is in possession and he is very starchy indeed. You might fire his pastry as shells and they would be most effective.

General Hickman who is one of my Brigadiers told the C in C that he thought he could be more useful as a member of Parliament at home than in command of a Brigade out here. He is a member. The C. in Chief said 'If I were you, I should put no obstacle in his way of returning to his parliamentary duties'. I told him I certainly would not and it would be such a relief to me to get rid of him without having to push him out. He will be the last of the politicians. I like him personally but I shall be glad to be quit of him.

FC, D/3835/E/2/9

53
Nugent to his wife

[Holograph] [Hedauville]
14 May 1916

It has been such a cold raw day today. I have taken a rest from trenches and inspections but spent the whole day at my table instead, not much of a change.

Poor wretched Dublin, what a country and what a people. The man who ought to be shot is Birrell.[41] He is as directly responsible for the destruction and murders as if he had planned them. Weak miserable buffoon. I hear a battalion of my reserve brigade came down from Belfast and were rather happy in having the chance of meeting their natural enemies.[42]

FC, D/3835/E/2/9

54
Nugent to his wife

[Holograph] [Hedauville]
16 May 1916

There was a tremendous bombardment last night just on our left. The night was very still and clear and it sounded terrific. It began about 12.30 am. I thought it was in our lines and jumped out of bed and rushed to the window, but when I watched the flashes for a while I was satisfied that it was just north of us and so went to bed again and went to sleep. It made this house absolutely rattle. We heard this morning that the Division on our left had been attacked. The Boches got into the trenches and took away some prisoners. I expect they will have a go at us before long. They owe us one.

Arthur came back yesterday, poor old fellow, he looked so white and sad.[43] On the whole I think it is best for him to be at work again with a change of scene. We had a long walk round the trenches this morning which were horribly muddy after all the rain.

Today has been beautifully fine and hot and there have been a lot of aeroplanes up and a lot of bombarding of them. The Germans do not come over our lines very much now and when they do come are generally driven back by anti-aircraft guns. Our men are constantly over the German lines and we do lose men and machines more than the Germans do, but that is inevitable as they are more enterprising than the Germans.

FC, D/3835/E/2/9

55
Nugent to his wife

[Holograph] [Hedauville]
22 May 1916

I have had such an interesting experience. I have thought for a long time that I would like to know much more of the German lines than I do, so today I went over them in an aeroplane. I had decided to do so some days ago but I did not tell you lest you should be jumpy. It was the most interesting experience.

The actual flying was nothing. I confess to being in a blue funk when I got into the machine and for the first minute while we were rising, afterwards I got so interested I never thought about being in the air. We went up to 7000 feet and we cruised up and down the line. I am sure every Divisional General ought to go up and see his own lines and the German lines in front of him.

I had a fright once. I wanted to look down into a wood which I hold and I waved my hand towards it. My pilot turned in the required direction and as I did not think of waving to him to go round after I had seen what I wanted he went on and I suddenly realised we were well behind the German lines and still going on, I frantically waved to him to turn and retreated back over our lines. He thought I wanted to make an excursion into the German territory.

I don't think they fired at us, but there is such a row in the air between the roar of the wind and the noise of the engine that I don't think one would know if the Germans were firing at the aeroplane unless one actually saw the shell burst or got hit. Being in the air is exactly like looking down on to a coloured map.

It did not make me in the least giddy. The most interesting thing is to note how we show ourselves and the Germans seem to conceal everything. The roads behind our lines were full of motors, and men and constant movement whereas in the German area one could see no sign of anyone moving.

The country does not look nearly so green from above as it does on the ground, because one sees the brown earth through the grass when looking down from a height.

There was nothing in the sensation of flying particularly exciting, possibly I was too much occupied to think of it, but it made my ears and head ache coming down so rapidly from a height to the earth again.

FC, D/3835/E/2/9

56
Nugent to his wife

[Holograph] [Hedauville]
26 May 1916

I don't think it is worth worrying yet about whether it would be safe to go to F[arren] C[onnell] or not in the summer. No one is able to take a proper view of the situation as yet because it is not sufficiently cleared up. I would not set too much value on old Neills' opinion.[44] He is oldish and his nerves are probably a bit shaken and he has always spoken in much the same way. Most North of Ireland men look upon the RCs and the South of Ireland in much the same way as Neills does and think they are hankering to go out and kill a protestant. One should remember that the rebellion was confined to the worst elements of Sinn Feiners and Dublin roughs. It was reprobated by the decent majority of Nationalists and as far as our part is concerned, the Sinn Fein movement has not taken hold. Before deciding however one way or the other, I will write to the Resident Mag[istra]te

Walker and ask him. He will know the conditions in the country and will be able to say just what they are. My own impression is it would be just as safe as at any time but I would not act on my impressions in such a case. There is really plenty of time to let things settle down and enable people to get a clear perspective. We have to remember that the late rebellion was practically confined to Dublin. I would not for the world that you should go home and feel a strain all the time.

FC, D/3835/E/2/9

57
Nugent to his wife

[Holograph] [Hedauville]
28 May 1916

I had no time to write yesterday as I was out all day going around trenches. Fine and a cold wind. Henry one of my ADCs went for a fly today and enjoyed himself much and was fired on by the Germans which he enjoyed less. I could not help feeling once when I was flying the other day, Suppose the pilot fainted or was killed, what could I do. I could only sit and wait. However he wasn't killed and didn't faint.

Well I wonder what Lloyd George will make of the Irish situation. It is the chance which may never occur again, but I have no confidence. The Ulstermen may reasonably say that Redmond and his party have proved that they have no real influence in Ireland and are not entitled to speak for their side. I am afraid the two parties are too fundamentally wide apart for any human being to bring them together.

What Ireland wants is Government, real Government.

Sir Wullie Robertson turned up yesterday. He was travelling to Paris to meet Joffre and he came to see me and stopped to tea . . .

FC, D/3835/E/2/9

58
Nugent to his wife

[Holograph] [Hedauville]
1 June 1916

I wonder if anyone seriously supposes that we shall be able to drive the Germans out of France, Belgium and Poland by force of arms. If they do they misread current events. The Germans have been hammering at the French at Verdun for 100 days today and have expended tens of thousands of men and what have they done. We shall never sacrifice life in the way the Germans do and we are not likely to be more successful than they have been. The combined pressure of the naval blockade and the Allied armies may do the business. There is such grave doubt in people's minds whether the Navy is being allowed to exert its full powers in blockade . . .

I shall be curious to hear if your Committee refers to Lady MacDonnell's gift of £500 to this Division and if so in what terms. I daresay some of them would like me to send it back with a letter to say that I scorned to take money from a Nationalist woman . . .

My parsons give me some annoyance. The Presbyterians and the Church of Ireland chaplains will not coalesce as they ought. I had to talk to them so I hope to see an improvement.

FC, D/3835/E/2/9

59
Nugent to his wife

[Holograph] [Hedauville]
3 June 1916

I have a raid coming off shortly and was at a rehearsal of it this morning. Such a variety of weapons that we never dreamed of 2 years ago. The party will be armed with rifles, daggers, bombs, hatchets, bludgeons studded with nails and a spike at each end to help prisoners along, handcuffs and ropes. They will all wear steel breast and back shields and steel helmets. It's a curious war and the latest from Verdun is not too reassuring . . . Arthur has been allowed to go home and advise Lloyd George how to settle Ireland! I say they ought to send for me too. I know as much and more about Ireland than Arthur does. I expect they really want to get the Ulster members of both houses together for a consultation as all my Ulster MPs have been sent for, by way of advising Ll George, which is of course nonsense. He can't want to consult them all so I suspect it is really Carson has got them sent for to support him.

I wonder if we shall get a settlement. I fear not. I do not see how two such incompatible ideals as Nationalist and Ulsterist can ever be brought into harmony. But oh what a blessing it would be to feel that we could return to our homes in peace. I dread the prospect of returning to the welter of Home Rule politics after this.

Hot sun and cold wind today. Morland the Corps Commander was so fired by my example that he too went up for an aeroplane reconnaissance yesterday and was much pleased with himself. Not half so frightened as he thought he would be.

FC, D/3835/E/2/9

60
Capt W. B. Spender to his wife

[Holograph] [Hedauville]
3 June 1916

Your news is most disquieting.[45] I could not have believed it would have been possible that many whom we know would have been ready to sacrifice their pledged word. Solemn covenants, old principles, calls of patriotism all count for nothing . . .

I would give a great deal – even my Military Cross!! ye gods – to get home for 2 days and speak out. I should not have many so-called friends left afterwards, but I do not think they are worth retaining . . . I am almost glad that I have no son to see the downfall of the Empire which is sinking through inertia, and whose decay will not even be delayed by the wholesome surgery of this great war.

Douglas[46] said to me last night, before we heard any rumour of this betrayal, the boys intend to wake up the Falls road when they get back. I shall not raise a finger to restrain them. One's only hope now as far as I can see is Devlin[47] who may yet save one from one's friends. What a splendid victory for the Sinn Fein martyrs, who will have died not in vain indeed for they will have won their cause. Apparently their power of self sacrifice was greater than ours.

SP, D/1633/1/1/295

61
Nugent to his wife

[Holograph] [Hedauville]
4 June 1916

The news is bad everywhere. The losses in the North Sea are very serious compared to what we seem to have inflicted.[48] I fear it will have a very bad effect upon neutrals.

I suppose we shall not be allowed to hear what really happened and will get nothing more definite than rumours . . .

Comyn of my staff had a letter from an uncle in Ireland today. He says the Inspector RIC who took Asquith to Richmond Prison in Dublin to visit the rebels who were awaiting trial, told him that Asquith shook hands warmly with the rebels and absolutely took no notice of the soldiers or RIC who were there. He inquired from the murderers and Sinn Feiners most solicitously after their comfort and then turned round to the Inspector and asked how they were being fed. He replied 'Precisely the same rations as the Military get' whereupon Asquith ordered their food be improved at once. It is inconceivable but the authority for the statement seems authentic. Fancy such a man being responsible for the government of Great Britain and Ireland . . .

The Germans scored off us last night. There was a raid on their trenches by the Division on our left and when they got into the German trenches after an hour's heavy bombardment, they found absolutely no one there, not even a piece of string. The Boches had simply retired out of reach and we spent an immense amount of ammunition to no purpose. When the raiding party returned to their own trenches, the Germans quietly came back to theirs.

FC, D/3835/E/2/9

62
Nugent to his wife

[Holograph] [Hedauville]
6 June 1916

We had a successful raid last night carried out by the 12th R Irish Rifles of this Division.[49] We got into the German trenches and found the Germans had retired all except 3 men who bolted into a tunnel. They were followed up some way, but the tunnel went on down into the earth towards our lines and I suppose the party who were going down it did not like the idea of being buried in the earth if the Boches suddenly came back, so they went no further and the tunnel was blown in.

The party then blew up all the dugouts they could find, including an officer's. I inquired how they knew it was an officer's and the answer was because it was hung with highly improper photographs. No doubt it must have been a <u>German</u> officer's residence.

The party had gone out well supplied with high explosives because I suspected that the trenches might be found deserted, as a raid of another Division nearby 2 or 3 days before had found the Germans all gone and I determined to do all the harm I could if I couldn't get any Boches. I am sorry they did not explore the shaft further as I have suspected mining towards my trenches, but the mining expert said there was no mining going on, but events have shown he was wrong.

I heard from one of my Colonels, who came back yesterday from Ireland that Carson is to have a meeting of the Unionist Council in Belfast and that he is sincerely anxious to find a solution but that the extremists of the Unionist Party in the North of Ireland will probably throw him over if he proposes any compromise. I must say I see no hope. If Redmond gives way the Nationalists would throw him over and the whole business would get into the hands of the extremists on both sides.

I always maintained that the physical force movement was a mistake and the arming of Ulster a still greater mistake. It gave the other side a lead and now neither side will disarm and we have no government strong enough to enforce disarmament.

I hear James Craig told Colonel Ricardo that he had no time to talk about recruiting, but the H[ome] R[ule] question must be settled first. He ought to be shot if that is true.

FC, D/3835/E/2/9

63
General Sir William Robertson to Sir Edward Carson

[Holograph] War Office
7 June 1916

There is no intention of breaking up the Ulster Division, and I hope there never will be. I do not think there will be. There is some difficulty regarding the provision of drafts, and on this question the Adjutant-General hopes to see you very shortly. I saw the division about a fortnight ago. It was looking very well and, as might be expected, has a very good esprit de corps.[50]

I am a little anxious just now, as you can imagine, with regard to the successor to Lord Kitchener. The selection of a suitable successor is a very important matter.

Carson Papers, D/1507/A/17/10

64
Nugent to his wife

[Holograph] [Hedauville]
8 June 1916

Yesterday afternoon we heard the news of the tragedy of the *Hampshire*.[51] It is a tragedy indeed. 'K'[itchener] was such a personality and one feels that there was not lately the loyalty to him that was his due. He no doubt made many mistakes, but it was he who realised at the beginning what this war was going to be and who taught the country to think in vast numbers. He was a great man and a very great loss to the Empire. What I cannot help thinking is that the Germans may have known by some means or other. It cannot be only a coincidence. I think so important a mission should never have been allowed to go in a ship unattended by another. If there had been a 2nd ship, K might have been saved and most of the crew too perhaps.

I suppose the politicians will fight over his vacant chair now. I think Lord Milner would be a good man but no doubt Lloyd George will claim it. At any rate I hope it will not be our Winston. I think the public would not stand that . . .

I hear the Irish question is to be settled by the exclusion of Ulster, except Cavan, Monaghan and Donegal, but that Devlin insists on the whole of Ulster being excluded or none and it is Craig and the politicians of Belfast who want now to cut out those 3 counties because they realise as Devlin does that if they are included in Ulster, there is a very good chance of a Nationalist majority in Ulster which would certainly not help the solution of the Irish Question.

The solution whatever it is will not settle anything and won't give any peace to Ireland.

Ricardo says it was touch and go whether the whole of nationalist Ireland rose the other day. If things had gone well with them at first they would have done so. Now it is probably about settled down but a little more shooting wouldn't do them any harm.

FC, D/3835/E/2/9

65
Nugent to his wife

[Holograph] [Hedauville]
9 June 1916

I believe the Irish question will be settled by excluding all Ulster except Cavan, Monaghan and Donegal and the Belfast people won't hesitate to chuck us over. I see Arthur spoke against excluding Cavan but what is the use of talking about it. It won't stop it if the Belfast people want us to be handed over in order to save themselves. The only thing that is certain is that it will not satisfy the nationalists.[52]

FC, D/3835/E/2/9

66
Nugent to his wife

[Holograph]

[Hedauville]
10 June 1916

I hear from Arthur that it is definitely decided to bring in H[ome] R[ule] at once, to exclude Ulster, except Cavan, Monaghan and Donegal, so you and I may as well join the Sinn Feiners at once.

The situation at Verdun is supposed to be very critical. The French are weakening and we may have to move very soon to help them. Meanwhile Russia seems to be doing well and to be making quite a good bag of Austrians, but Austrians are not the same as Germans. Still one does hope they are losing pretty heavily too. I am afraid they have inflicted pretty heavy losses on us at Ypres. I wonder what that attack was done for. Possibly to see if we had moved a lot of men away from Ypres to other parts of the line, or to make us think they were going to make their big effort there.

They are wily people and don't as a rule do things without an object . . .

I have just been to a lecture this afternoon by an officer of Rycroft's Division who had the extraordinary luck to be staying on the *St Vincent* and was in the naval battle.[53] The fleet sailed, ¼ of an hour after he got on board. He did not see a great deal as the haze was very thick, but he saw the *Defence* blown up and saw the *Marlborough* hit by a German torpedo and he saw 2 German battleships being knocked to pieces, one of which he saw sink but not the 2nd.

My trenches were raided last night by the Germans on a part of my line. They levelled them flat and then attacked with infantry.

We beat them off. 5 men reached the front line but never actually got in. We had 65 casualties however, including 3 officers 2 of whom were killed and the 3rd is dying I am afraid . . .[54]

I gather that if our battle fleet had been an hour earlier on the scene, it might have got the whole German fleet. We have no luck, but the Germans did not wait and small blame to them . . .

The lecturer, a Major Wallace, today said that when the whole of the 12" guns of the *St Vincent* were fired together as they do, it was like nothing that could be described. The whole of your inside rubs up against each other, it knocks men down and absolutely flattens you out. The wind of the concussion is like a hurricane.

I have taken to a steel helmet now for my journeys in the trenches as the shelling is getting so persistent. Formerly one could generally count on the Germans doing nothing out of their ordinary practice but lately they have taken to shelling at all hours.

FC, D/3835/E/2/9

67
Nugent to his wife

[Holograph] [Hedauville]
17/18 June 1916

Arthur tells me that Somerset Saunderson would like to come very much, but I am not so sure that I should find him suit me. He is a restless sort of person full of fancies and can be very unpleasant, also I do not know how he would like the constant work which never gives a man a minute to himself.[55]

I should like to have an Ulsterman and a man from Cavan but I have grave doubts of Somerset being the man.

Fine today but cold. I spent the morning in the place partly underground and partly above ground where in case we make an attack from our present trenches, one of my staff will watch its progress and telephone a report of it to me. It is cunningly concealed in a lot of chalk with two slits inside a steel box through which one looks and down in the bowels of the earth is the little place where the telephone operator sits, fairly safe from shells I should say.

18th. We have some of the French 75s here with us now, most wonderful queer . . .[56]

Somerset is really anxious to come, Arthur says, and told him to tell me that I might try him and if he didn't suit I could send him home. Rather touching of him. I won't make up my mind about him yet . . .

Arthur showed me a letter from Somerset in which he said he'd been to see Walter Long[57] and WL told him Lloyd George had told Carson that the Cabinet were decided about Ireland whereas they had never even been consulted and the Unionists were astounded at Carson's speech in Belfast, in which he told Ulster Unionists that they must make up their minds to accept what they could get. Carson seems to have been completely fooled by Ll G who had no authority to offer anything apparently. I thought the man was growing honest. I think Carson must have lost some of his mental power.

FC, D/3835/E/2/9

68
Nugent to his wife

[Holograph] [Hedauville]
23 June 1916

I hoped to be back from the trenches in time to write a longer letter to you than yesterday, but I got caught up in a regular water spout while I was out. I never saw such a downpour. In 3 minutes I was absolutely drenched to the boxes. The rain beat the mud off the top of the trenches so that it came over us in a shower of mud and water. You never saw such a sight as we were. It was pretty weird, because there was a thunderstorm at the same time and it turned very dark, a regular tornado of wind blew at the same time stripping leaves and branches off the trees in the wood and between the wind and the darkness and the thunder and the bursting of our shells and German shells and the noise of the guns on both sides, it was about as stirring an afternoon as I have had, a fitting prelude.

The men of the Ulster Division are as fit and as keen as men can be. There will be no hanging back on their part I'm very sure when the hour strikes . . .

I don't suppose Sir E C[arson] can make any use of the story about Asquith and the Sinn Feiners, but I don't think the British public would quite appreciate it. Asquith's excuse would be that in this crisis in our affairs we must do nothing to create new enemies and apparently he was and is very much afraid of American opinion.

FC, D/3835/E/2/9

69
Nugent to his son St George

[Holograph] [Hedauville]
27 June 1916

I was so pleased to read in one of your letters to Mummy that you had been doing really good work at cricket.

It was really a good performance to make runs in 2 innings and take 5 wickets as well. Tip top! You will be a cricketer yet. I have not flown again as there has been no need for it, but we made two very successful raids on the German lines, one last night and one that we did about a fortnight ago. That was very thorough though we unfortunately got no prisoners. A rather over-zealous Engineer officer went out on that raid with a large amount of high explosive done up in tins and though there were Germans in all the dugouts the party raided, he gave the wretched Boche no time to come out but blew them into small pieces and brought their dugouts down on top of them and buried their remains. One Boche was seen in a dug-out in which there was a candle, which the Boche had apparently forgotten to blow out. An officer went up to the window and shot him through it and then the Engineer man threw in a bomb so he was buried too. It was however important in one respect as we found a mine shaft leading under our lines, or at any rate in the direction of them with high power electric wires leading into it. The party could not explore its whole length as it was too long, but we have suspected mining for some time. Now we're pretty sure of it. We expect the Germans to touch it off any day. However we have taken precautions to minimise the results.

Last night's raid was very good. We got in and found the Germans sheltering from our bombardment in their dugouts. The men had been taught the German for 'Hands up, come out and you will be well treated' and at each dug-out they shouted this down. As a result several Germans came out and surrendered, those who didn't were bombed in the dugouts and fearful screams rent the air. We captured an officer, a sergt major and eleven privates and brought them in. We lost six men killed and seven wounded, but they were all dead and wounded brought into our lines.[58]

This afternoon I pressed the button and let off a 15" howitzer which coughs in my area. It is a most appalling roar, but nothing to the effect of the shell when that bursts. It weighs 1460 lbs and demolishes half a village at a time.

I have a crow's nest sixty odd feet up in a tree from which I can see the German lines well back behind their front line and it is there I shall be sitting one day very soon, I expect, watching through my glasses the Ulster Division in advance to the assault.

I hope your gun was just as you wanted it. Much love my son and God bless us all.

FC, D/3835/E/2/9

70
Nugent to his wife

[Holograph]

[Hedauville]
29 June 1916

Yes, dearest, it was lovely to think of you all praying for a blessing on me and my men.

I spent a long time this afternoon up my tree watching the bombardment. This morning I went round to see three of the battalions, Ricardo's and Pakenham's and Blacker's to wish them success.[59]

Bob Maxwell was wounded last night, but very slightly, a piece of shell in the shoulder. He will I hope be out again almost at once. He has gone to the nearest Field Hospital. A shell burst in the middle of a party of men starting off to the trenches, killed 14 and wounded 44. It was the worst piece of bad luck. Bob Maxwell was standing close by.[60]

What do you think of enclosed?[61] I think the men all liked it.

Good night my beloved and love to you all. You should get this letter on the 1st July. Think of us.

FC, D/3835/E/2/9

71
Nugent to his wife

[Holograph] [Hedauville]
30 June 1916

Bob Maxwell has been sent down to hospital at the base and so will be out of it. I expect he will be sent home, there is nothing the matter but a flesh wound, they won't keep anyone out here now. They must keep the hospitals clear. Mrs M will be relieved I'm sure, but it will be a great disappointment to him . . .

It has not rained now for two days and there has been a strong wind all day which has dried up the ground, so I hope weather conditions for tomorrow will be favourable.

This last 24 hours is rather trying. There is nothing to do to keep one's mind busy and we are all strung up to the highest tension.

I shall go to my tree tomorrow at 6.30 am and stay up there as long as I can see events and then go to my battle headquarters, which are dug into the side of a hill not far from the front, but from which I can see nothing. I expect to spend the night there tomorrow and I wonder where I shall be the following night. Can it be possible it may be under a tree or in a ruined village behind the German lines.

Certainly if it is possible for men to get there, mine will go.

FC, D/3835/E/2/9

72
Nugent to his wife

[Holograph] [Hedauville]
2 July 1916

Just a line to say Arthur and I and my staff are all well. Yesterday was terrible. Our losses I fear very heavy.

My dearest, the Ulster Division has been too superb for words. The whole Army is talking of the incomparable gallantry shown by officers and men. There has been nothing like it since the New Armies came out. They came out of the trenches, formed up as if on the barrack square and went forward with every line dressed as if for the King's inspection, torn from end to end by shell and machine-gun fire.[62]

We are the only Division which succeeded in doing what it was given to do and we did it but at fearful cost.

We are fighting today but we have so few men left.

I am hanging on till dark when we are to be relieved by a fresh Division for the fresh attack tomorrow.

The Ulster Division no longer exists as a fighting force and we shall probably go back behind the line to refit and be made up again in numbers. I do not know the full tale of losses yet, but think we have lost about 150 officers and about 6000 men, not all killed and in fact I hope that there are a large number of not serious wounds.

The Ulster Division has proved itself and it has indeed borne itself like men. I cannot describe to you how I feel about them. I did not believe men were made who could do such gallant work under the conditions of modern war.

The Division took nearly 600 prisoners themselves in the first rush. The Germans were absolutely cowed and flung themselves on their knees asking for mercy.

No time for more. I am very proud but very sad when I think of our terrible losses.

The 2 Divisions on our right and left failed badly and left us exposed to attack from both flanks. We could do nothing but just stick it out far in front of everyone else and we are still sticking out.

FC, D/3835/E/2/10

73
Nugent to his wife

[Holograph] [Hedauville]
3 July 1916

There is a lull on this front.

The losses of the Ulster Division are 210 officers and 5200 men, of whom I hope about 2000 will eventually rejoin us.[63]

The more one hears, the more sublime seems to have been the courage and devotion shown by the men. They simply marched straight over every obstacle, cheering each other on. Nothing could stop them.

The 29th Division on our left and the 32nd on our right which should have reached a certain line to bring our advance in harmony, failed entirely to even capture the German front lines opposite to them. The result was that the Ulster Division marching far in front over absolutely open ground was shot at from in front and from both sides. When it gained as it did the line to which it was told to go and where it was to halt, it was absolutely isolated far in advance of the whole Army without support and every man I had had been already sent forward.

The Germans then turned every gun and machine gun they had on to us and for the whole long afternoon the Division was pounded and hammered. We could get nothing up to them and they could get no messages back. Just after dark the Germans made an attack on the rear of the line we were holding. By that time the men were completely exhausted and were running out of both bombs and ammunition. Nearly all the officers were killed or wounded and we could do nothing. To have stayed out where we were without supports and with both our flanks exposed would have simply meant annihilation next day and the senior officer out in front took the responsibility of withdrawing. I don't say he was right or wrong yet. It has to be inquired into. I did not order a withdrawal, but I think it may have been the only thing to do.

The men came back just as steadily as they had gone forward and held the next line of German trenches until last night when we handed over to the 49th Division and the remnants of the Ulster Division are now behind the lines.

Anyhow nothing more has been done here. I so much fear that credit will not be given to this Division for its magnificent attack.

Nothing finer has been done in the war.

FC, D/3835/E/2/10

74
Nugent to his wife

[Holograph] [Hedauville]
4 July 1916

I assembled the remnants of 2 of my Brigades today and thanked them for the work they had done. I am going to see the other Brigade tomorrow. We are behind the lines now but these are not matters I can discuss. I enclose you the order I published to the Division last night.[64] Do you like it? One will never get to hear all the particulars but I believe there were numberless extraordinary feats of heroism performed in the course of the day or 2 days during which we were fighting. We have heard no news of what is happening along the front. At this particular point it is very quiet today, but that is how it goes at one moment quiet and at the next a terrific attack is suddenly launched. It has been very hot for the last 2 days and the dust was fearful, but it has rained most of the day.

FC, D/3835/E/2/10

75
Nugent to King George V

[Holograph] [Hedauville]
4 July 1916

Your Majesty desired me to tell you how the Ulster Division bore themselves in their first real encounter with the Germans.

That came on the 1st July. We have had several small affairs since we have been in the trenches, either raids on our part into the German lines or attempted raids on the part of the Germans. I am glad to say that whereas we have been successful in every raid we made, we have never let the Germans once get into our trenches.

The men were in splendid heart when we advanced to the attack on the 1st July although they had been living under heavy artillery fire for 5 days and had had a considerable number of casualties in the trenches.

The 1st July is the anniversary of the Battle of the Boyne and that had a special effect on the bearing of the men.

Our trenches were for the most part diagonal to the German trenches opposite and from 300 to 500 yards apart.

In order to attack square to our front, the leading lines of the attack had to come out of the wood in which our right trenches were and we had to do the same thing on the left in order to reach the German lines without changing direction after we began the advance.

Our left was separated from my centre and right by the river Ancre and about 300 yards of marshy ground.

I cannot attempt to describe in adequate terms the extraordinary gallantry and discipline displayed by every battalion in the Division.

I had a crow's nest in a tree which gave me a view over the whole of our front but the morning was foggy so I could not see, but artillery officers and other observers from a hill nearer the firing line told me that they had never believed troops could have behaved so magnificently.[65]

The moment the first line came over the parapet the German machine guns began to shoot. Notwithstanding continual casualties the men formed up outside their trenches in Noman'sland in successive lines as steadily as if they were on the barrack square.

They advanced at a walk, racked from end to end by machine gun fire and before they had got half way over the German artillery had found them. Nothing could have stopped them. On the right they carried the 1st 2nd 3rd 4th and 5th lines of German trenches and reached the objective laid down for them on the stroke of the hour at which it was thought possible they might get there. We suffered very heavy losses from machine gun fire from both flanks and in front. We captured nearly 800 prisoners, but were only able to get 550 of them back to our lines. We actually gained 2000 yards of ground to our front and all seemed well when the disappointment came that the 29th Division on our left and the 32nd Division on our right had been unable to advance in the face of the German fire and were back in their own lines again.

The effect was that the Ulster Division was isolated 2000 yards in advance of its own trenches and with both flanks in the air. The Germans soon realised the situation and from about 10 in the morning till late at night they kept a ceaseless bombardment on our lines and a cruel machine gun fire.

We could not communicate, we could get nothing up. There were no more reinforcements in the Division and most of the Officers had been knocked out and more than half the men.

There was no hope of being able to remain on without support and it was impossible to support us and so after dark we had to come back. It was a most bitter disappointment that such a gallant effort should have spent itself in vain.

Out of 240 Officers and about 9000 men that went over the parapet, only 30 Officers and 3800 were left at the end of the day.

It was a magnificent example of discipline, self devotion and courage of the highest quality.

I am sure, Sir, that you would have been satisfied with these incomparably gallant men, could you have seen their attack and their absolute disregard of personal danger.

We shall no doubt be made up again but I fear we shall never have men of such splendid qualities again.

RA, PS/GN/Q832/270

76
Nugent to his wife

[Holograph] [Hedauville]
5 July 1916

I think the Ulster Division will get their full recognition when the story of their attack is known. Everyone outside the Division is full of it. The Press Correspondents too have begun to get hold of it and the Higher Powers are beginning to realise that it was the finest thing that has been done in the whole Army engaged in the present offensive.

We don't really know half of the facts yet. Yesterday 4 of our men staggered into our lines dry with thirst and weak with want of food. They were 4 of a party of 8 men who had pushed on alone far in advance and found themselves isolated in a German trench. This was on the 1st July. They stayed on absolutely cut off till yesterday, 4 whole long days. Then having been without food or water for 2 days they determined to divide into 2 parties and try and get back and 4 of them managed to work their way through the Germans and fetched up again in our lines.

One battalion formed up in successive lines out in the open and marched up to the German trenches cheering and captured them, but when they got in there were only 40 men left.

A young officer went into a dugout and found 30 Germans in it. One man put up his rifle to shoot him but our man shot him dead and ordered the rest to put their hands up, which they did. Then as he had no men with him to send as an escort, he kicked the whole batch over the parapet and told them to go over to our lines and give themselves up, which they set out to do, but were most of them killed by their own machine gun and shell fire before they got there. Some parties of men during the advance took batches of prisoners in various trenches and as they did not know what to do with them they made them come along with them in their advance and they did, whining and pawing their captors and calling them 'Kamerad' and begging to be sent into safety. Our men were just tuned up for this day. They were inspired, the Anniversary of the Battle of the Boyne and also poor fellows they did not know what they had to face.

FC, D/3835/E/2/10

77
Sir Edward Carson to Nugent

[Typescript] London
5 July 1916

I have heard with great pride of the magnificent and heroic conduct of the Ulster Division in the fighting on Saturday, and I should like to say how deeply moved both I myself and my Ulster colleagues in the House of Commons have been at reading of their brave actions. We are of course much distressed and saddened by the knowledge of the heavy losses that must have been incurred through the fact of their being selected for an operation of great danger and difficulty and we all deeply sympathise with those who have joined the Roll of Honour or who are suffering from wounds through serving their King and Country. I have never doubted that when the moment came these brave men would be prepared for the great sacrifice, but I feel I have myself lost a great number of men whom I may say I always counted as personal friends. Perhaps you may have some opportunity of letting the Division know that I and my colleagues are thinking much of them and of the pride we feel in all they have done and suffered.

FC, D/3835/E/10/3B

78
Nugent to his wife

[Holograph] [Rubempre]
6 July 1916

We are now back to rest and rebuild in company with other shattered Divisions.

Dear old thing, I never thought the Ulster Division would fail in the hour. I was much more afraid of my failing them.

I think we did all that was humanly possible. The reasons of [*sic*] our losses were that the Divisions on our right and left failed us. We went on capturing line after line of trenches, losing more and more men at every stage and getting further and further away from support.

Then the Germans having nothing much to distract them on either side, turned all their guns and machine guns on to us and we suffered most terribly. I am so glad however to see the Times refer in its leading article so nicely to us, though the expression 'mournful admiration' is rather lugubrious.

You mustn't really have any pride overweening or otherwise in me, bless you. As Alison said of herself I am just ordinary and do my best.

You need not imagine the Correspondents allowed out here are going to tell you much. They can only write what they are allowed. It would never do to give them a free hand.

As to our movements, I can say nothing for I don't know. We may move off again at an hour's notice.

FC, D/3835/E/2/10

79
Nugent to his wife

[Holograph] [Rubempre]
8 July 1916

We have just got orders that we are to be sent off north to Belgium I fear. It is of course to enable fresh Divisions to be brought down. Most of the Divisions which have suffered severely, have already gone or are going, but how I loathe the idea of Belgium again. However it may not be Belgium because the 2nd Army to which we go holds ground in France as well as Belgium.

This bit of information must not be mentioned. Perhaps when we are rebuilt and refitted we shall be able to get back to something more exciting than Belgian mud . . .

I hope to goodness the politicians won't try and make political capital out of us. I should hate that and so should we all I think. We are quite satisfied with the knowledge that the Army and the people at home know what we have done, without politicians using us as stalking horses.

I carried out the King's command. I have written to him and told him how well we did, but I daresay he will read it in the papers.

I also heard from Sir E C[arson] today with a message of congratulations from himself and his Ulster colleagues in the H of C and asking that its contents be communicated to the troops. If you see Lady C you might tell her I got his letter and am very pleased and that I will see it is made known, but I am not going to hurry about it. I have my doubts about Sir EC now. Anyhow I think he sold us over Cavan.

FC, D/3835/E/2/10

80
Nugent to his wife

[Holograph] [Bernaville]
11 July 1916

The country has the same heavy flat look that Belgium has and I hate it and shall be glad to be out of it. I simply loathe the thought of Belgium, its dirt, trenches, flies and inhabitants.

I am greatly annoyed at my letter to Sir G Richardson being published . . . One cannot even write a private letter without having it stuffed into the papers. It is all politics of course . . .

Dearest, the question of why my Division was told to go on when the Divisions on the right and left of them failed is one of the things which will be inquired into later on, I hope. I can only say that as soon as I saw how things were going on either flank of us I wired at once that in my opinion any advance beyond a certain line would leave us dangerously exposed. The answer was, 'carry out the programme'. I could have stopped it then.

An hour later a message came approving my proposal and telling me to stop further advance but it was too late then, even if I could have got a message through.[66] People at home may imagine COs and Generals can alter or change a plan once put in operation. It is impossible. Once troops begin to move under such conditions as the Division encountered on 1st July nothing can be stopped or changed.

Nearly every messenger sent forward was either killed or wounded. We were really almost surrounded by the Germans owing to the failure of the Divisions on either side of us. We were attacked from 3 different sides and a fly could hardly have got across no-man's-land to the first line of German trenches owing to the German machine gunners and Artillery. Everything was turned on to us. Nothing but the most determined fighting enabled the remainder of the Division to be withdrawn after dark. Nothing could be done during daylight. The COs were not allowed to go forward with their men. They could have done nothing if they had and in trying to do something would all have been killed or wounded. I absolutely forbid them to go beyond Thiepval Wood. Now at any rate I have the COs to start rebuilding their battalions. They all protested when I told them, they were not to go forward, but they all realise now, they could have done nothing and they are far more valuable as live men than dead heroes.[67]

A month before the attack I had dug an exact plan of the German trenches, on the full size scale, taken from aeroplane photos, on ground behind our lines and the battalions and Brigades were practised day after day in going over them. Every company and every man always went to the exact same part every day until they were so drilled into the exact piece of the programme each man was expected to carry out that they went instinctively when in the attack to where they had been trained to go.[68] The faults committed were those of the higher authorities in underestimating the difficulties and in giving us an impossible task.

I knew that unless everything went like clockwork on all sides of us, there was certain to be a failure. I pointed out in the strongest possible way that we were asked to do impossibilities and I was told I was making difficulties. It is all on paper, my objections and my reasons, but naturally when they were overruled there was nothing more to say but go ahead and look cheerful.

The man I loathe is Harry Rawlinson, the Army Commander whose senseless optimism is responsible for the practical wiping out of the Division. He is the only man too who has never sent the Division one word of acknowledgement, thanks or praise for what they did for him.

FC, D/3835/E/2/10

81
Nugent to his wife

[Holograph] [Tilques, nr St Omer]
13 July 1916

I enclose you a letter from Hubert Gough, which is very nicely expressed. We hear that both the Corps commanders, our late Corps commander and the one on our left are very shaky and may possibly be on their way home soon.[69] It is also rumoured but must not be repeated that Allenby is not unlikely to be going home too, but none of these matters may be even whispered.

FC, D/3835/E/2/10

82
Nugent to his wife

[Holograph] [Tilques]
15 July 1916

Do you find the women of the North very difficult? You can't find them more difficult than I find the men. They are the most self-centred people I have ever met. If you are not Ulster and if you don't subscribe to every Ulster prejudice and if you are not as intolerant as they are, they will have nothing to do with you.

They simply won't accept you. I have found that for 10 months and I feel today no nearer them and no more in touch with them than when I came.

I'm merely the Divisional Commander, a person who has to be obliged and who can be very disagreeable if he isn't, but I'm merely an incident and anyone who followed me would be merely an incident. They are magnificent soldiers but very hard to know.

They think nothing of and know nothing of the months of unceasing preparation and organisation for their attack. Well, all the preparation and organisation in the world would have been useless if there had not been their splendid courage and determination to carry them through. All the same they are not lovable but I daresay I am not either.

Now that figures are becoming obtainable the actual losses in killed and missing are not so bad. The total was 5500 in killed, wounded and missing. Of these 4800 passed through the Field Ambulances and we know that 3000 of these were only slightly wounded and of the remaining 1800 the great majority will recover, so that I hope not more than 700 to 800 will be the total of dead and missing. Of these we know a number of wounded had to be left behind when we retired and we must believe the Germans would treat them properly . . .

FC, D/3835/E/2/10

83
Capt W. B. Spender to his wife

[Holograph] [Tilques]
16 July 1916

I have just had d[evil] of a row. Either Genl P[owell] or Sir G[eorge Richardson] published the letter I sent them, to which the abbreviated version is 'the GOC now confirms he has got excellent troops'. He is perfectly furious and swears all kind of threats. I can quite see his point of view in this as it makes an implication – not intended – that he did not appreciate them before, and he thinks I have been criticising him behind his back. I find it a little hard to forgive Sir G who I suspect is the culprit and who as a soldier ought to have known better.

I have saved Farnham and Singleton by getting Henry[70] to suppress his paper in which letters written by them appear . . . The G never forgives and we at present loathe the sight of each other, tho' I do see his point of view.

You may as well be very careful in your dealings with Mrs N[ugent] and all who are likely to pass things on to her. I rather wish I were going to the 24 Div tomorrow and get things over as the atmosphere is sultry and P[lace] does not help much – au contraire he is coming by his own and will make the most of it . . .

I fancy I am now on the Genl's nerves . . . in which case it may be as well if I leave which is what he has in mind. In many ways I shall not regret it as there are disadvantages in being with 'one's own children' in a battle and I quite see them. At the same time it will be a bit of a wrench and will be one of the other things which one will not be able to explain after the war, tho' perhaps then – but not now – I shall drop a hint to Craig of how it has happened.

SP, D/1633/1/1/347

84
Nugent to his wife

[Holograph] [Tilques]
18 July 1916

I fear we are for the Ypres Salient. In fact I know we are and we shall probably be about where we were this time last year. Too disgusting.

People no doubt talk a lot of ignorant rubbish. I suppose they think I ought to have refused to obey orders for fear someone should get hurt. Don't they understand that I have to carry out orders just as the men under me have to try to carry out theirs. I get my orders how far I am to go and then my job [is] to work out how we are to do it. Do they think I started the Division off on its own into the German trenches. I am afraid Ulster women are a narrow-minded clique and I dislike them all intensely though I don't know any of them and don't want to . . .

Our drafts are coming in very slowly and we shall be a long time making up our numbers if they don't hurry up . . .

Sir H Plumer the 2nd Army Commander was round this morning meeting some of my COs.

I am writing to Somerset to tell him to come out as Arthur's CO wants him to join and I can't in decency keep him any longer. I shall miss him horribly.

FC, D/3835/E/2/10

85
Nugent to his wife

[Holograph] [Esquelbecq]
20 July 1916

We move again the day after tomorrow and go into the line. I am much annoyed as I want them to reinforce the Division . . .

Anyhow there are none [Corps] vacant at the moment and if there were, there are dozens of generals senior to me. I expect it's no more than that someone said that I could be given a Corps, merely for something to say.

I would not care to leave the 36th Division, knowing of course that it would be considerable promotion.

Spender is leaving. He is going as GSO(1) to the 4th Army with the rank of Lt Colonel. Promotion for him. I am glad and I think he will be better away. He is too much mixed up with the politicals in Belfast and talks and writes too much to them.

I have not been able to speak to him for the last week since reading a letter of his in a Belfast paper in which he took it on himself to say 'The General now knows he has commanded the best troops in the world and confesses it'. It implied that I had commanded them for 10 months without knowing whether they were good or bad, the men I had been training for 10 months! 'And confesses it', as if I had been crabbing them all the time and now confessed that I was wrong.

The impertinence of one of my staff daring to put expressions into my mouth and the disloyalty of it. I have been so angry that I have simply not been able to speak to him for fear I should let myself go. Of course I have spoken to him, but I told him I simply was afraid to let my feelings have vent.

FC, D/3835/E/2/10

86
Nugent to his wife

[Holograph] [Mont Noir]
25 July 1916

I recommended a man today for the posthumous conferring of the VC for almost the finest act of self-sacrifice I have ever read of. He was giving out bombs just before the attack on the 1st July to a number of our men in a trench. He was walking along the top giving them out of a box. He slipped and the box fell out of his hand into the trench and the jar set off the fuzes in 2 of the bombs. The trench was full of men. Without a second's hesitation the man jumped down into the trench and threw himself down onto the bombs and covered the burning bombs with his own body. He was blown to pieces, but he saved the lives of all the men in the trench. He knew what he was doing as he was a bomber. His name was W J McFadzean, 14th R I Rifles. It was a sublime act and he will get the VC for it I am certain.

FC, D/3835/E/2/10

87
Nugent to General Sir Edward Hutton

[Holograph] [Mont Noir]
27 July 1916

I have been rather busy lately so that is my excuse for not thanking you sooner for the Chronicle.

I have sent it to Morland to read.

We had a week of very heavy work and the Division is now out of it and gone up North to replace a Division sent down in relief. In fact many Divisions are out of it and I think there are very few Divisions in France which will not take their share in this offensive.

The losses are formidable. My own Division came out after sustaining over 60 p.c of casualties. I am glad to say most of the casualties were from machine gun fire and are not severe, but latterly shell wounds are getting more numerous.

There is no doubt the Germans are using their reserves rapidly. If it were not for their machine guns we should have them on the run, I am sure.

Their skill in organisation of defensive localities enables them to check us long enough to create fresh lines behind, so the process goes on. It is really a question of endurance now.

Though I say it my Division made a truly magnificent attack on the 1st July. I think we were the only Division to reach the objective laid down for the day. We took 4 lines of entrenchments to a depth of 2000 yards. Unfortunately the Divisions on our right and left could not get on and we were isolated and later in the day were attacked in front both flanks and rear and had to fight our way back to the German 2nd line which we held against all attacks until we were relieved by another Division and sent out to recuperate.

As far as I can gather we have used up about 12 Divisions for the time being. There is no doubt with few exceptions the New Armies are fighting superbly, but none could have done better than my Ulstermen. I am very proud of them. I hope we shall be restored to strength soon. I want to get back to work again.

It is pretty bad fighting. There is not much quarter and the feeling is pretty bitter. The Germans are treacherous as ever.

The great secret in assault is to keep close up to our own shells so as to be in directly the Artillery lengthens.

It is the only chance. If the Germans get their M.G.s going it is impossible except at very heavy cost to make any advance.

I really do believe that the Germans have no more reserves. We know of 12 Divisions on this front which have been moved to the Somme and more from the interior of Germany. Next summer will I hope see the end.

BL, Hutton Papers, Additional MS 50098

2

Messines and Third Ypres, August 1916 to August 1917

Introduction

In the autumn of 1916 the Ulster Division and the 16th (Irish) Division, which had suffered heavy losses at Guillemont and Ginchy in early September, faced a new threat. Not enough Irish replacements were available to bring them up to strength. The manpower crisis long predicted by Nugent and others had at last arrived.

Irish recruitment was a controversial political issue throughout the war. In terms of overall numbers, the best estimates suggest that around 21,000 regular Irish soldiers in August 1914 (along with 5,000 sailors and 2,000 officers) were joined on mobilisation by 30,000 reservists. During the war a further 134,000 men enlisted in the Army, together with 10,000 recruits to the Navy and (from April 1918) the RAF and about 4,000 direct commissions to the armed forces. This total of 206,000, which excludes wartime Irish enlistments in Britain or overseas, represents, in David Fitzpatrick's words, 'the greatest deployment of armed manpower in the history of Irish militarism'.[1] Significant though the total is, however, it still represented enlistment levels proportionately much lower than in Britain, and it was the profile of Irish recruiting as well as the total numbers that posed such acute problems for the Irish divisions.

Between August 1914 and December 1915 around 90,000 men enlisted in the Army (about 8 per cent of Ireland's male population between the ages of 15 and 49; the equivalent rate for England and Wales was 24 per cent, and for Scotland 27 per cent). In the absence of Irish conscription only 44,000 more enlisted in Ireland after January 1916 (less than 4 per cent of men aged 15 to 49: the figures for England and Wales, and Scotland, underpinned by compulsory service, were 22 per cent and 15 per cent respectively). The recruiting slump predated the Easter Rising, often blamed for the collapse of recruitment over much of the country.

The pattern of recruiting reflected various factors. Political allegiance was certainly one, and it was to this that Unionist politicians attributed the fact that Irish Protestants – most of whom lived in Ulster, and nearly all of whom were Unionist – were disproportionately represented, providing, according to one estimate, around 45 per cent of recruits despite comprising only 25 per cent of the island's population. (During the first six months of the war predominantly Protestant Antrim, Down and Armagh were the only Irish counties, with over one-fifth of eligible men enlisting, to match recruitment levels in Britain.) In fact, however, there was no simple correlation between political or religious affiliation and willingness to serve. After the initial surge recruiting fell away in Unionist areas almost as markedly as in Nationalist ones: indeed, more Catholics than Protestants enlisted in Ulster in 1915. Regional and occupational variations demonstrate the central importance of social and economic factors: men of all religious denominations were more likely to enlist in the industrialised north than elsewhere in the country; throughout Ireland urban workers were more likely to enlist than agricultural ones; and membership of collective organisations like the Ulster or National Volunteers or the Orange Order appears to have been a positive factor in individuals' willingness to enlist. By November 1914, while rural southern and western Ireland had produced fewer recruits than any other region in the United Kingdom, recruiting levels in the north and east of the country outstripped agricultural areas of England like East Anglia and the west country. The gap between the Irish and British experiences prior to the introduction of conscription was not as great as the headline figures suggest.[2]

Whatever the underlying reasons for the decline in Irish recruiting, the practical consequence was that by mid-1916 the 54 Irish battalions at the front could not be sustained in the face of mounting casualties.[3] The crisis came that autumn because of the coincidence of the losses of the 16th and 36th Divisions on the Somme with the decimation of the 10th (Irish) Division by malaria in Macedonia. In late September the Army Council concluded that 'as recruiting in Ireland had almost ceased, so that the maintenance of as many as three Irish Divisions had become impossible, steps must be taken to reduce the number'. It directed that the 16th and 36th should be amalgamated and that Edward Carson and John Redmond be informed.[4] In October the Adjutant-General, Sir Nevil Macready, followed this up with a paper to the Council reporting that Irish infantry units were already 17,000 under strength and projecting that the shortfall would rise to nearly 50,000 in six months. It outlined five possibilities: introduction of conscription in Ireland; amalgamating the 16th and 36th; reinforcing all three Irish formations with non-Irish drafts; allowing them 'gradually to die out'; or transferring to them Irish regular battalions from other formations.[5] Macready's own preference, assuming no Irish conscription, was amalgamation.

Both Redmond and Carson were horrified by this prospect. Redmond pointed out that such a step would have a disastrous effect on recruiting by removing the only distinctively Nationalist contribution to the war effort;[6] Carson too was vehemently opposed [98]. Macready also consulted Nugent, who was in London on leave. True to his hope that the war might act as a reconciling experience, Nugent believed that if the 16th and 36th could not continue as separate entities they should be amalgamated with each other. He argued this strongly with Carson, while at the same time pressing yet again for Irish conscription [95, 96, 101].

On 19 October the War Cabinet decided for political reasons to keep the three Irish divisions going by a combination of English drafts, breaking up Irish units to provide replacements and transferring in regular Irish battalions. This decision determined the character of the Irish formations for the remainder of the war. The arrangement worked, to the extent that Irish infantry units continued to contain a majority of Irishmen for the next 18 months: for example, the proportion of Irish soldiers in the Ulster Division's battalions at Messines (June 1917) was 61 per cent, at Langemarck (August 1917) 59 per cent, at Cambrai (November/December 1917) 67 per cent and during the Kaiserschlacht (March 1918) 60 per cent. The Irish infantry was, though, a wasting asset. The Irish divisions only received large drafts of English troops in early 1917: there was political opposition in Britain to Irish units being 'bailed out' by British conscripts, and from the summer of 1917 onwards they depended increasingly on disbanding their own service battalions to maintain their strength. By the spring of 1918 the supply of units had been exhausted – two-thirds of Irish wartime-raised battalions had been broken up and all but one of the Irish regular line battalions had been transferred to the Irish divisions – and by mid-1918 both the 10th and 16th Divisions had ceased to be Irish formations.[7]

For Nugent the War Cabinet decision at last brought the prospect of bringing his division back up to strength [106]. Initially, however, reinforcements were slow to arrive (though when they did Nugent where possible greeted them in person, sometimes being surprised by his reception [109]); and when in December 1916 the *Belfast Newsletter* invited him to contribute a Christmas message to people at home, his frustration showed [117]. The reaction was immediate: Ulster Unionists were outraged by criticism which they regarded as unfair as well as politically damaging,[8] and the episode ended what remained of an unrepentant Nugent's relationship with James Craig [127, 142]. In January 1917, indeed, Spender heard that 'Belfast's main topic of conversation is ON's unpopularity and that this is mainly responsible for no more men coming forward now'.[9]

By April 1917 the Ulster Division was back up to strength. But while the proportion of Irishmen in the infantry battalions stood at around two-thirds, when supporting arms were taken into account – the Divisional artillery was not recruited in Ireland – the overall proportion in the Division had fallen to around 50 per cent. At the end of April Nugent received an unwelcome message from Haig inviting him to offer to drop the 'Ulster' title [131]. Nugent was appalled, less by the possible loss of the title than by Haig's attempt to get him to take the blame for suggesting it. After consulting Plumer and his COs he responded formally that the decision rested with the higher command [132–7]. Faced with this GHQ dropped the proposal, but Nugent had done himself no favours with Haig.

Meanwhile the war went on. Manpower problems notwithstanding, the Ulster Division maintained its reputation for aggression, carrying out ten raids between 15 September and 16 November 1916 as Second Army tried to prevent German units being transferred south to the Somme [94, 99, 105, 108, 110]. Nugent's admiration for Plumer, the Army commander, and his chief of staff, Harington, was unbounded [153, 172] and the regard was reciprocated – it is no coincidence that Plumer later wrote the foreword to the Divisional history, or that in it he paid particular tribute to Nugent.[10] The free exchange of ideas in Second Army is illustrated by Nugent's comments on Harington's report of his conversations with battalion commanders early in 1917 [123]. The BEF was developing new unit and sub-unit tactics to take advantage of weapons and techniques optimised for trench warfare: during the winter Nugent's training plans had been hampered by manpower shortages [121] but in the spring the programme intensified. This included trying to pick up tips from others, and the comments of Brigadier-General Ricardo, now with the 37th Division, offer a comparison between the Ulster Division and another New Army formation during this period [113, 118].

Nugent had progressive ideas about tactics, illustrated not only by his innovations on the Somme and the different assault formations the Division experimented with in each of its 1917 battles, but also by his perceptive analysis during Third Ypres of the problems of attacking defences sited in depth (he advocated strengthening the barrage covering the advance at the expense of counterbattery work, on the grounds that once in the German position the full force of their artillery could not be unleashed for fear of killing their own men; and deploying the attacking infantry in 'mobile company columns echeloned in depth on a narrow front' rather than linear formations, which broke up under fire or in difficult terrain).[11] Crozier regarded him as a highly competent commander with whom 'every man knew where he was, and that the objectives would be taken with as little loss as possible'.[12] One can therefore take with a pinch of salt a comment by Spender (an ex-gunner) in January 1916 that his forthcoming course on artillery tactics was 'most important as the General knows very little about them', but there is no reason to doubt his report that Nugent believed 'that Gunner and Sapper Generals are a mistake': Keir, the corps commander at Hooge, had been an artillery officer.[13]

In late September 1916 the Ulster Division had been joined in IX Corps by the 16th Division. Nationalists like John and Willie Redmond had long lobbied the military authorities to create a permanent Irish formation, like the Canadian and Australian Corps, which they hoped might form the basis of a 'national army'; Unionists like Spender opposed the idea for that very reason. Spender attributed this move to Nugent, but the timing – the two divisions were brought together when their amalgamation was being actively considered – suggests more probably contingency planning by GHQ. Whatever the reason the two Irish divisions served together for the next eight months and relations between them proved to be very good at officer level and generally so amongst the soldiers, though there were occasional frictions.[14] Nugent and his opposite number Hickie worked hard to develop good relations, presenting cups, holding competitions, and arranging social events [107, 115]. Nugent also met, and like many of his military colleagues was impressed by, Willie Redmond [111, 143].

The first battle in which the two divisions fought together was Messines in June 1917, a limited 'bite and hold' operation mounted with all the care and attention to detail that Plumer and Harington could bring to bear – Nugent later described it as 'a perfect example of trained effort in which nothing essential to success had been overlooked, in which cooperation and mutual help between units and between the man in the field and the Army Staff reached its fullest expression'.[15] The 36th and 16th, part of an assault force of eleven first-wave divisions, attacked the southern part of the ridge opposite Wytschaete in a highly symbolic operation.[16] Politically the timing was important, with the Irish Convention meeting in Dublin, and America with its influential Irish-American lobby having recently entered the war.

At 3.10 a.m. on 7 June, 19 huge mines were detonated under Messines ridge, three of them on the Ulster Division's front: as they went up Nugent's leading troops began their advance. He attacked with two brigades (the 16th Division was on his left flank, the 25th on his right): the objective, the Black Line, lay 2,000 yards in front just over the crest of the ridge. Four tanks supported the Division, their first experience of working with armour.

The assault, famously, was completely successful [149–52]. Most of the forward defenders had been killed or were in shock and the wire had been completely destroyed. Where isolated posts held out the new platoon tactics enabled them to be quickly dealt with, in one or two cases with the assistance of the tanks. Wytschaete was captured in cooperation with the 16th Division, and by mid-morning all the Division's objectives had been taken. On the night of 9 June, after enduring two days of German shelling, Nugent's men went into reserve. At a cost of just over 1,100 casualties (about 700 in the assault itself), the Ulster Division had captured 1,200 prisoners and taken all its objectives. Nugent was delighted by the success both of his own troops and of the 16th Division, marred only by the death of Willie Redmond: he made a point, in the face of some internal opposition, of making a contribution from divisional funds to Redmond's memorial fund [169].

Despite the triumph, however, for Nugent personally Messines had a sour aftermath. Of the commanders of the 11 leading divisions on 7 June, all except Nugent were knighted or had existing knighthoods 'upgraded' for their part in the victory, eight – including Hickie – in the new year's honours of January 1918 (the other two, who had less than 12 months' experience in command at the time of the battle, were knighted in 1919). Nugent was similarly recommended by his corps commander and Plumer but the recommendation was not forwarded to London. Only Haig personally could have blocked it. The dismay of both Hamilton Gordon and Harington when they found out was unconcealed [196, 228]. One does not generally think of Haig, whatever his failings, as a petty man, but this mean-spirited action clearly reflected his dislike of Nugent [138].

In early July the Division left Second Army for Gough's Fifth Army, moving north to prepare for the coming offensive at Ypres. The 16th Division moved too, and both now came under the command of XIX Corps. Nugent's initial meeting with Gough was pleasant enough [161], but the next battle was to be an unhappy contrast with Messines.

The Third Battle of Ypres, or Passchendaele, has become synonymous with the worst aspects of the Western Front. Certainly it was a low point for the Ulster Division during the war. Gough and his Fifth Army staff, directing its opening phases, earned an unenviable reputation for poor operational planning, sloppy staffwork and an uncaring attitude to those under their command.

The offensive opened on 31 July; that evening the weather broke and it rained unceasingly for the next few days (the rainfall that August was almost double the seasonal average). The Ulster Division, like the 16th Division on its right, moved into the line on 2 August near St Julien, expecting to attack soon. But already the offensive was getting bogged down, literally, and the Division spent the next 12 days under intense shellfire in waterlogged trenches [159–62]. By 15 August the Division had lost over 1,500 officers and men, mostly from the infantry battalions, and was exhausted. The 16th Division was in a similar condition. Despite this, Gough decided to use them in the assault rather than put in fresh troops, and at dawn on 16 August the Ulster infantry clambered out of their trenches and advanced.

Nugent once again attacked with two brigades; their objective was 2,000 yards away with an intermediate line halfway. The story is soon told. The ground was a bog, the mud being waist-deep in places; the wire was uncut; the enemy machine-guns had not been neutralised; and the German artillery was unsuppressed. Despite this an advance of a few hundred yards was achieved before a heavy German counter-attack sent the survivors reeling back. The attack cost the Division a further 2,000 casualties and was a virtually complete failure. Gough wanted the attack renewed immediately: Nugent pointed out that this was impossible, whereupon Gough decreed a further attack next day. Nugent's letter home that night reveals his despair [163]: in the event, the Division was withdrawn the following day. Nugent never forgave Gough for this disaster [164–6].[17]

At the end of August the Ulster Division left Fifth Army, without regret, to join Byng's Third Army opposite Cambrai, where it spent the next few weeks slowly rebuilding its strength. The 16th Division moved too, but to a different corps. Whether by accident or design the battle of

Langemarck had brought to an end the experiment of operating the two Irish divisions side by side. Spender, for one, anticipated the change with relief, telling his wife shortly after the attack:

> I am afraid the 36th has been very badly hit again, due so they say to the 16th in a large measure but I do not know the facts. I imagine the stupid experiment of the partnership will now be given up – another of ON's awful mistakes by a man who said that he would have nothing to do with politics.[18]

88
Nugent to his wife

[Holograph]

[Mont Noir]
5 August 1916

Alick Godley[1] invited me to come and see a Maori war dance this afternoon given in honour of General Plumer, the 2nd Army Commander. It was very quaint and quite interesting. It was more chanting and yelling with rithmic [*sic*] swayings of the body than dancing but part of it consisted in making the most awful faces and giving utterance to blood-curdling yells and groans, supposed to represent the shouts of the victors and the screams of the victims being tortured. Other parts represented eating the vanquished. The faces were to frighten the enemy. It was very quaint to see Plumer, a man with a most wooden expression, solemnly standing in a circle of howling naked savages, who pretended to stab with sticks and put out their tongues at him. Afterwards they sang Maori songs which were beautiful and most unusual and soft. I spent all morning inspecting schools and transport today, very tiring.

FC, D/3835/E/2/10

89
Nugent to his wife

[Holograph]

[Mont Noir]
10 August 1916

I got a letter from the Grand Master of Belfast Orangemen saying the brethren were proud of the Division and that their hearts went out to them. I thought this was about the limit, considering that none of them are enlisting, so I replied that if their bodies accompanied their hearts, it would be much more to the point. I think it is sheer impertinence to write flapdoodle of that kind at the present time.

I did not visit the trenches today but went to the 2nd Army school of instruction near St Omer instead to see what I could pick up in the way of hints for my school. I have got Colonel Pakenham staying here for a couple of days which I think is very nice of me, but he has not been well and may have to go home, at any rate for a time. He is a great friend of Somerset's.[2]

Kennerley Romford is working in a Motor Ambulance close to here. I shall ask him to sing at my Follies one night. We have quite a good troupe now who perform nightly to appreciative audiences.[3]

FC, D/3835/E/2/10

90
Nugent to his wife

[Holograph] [Mont Noir]
11 August 1916

I am in command of the V Corps at present, but it is only temporary. It may be confirmed but as to that I can't say at all. We are in the V Corps so I have made no change at all and am continuing to command the Division. It would not be worthwhile to move to Corps HdQrs which are only 2 miles from here until things are clearer. The Corps Commander has been ordered to go south to take command of another Corps, also temporarily. He may or may not come back and if he does not come back I may or may not get the Corps. I think probably not so there is nothing in it at present.[4]

FC, D/3835/E/2/10

91
Nugent to his wife

[Holograph] [Mont Noir]
14 August 1916

I have had quite a pleasant day moving in circles of the highest kind (!!). I lunched with the King, the Pr[ince] of W[ales], Army

Commander and various Corps Commanders, Lord Stamfordham, Clive Ingram. The K was most affable and talked quite a long time to me both before and after lunch.[5]

He thanked me for writing and I explained that I had not dared to make his letter known to the Division because they were so indiscreet. He said I was quite right. He would talk and so did Lord Stamfordham of the Ulster Divn as the Irish Divn and I had finally to explain that we were the Ulster Divn and that there was an Irish Divn so he said he thought it was a pity we were not called the Irish Divn too as he thought 'Ulster' savoured of politics. I firmly and gently put him right and said there were no politics in the Ulster Division. When he left he told me he was very glad to have seen me again and wished me the best of luck and said he was sure the Division would continue to do well.

I had 30 officers and men who had most distinguished themselves in the garden and I took him round after lunch and gave a short account of what each officer and man had done. He was much interested and said a few words of congratulations to each and shook hands with the officers.

I can't think why no one ever thought of doing that before. It will have such a good effect.

FC, D/3835/E/2/10

92
Nugent to his wife

[Holograph] [Mont Noir]
21 August 1916

My institution of COs visits is quite a success. They all seem to enjoy themselves and like the place and the surroundings. I get a chance of knowing them too better than if I only see them in the trenches.

The Corps Commander, Hamilton Gordon, came to lunch.[6] Food is wasted on him I fear as he has no taste and can't tell any difference between bootlaces and macaroni . . .

[My mother] will be thrilled to the very marrow, and how she vill love telling everyone that the King is very fond of my son – he ommands the Ulstermen – they were in the battle – they won't ave Home Rule.

The hardest thing I have to do now is to apportion the ecommendations for rewards. There are only a limited number hey will allot to each Division and there are 3 times as many cases leserving of reward as there are decorations. So much depends on ow COs word their accounts. Some who can't write grammatical English would never get a reward for their men because they can't lescribe the occurrences. Others write vivid stories which are too picturesque to be entirely true and then one has to sort them so hat each battalion gets its fair share. I'm still at it.

'C, D/3835/E/2/10

93
Nugent to his wife

Holograph]

[Mont Noir]
22 August 1916

went to the trenches today by a shorter road than I usually travel out which unfortunately was in view of the German lines in places. The Boche evidently spotted us and shelled the road for half an hour where they must have thought the car was. We were not there but on the way back the road was pitted with shell holes and broken branches where he had sent his affectionate love and best wishes. I don't think I'll use that road again. It isn't good enough . . .

I wish they would make us up again to strength. We shall not get another chance until we are made up. The recruiting in Ulster s an utter frost. No one took any trouble to give the party I sent home a welcome and in Belfast they did not even know we had sent a party. The people we wrote to had done nothing.[7]

Such a shame and I am so angry about it. I loathe the people of Belfast.

FC, D/3835/E/2/10

94
Nugent to his wife

[Holograph] [St Jans Cappel]
17 September 1916

We made 2 raids the night before last on the Germans, both very successful.[8] We killed a lot and took prisoners and only lost 2 men. Audley Pratt's battalion did one of them. The men are very pleased in consequence. I must write to St G[eorge] and give him more particulars of them.

Yesterday I gave a part of the German trenches from which they have been giving me great annoyance a real doing, 2 hours in the morning and 2 hours in the afternoon. I had every big gun I could borrow 9", 6", and 4.7". I looked on and it was most pleasing to see the German trenches and dugouts going up into the air, trenches and beams and corrugated iron and one German who went up like a Catherine wheel and came down more or less in pieces on to their wire where he was hanging all yesterday. The Boche made no response which is most unusual and I can't think what they are up to. I fully expect something awful in a day or two.

FC, D/3835/E/2/11

95
Nugent to General Sir Nevil Macready

[Typescript] [St Jans Cappel]
6 October 1916

You may remember telling me that Carson had said he would prefer to see the Ulster Division absorbed in a Highland Division instead of seeing them amalgamated with the 16th, should the necessity arise. I have thought this over, and I am sure it would be disastrous from the point of view of Ireland.[9]

It would mean the complete disappearance of two Irish Divisions and it would be read as an admission that the two Irish Divisions could not combine, that Irish creeds and politics were carried into the fighting line. It would be a libel on both ivisions. There are no politics whatever, and I am sure there ould be no better cure for Irish home troubles than that rotestants and catholics should fight together in the same unit.

If we do get compulsory service in Ireland, I sincerely hope the lster Division will not be exclusively supplied from one creed. I ope that all creeds and politics will be drafted into it. It will then e really representative and not as at present with too much avour of a time which is I hope dead and buried.

If, however, the question of amalgamation becomes imperative, hope the 16th and the 36th will be amalgamated so that there ay be at least one Irish Division.

arson Papers, D/1507/A/19/16

96
Nugent to Sir Edward Carson

Typescript copy] [St Jans Cappel]
[n.d. but 7 or 8] October 1916

was in London on my way back from leave and I saw the djutant General on the subject of reinforcements for the ivision.

The position is very unsatisfactory, but what surprised me was hat he told me he had seen you and asked your views on an malgamation of the 16th and 36th Divisions to form one omplete Division, and you said that you would prefer, if it ecame necessary, to see the 36th Division amalgamated with a ighland Division.

In my opinion this would be a most disastrous mistake. I am ost desirous, if the two Divisions have to disappear as separate nits, that they should be merged in each other.

I can imagine no cure for political differences so radical and ffective as that all Irish creeds and politics should be represented n each Irish unit and blend in the fighting line.

I am certain that this would be the opinion of every soldier in he 16th and 36th Divisions who had the interest of Ireland at eart.

Your suggestion would mean that both Irish Divisions woul disappear and it would be universally interpreted as meaning tha racial and political differences in Ireland were carried into th ranks of the Army out here and that the two Irish Divisions coul not be trusted together.

This would be a libel on both Divisions. Let us be Irish as lon as we can, even if it does mean the amalgamation of the Division . . .

Compulsory service now would be the moral regeneration o the country. Most Irishmen have a wholesome respect for th machinery of the law when it is handled by men who mean to b obeyed. Believing as I do that disloyalty in Ireland is to a grea extent a political pose, that Irishmen have always been amenable t strong even-handed government and that there is a large body o self-respecting Irishmen who would gladly see their countr fulfilling her destiny as a unit of the Empire, I feel that the presen Government will commit an unforgivable crime against the goo name and honour of the country if they allow themselves to b swayed by the clamour of an unstatesmanlike and shortsighte political party into inflicting upon Ireland a stigma which wil stick to her for generations and which is opposed to every Iris interest.

It is nonsense to talk, as people in Ireland do talk, that she ha given her share. She has done nothing of the kind and no more i one part of Ireland than in another.

FC, D/3835/E/2/10/8

97
Nugent to his wife

[Holograph]

[St Jans Cappel
8 October 191

Notwithstanding the clamour of the rival factions in Ireland I an certain compulsory service can be introduced into Ireland wit much less trouble than is anticipated. If the Govt only have th pluck. There are lots of Irishmen who must realise the shame an disgrace which will attach to the name of Irishmen after the war if they refuse to bear their share of the burden of Empire now.

Compulsory Service might kill politics for all time in Ireland and what a blessing that would be.

I have written to the Adjt Genl to urge that if Compulsory Service is brought in for Ireland that I hope the 'Ulster' Divn will be made 'Ulster' in the broadest sense and that Ulstermen of all creeds and politics should be sent to it so that it will no longer be a sectarian Division.

Do not breathe a word of this to your Committee else they will throw fits in every corner of the room and probably get up a deputation to the govt to ask for my removal.

FC, D/3835/E/2/11

98
Sir Edward Carson to Nugent

[Typescript] London
10 October 1916

I am in receipt of your letter of the 7th. I am very sorry I did not see you when you were at home; I made several enquiries but could not find you. The conversation I had with the Adjutant General was very short though I had a longer one with the Secretary of State and I urged that the real thing to do was to impose Conscription, though I have not the slightest hope that the Government will take this course.

With reference to the amalgamation of the Divisions, whilst there has been a great deal said about the good effects, I do not think myself in present circumstances it is really a feasible course. I am told that the amalgamated Division will be called the Irish Division and the name of Ulster will disappear, as none of the regiments have an Ulster denomination as in the case of the other provinces. I feel perfectly certain that there would be great disappointment in Ulster, and indeed resentment, particularly as the 16th (Irish) Division was never really a Division at all and is now only little more than a brigade. There are many other matters which I cannot discuss in a letter, but I have called together the Ulster members tomorrow to consider the whole situation.

FC, D/3835/E/10/8

99
Nugent to his wife

[Holograph] [St Jans Cappel]
12 October 1916

We had 3 raids last night, 1 failed to get in as the Boche were too much on the alert, the other 2 got in, in one the Germans bolted and they got none of them but the other raiding party killed 30 Germans and brought back some prisoners.[10]

The German trenches in front of my Division are pretty well knocked about. We are always hammering them with artillery and mortars and I think the Boche is having a pretty rotten time here. I don't know what is the matter with him. He hardly retaliates at all. I don't think it is like him and I fully expect he will do something horrible as soon as he has a little spare time.

He is pretty busy in various places just now. I am very depressed all the same. I see no chance of getting any men and in consequence of being short handed the men are over-worked and over-tired and there is a lot of sickness.

Every other Division almost has been back to the Somme, some 3 times, but we are sidetracked and forgotten. It is very disheartening.

I heard from Congreve the other day.[11] I wrote to give him my sympathy and I told him of the story you told me of Mrs Congreve and the tree climbing. He was interested and told me he had sent my letter on to her. I hope they are a little nearer to each other than they have been for years I am afraid.

We had a good many casualties last night I am sorry to say but they are more or less inevitable. Unfortunately they were mostly caused by our own Artillery which for some unaccountable reason was short.

FC, D/3835/E/2/11

100
Nugent to his wife

[Holograph] [St Jans Cappel]
15 October 1916

The Boche gave us another heavy bombardment yesterday and knocked us about considerably. It is very inconvenient as it entails so much work on us. It was all right while we were knocking him about but the dirty worm has turned and I shall have to hammer him again severely.

Somerset and I went to lunch with Colin Mackenzie who commands a Division near here. He has got Singleton[12] now who was promoted to a higher staff appointment out of this Division.

The question of the future of this and other Irish divisions is coming near crisis. I don't know what the future will be but as all the Irish Divisions are dying out something will have to be done soon. I may be coming home one day, this Division having been absorbed by some other Division. How dreadful it would be to have me as a half-pay General filling up the bungalow. They might perhaps give me another Division, but on the other hand they mightn't.

Our miserable little country. If only they would govern it how happy we might all be.

Duke I am told is just Birrell without the humour.[13] I am sick of Irish problems or hearing of them. I would like to drown or shoot all politicians or any rate get them out here into the trenches.

FC, D/3835/E/2/11

101
Nugent to Sir Edward Carson

[Typescript] [St Jans Cappel]
16 October 1916

I am truly sorry to read from your letter of the 10th instant that you think there is no hope of compulsory service being extended to Ireland.

The position therefore as regards the future of the Irish Divisions and Regiments appears to be one of the following alternatives :–

1. Amalgamation.
2. Drafts from Great Britain.

As to amalgamation, it is sincerely to be hoped it will not be found necessary . . . It is simple in principle, but presents many difficulties in practice. It obviously entails the disbandment of some units for incorporation with others. In the case of larger organisations such as divisions, it would mean the breaking up of an organisation which has found itself by trial and error, which is a going concern and which would have to be replaced, because the division is the fighting unit of the Army.

In the case of the Irish Divisions, I think we must face the fact that amalgamation, whether of Divisions or of Battalions of the same Regiment, can only be a temporary arrest of decay, because the flow of recruits from Ireland has practically ceased.

If we were to take all the Irish Battalions in the Army and halve the numbers by rolling two into one, I believe we should still find the remaining Battalions short of their establishments and we should still be faced by the fact that there were no reserves behind them.

It is a question of policy to be settled by the Army Council, but if it is adopted I should myself prefer to see Irish units retain their individuality as long as possible, even at the cost of the disappearance of some of the Battalions which have established such a fine record as have those of the Ulster Division.

This is my personal view. I have not been asked for it officially. If I am, I should consult Officers in the Division who from longer residence in Ireland and closer association with the people have a better claim to speak with knowledge than I have.

Your point that amalgamation would mean the disappearance of the designation 'Ulster' would be equally applicable to amalgamation with a Highland or English Division.

As regards the second alternative, I am told that the Secretary of State objects to drafts from Great Britain being sent to Irish Divisions.

It must be conceded that if we are to be kept going by English or Scotch recruits we cannot claim to be Irish.

It is better for the State that we should continue to live as a fighting unit of the Army than die out as the 'Ulster' Division.

Perhaps if we dropped a claim which our own people are unable to maintain, and content ourselves with being merely the 36th Division, the objections to giving us drafts from Great Britain might lose their force. We cannot have it both ways and the good of the state must come first.

As a final suggestion. Why not move to include Ulster in the Compulsory Service Act? Both parties are fairly evenly balanced in Ulster, so that the incidence of service would fall equally on both. It would ensure that the Ulster Division at any rate was maintained, and it would be the best and most unanswerable reply, now and in the future, to the accusation that Ireland as a whole did not do her duty.

Carson Papers, D/1507/A/19/19

102
Nugent to his wife

[Holograph] [St Jans Cappel]
25 October 1916

I had a weary tramp through deep mud all morning going round horse lines of my artillery.

I wonder if Nationalists and Unionists would agree to give Home Rule a joint trial for say even 5 years if the Nationalists would pledge Ireland to accept Compulsory Service. If they could do so, I would gladly see the Compact but I have no doubt if I said so in Ireland the various loyal committees of Ulster would go into violent hysterics and call me a traitor.

How I do hate all politicians. Somerset out here continually asserts that he loathes politics whereas it is the breath of his nostrils and if he is not abusing someone of the Liberal or Nationalist parties, he would feel he had failed in his duty. These Ulstermen have an extraordinary narrow outlook.

FC, D/3835/E/2/11

103
Nugent to his wife

[Holograph] [St Jans Cappel]
27 October 1916

I heard from Somerset who had been to see Derby who said there was no apparent likelihood of compulsory service being introduced into Ireland. The Irish Divisions would probably be shortly reconstituted as English Divisions and Irish titles dropped and the battalions would be amalgamated 2 or 3 into 1 and English battalions added to make up the balance. I don't care which way it goes so long as they give us men.

The Govt as usual I suppose will funk the responsibility of insisting upon Ireland doing her duty.

FC, D/3835/E/2/11

104
Nugent to his wife

[Holograph] [St Jans Cappel]
1 November 1916

I went for a ride this morning to the snipers school about 3 miles off. I wanted to satisfy myself of the reality of the claims made by the artists who paint the camouflage suits for snipers to wear, that they are really invisible at a short distance. The dress is a long smock with a hood which covers the head leaving only 2 holes to see out of and gloves for the hands. They do most certainly do all that is claimed. Absolutely invisible. I was taken up to within 20 yards of men standing upright against a tree or lying beside a bush or tussock of grass that could not really conceal a sniper and even when they were pointed out to me I couldn't see them. It really was uncanny. The smocks are fresh light canvas splashed over with green and black and amber and they so blend with the surroundings that you might walk on a man before you saw him.

In the afternoon I went to inspect a vast system of dugouts constructed under a hill here, really long galleries. A wonderful piece of work and capable of holding 4500 men, a whole Brigade! Some dug out . . .

Neither of my raids last night were entirely successful, in fact they were failures.[14] The Boches were very much on the alert, so we couldn't get in. It is never the policy to lose men if it can be helped on these occasions so if the Boche is prepared we don't try to do anything.

FC, D/3835/E/2/11

105
Nugent to his wife

[Holograph] [St Jans Cappel]
2 November 1916

The Germans are the most miserable whining curs when they unbosom their secret thoughts in their diaries which we often take from them.

I read one today in which the writer, an officer, says of Thiepval 'This is a hell that no imagination can picture, many of the men look like corpses, wax yellow and without expression. In 2 to 3 days a company is wiped out. Warm food is not be thought of'.

They often write most bitter remarks of their officers which a short time ago no German would have dared to do . . .

This Division has received much commendation for its activity. We were told we were the best Division at strafing the Boche in the 2nd Army, which is satisfactory and encouraging. We certainly do give them a bad time. I have a weekly bombardment and blow his trenches to pieces and then he has to send up working parties to repair them at night and we hear or see them and fire on them with machine-guns and rifle grenades and Stokes mortars and then we send over smoke bombs and he thinks its gas and rings alarm bells all over his front and sits for hours in a gas mask and we constantly raid his trenches and blow up his dugouts. He really has a rather bad time with us. I examine his trenches often with a periscope and I can see the broken beams and wood of his dugouts sticking up in the air in every direction.

FC, D/3835/E/2/11

106
Nugent to Brigadier-General Hacket Pain, commanding 15th Reserve Brigade in Ireland

[Typescript copy] [St Jans Cappel]

5 November 1916

There is now no reason to fear that our men will go anywhere else than to the Ulster Division.

I cannot, however, undertake that they will be posted to any particular battalion. So far as possible they will go to the battalion in which their friends are, but it may be necessary to post men to other battalions of the same regiment in the Division.

I further told the Adjutant General that the feeling of this Division was that its continued existence as a fighting unit was more important than any question of the politics, creeds or nationality of the men comprising it and that the proper solution was that the Irish Divisions should, if necessary, drop any claim to be called by an Irish territorial title, retaining merely their numbers and getting their drafts from Great Britain.

This, I understand, is the policy which has now been adopted. The 'Ulster' designation, or 'Irish' as the case may be, will be taken away as soon as the Irish Divisions have more than 50% of men from Great Britain in their ranks.

This is reasonable. Anything which gives us men is better than the state of suspended animation in which we have lived for the last four months.

I have written to you this fully because I hear that it has been stated in Belfast that I proposed that the 16th and 36th Divisions should be amalgamated. The statement, if it has been made, is both true and untrue. It depends entirely on the meaning sought to be conveyed.

Your suggestion that men of Ulster parentage domiciled in England should be sent to the Ulster Division seems an excellent one. That is a point which might be raised by Ulstermen at home. I can hardly do it myself.

FC, D/3835/E/10/8

107
Nugent to his wife

[Holograph] [St Jans Cappel]
9 November 1916

It is very uphill work keeping Brigades and battalions up to the scratch and to my ideas of what is proper. The Division has been so long in the trenches, never out for general smartening up and drill and that sort of thing, so many of the best officers are gone, that the tendency is to get slack, Brigadiers as well as COs and I am obliged to put the screws on again and ginger them up.[15]

It is disappointing, one would have thought good habits would have become ingrained by now, but the New Army is not like the old and one must keep everlastingly at them.

We don't get much chance being always in the trenches.

The 16th Irish Division are alongside us and their men are very much smarter than mine are now and that fills me with indignation against the COs and Brigadiers for letting the men get slack.

FC, D/3835/E/2/11

108
Nugent to his wife

[Holograph] [St Jans Cappel]
17 November 1916

We had a most successful raid last night, rather a big one. It has been preparing for some days and last night we brought it off. I had 5 different parties out, 3 got in and 2 couldn't, but we fairly had tea with the Boche. Took him completely by surprise, took a number of prisoners and killed a lot, blew up dugouts and emplacements and carried off a lot of loot. Audley Pratt's battalion did it and did it very well. I went to see him this morning and found him so excited that he was foaming. His battalion is tremendously pleased with itself and cheered itself half the night after it got back.[16]

The Army was very pleased as they very much wanted prisoners to establish identifications of troops opposite us.

FC, D/3835/E/2/11

109
Nugent to his wife

[Holograph] [St Jans Cappel]
24 November 1916

The sinking of the Britannic is a nasty jar.[17] I think she was bigger than the Titanic. If we can't cope with the German submarines they will beat us. I am afraid opinion in England is not satisfied with the present Board of the Admiralty. I am afraid Balfour is too old. We really seemed to have done better with Churchill and Fisher.

The new conscript army is beginning to roll up. I got about 300 or more this week and inspected them yesterday. I found artisans of all sorts, cooks of all kinds, entree cooks, pastry cooks, plain cooks, and one great find, a music hall comedian. I asked him what line he did and he said 'I'm versatile, sing, dance or juggle', so I have said he is to be marked down for our Follies. I gave them an address and good advice and said I hoped they would be very happy and well looked after and at the end they called out 'Thank you Sir'! I nearly fainted. Such want of discipline, on parade too. Besides the idea of the British soldier thanking one for anything was too much.

FC, D/3835/E/2/11

110
Nugent to his son St George

[Holograph] [St Jans Cappel]
27 November 1916

We did a highly successful raid the other day, broke into the German trenches in 3 places, took several prisoners and killed nearly 50.[18] I was rather annoyed that the parties did not take more prisoners but our men wouldn't trust them. They had been had before by Boches holding up their hands and shouting 'Kamerad' while another man took a pot shot from behind him, so they killed everyone almost that they met.

They left behind a number of booby traps for the Boches when they returned. They pulled the pins out of Mills grenades and put them under dead Boches in the trenches, so that the weight of the body kept the lever down, in the hope that when the Boches came back and lifted up their defunct comrades, they would explode violently. I did not hear whether the traps worked, but they deserved to.

Barring weekly bombardments and occasional raids times are fairly quiet, but I never trust the Boche. He is full of fight yet and I see no end in sight yet.

FC, D/3835/E/2/11

111
Nugent to his wife

[Holograph] [St Jans Cappel]
5 December 1916

I had W Redmond to dinner last night. Congreve couldn't come. All I can say is that if all Nationalists were like him, I am not surprised that Chief Secretaries and Viceroys after a short time in Ireland become H[ome] R[uler]s. He is the most charming and delightful person I ever met. A most amusing person with a most fascinating voice, a soft Irish accent and slight drawl which is a charm in itself.[19]

He told us most amusing stories the whole evening of the H of Commons and his struggles to get things done there and the dodges and bargains he had to make.

Somerset was dying to talk politics, but I saw Redmond only wanted to enjoy himself and I squashed him each time he began.

Redmond thanked me so nicely after dinner and talked of the honour I had done him. I felt quite puffed up. I sent for him and sent him back in my car.

Now if H[ome]R[ule] comes and awful things happen, we have a friend in the Nationalist party.

FC, D/3835/E/2/11

112
Nugent to his wife

[Holograph] [St Jans Cappel]
7 December 1916

When we got the news last night at dinner that Asquith and the Government had resigned, we all cheered with joy.[20] I do hope L[loyd] G[eorge] will have his way and no more miserable compromises. I feel as if a load was lifted off our necks. If nothing comes of it and Asquith returns to office, I shall feel that we have definitely embarked on the down grade to ruin, to damnation and to defeat.

I can't think anything so terrible can happen as failure now to force a real war Government. The Germans are already shrieking with joy at what they think is the fall of LG. I pray that a nasty disappointment awaits them.

FC, D/3835/E/2/11

113
Brigadier-General A. Ricardo to Nugent

[Holograph] 37 Division
12 December 1916

I delayed writing to you until I had seen something of my Brigade.[21]

I have two Lancashire Battalions, a Bedford and a Warwick Battalion – all New Army, of course.

They are at about the same strength as we were in 109th but are being filled up with Derby men – who are on the old side 35–38.

The first Battn I saw was a Lancashire one and I was amazed to see the difference in their physique, especially height, when compared with our big boys; inches shorter as an average.

Generally speaking the NCOs are better than ours, but men not nearly as good in any way.

Officers better I think.

The transport is wonderfully good – as good as anything we had and all at a high level. I was surprised at this.

Battns have more material for 2nd in Comd and future COs than we had in 36th.

In this Brigade they all go in for clean buttons etc which I am glad to see. The M Gun Coy is good with a tip top Regular soldier in command – the T.M. Batt: as usual has poor rank and file but officers distinctly good – all volunteers for the job.

One F[ield] A[mbulance] and one Coy R.E. and one Coy of the train work permanently with the Brigade and consequently the personal bond between their COs and the Inf COs and Brig Staff is close.

My Brig Staff are all gentlemen and we shall get on together, they haven't much experience.

There is very little crime but march discipline and so on is a long way behind ours.

Not near enough has been done for the men – and the COs and Regtal officers are surprised at the possibilities of helping in men's comfort and cheerfulness and they are quite enthusiastic when given the ideas – but they haven't used their imaginations enough.

We are out resting and educating – the drafts have done little or no musketry (shooting)!!

My old groom from my beloved 9th arrived yesterday and his description of his trek with my mare was like a whiff of paradise, it was good to hear the northern accent again and made me feel homesick!

I find my job intensely interesting, especially in starting and organising a Brig school. And I have been reading a heap of literature on the later experiences on the Ancre.

So many points you contended for, getting out in front during the intense bombardment, getting close up to and following up close and quick etc etc are now laid down as indispensable to success.

I am always happy when I am busy and have my time filled with work that I can feel I can do and that is useful – but I'd give much to be back where I was with the men I've learnt to love so much.

And if I should by any chance find myself back in the Ulster Division I should be a very proud and happy man.

I never told you all I feel towards yourself personally. I rejoiced when I heard you were going to command the Division and I never for one moment at any time changed that feeling. I have always admired and respected you as a chief and you won my affection as an unfailing friend – you'd feel surprised perhaps to know how widely that feeling for you is throughout your Division – we are an inarticulate nation.

You should have had a Corps long ago and I hope for the Army's sake that you soon get one but it will be a black day when you leave the Ulster Division.

I send you a Xmas card with every good wish – and the fervent hope that I shall have the chance of serving under you again.

FC, D/3835/E/10/8

114
Nugent to his wife

[Holograph] [St Jans Cappel]
15 December 1916

We gave the Germans a terrible doing this morning. I concentrated something like 50 guns and mortars on a piece of his line and we literally blew it away.

Somerset and I went up to a hill from which a view is obtainable pretty close to the place and it was most inspiriting.

The whole of the part we were bombarding was a sheet of flame and smoke from bursting shells and timber and corrugated iron, earth and every sort of debris was flying hundreds of feet up into the air. I did think I saw one Boche soaring upwards. He was about 200 feet up in the air when I saw him and still going up. If it was a Boche he had lost his head and arms.

FC, D/3835/E/2/11

115
Nugent to his wife

[Holograph] | [St Jans Cappel]
17 December 1916

The 16th Irish Division next door to us is very friendly. They have presented 4 cups for boxing competition to be competed for by the Ulster Division. Quite embarrassing as of course we shall have to do likewise.[22] Still it's all for good and as I have no doubt L[loyd] G[eorge] means to give Ireland Home Rule all round as the price of men, anything which tends to promote good feeling will tell afterwards. Personally I don't care 2d as long as we don't have to go home to the never-ending political sordid squabbles.

I think Irishmen ought to be made to do their duty in their own interests. It will make them better men morally and physically. As things are now Irishmen from the South who go home on leave from the Army are reviled and spat upon and if only to protect them, all Irishmen should be compelled to serve too.

Imagine an Ireland without an eternal Protestant and Catholic question. I daresay I might be an MP for Cavan. What honour.

The Nationalists would shortly all be fighting with each other and with the Priests.

The French advance is even better than the first reports.[23] They have learned far more than we have in attack and know how to cover the advance of their Infantry with artillery fire much better than we can. Their 75 is a wonderful gun.

FC, D/3835/E/2/11

116
Nugent to his wife

[Holograph] | [St Jans Cappel]
20 December 1916

Well, the C in C (D Haig is his name. He's in the Army. He's had a brilliant career.) came this morning and saw some of my men. I rode with him for 3 or 4 miles while he was going through my area.

Nothing could have been more charming. He said 'I must thank you for all the splendid work done by your Division since it came out. You did magnificently on the Somme and I always think with regret that we failed to give you all the support we ought to have done'.

I thanked him and said I thought that perhaps we had all been rather optimistic as to what it was possible to do. He replied 'Well, we were all learning'. Anyhow that was really very nice saying [*sic*] and so far from my back hair standing up, I was almost purring.[24]

FC, D/3835/E/2/11

117
Belfast Newsletter[25]

[Printed] [Belfast]
26 December 1916

Major-General O. S. W. Nugent, D.S.O. (A.D.C. to his Majesty the King), the General Officer Commanding the Ulster Division, has sent the following message to the people of Ulster through the medium of the 'Belfast News-Letter':–

> You have done me the honour of asking me to contribute a message as representing the Ulster Division.
>
> A message to the people of Ulster from Ulster's Division must contain, besides greetings and good wishes, some hard truths.
>
> For this is the position as it stands today between the Ulster Division and those of its own kin at home.
>
> When the people of Ulster in 1914 promised a Division to the service of King and country, no finer body of men than those who redeemed the promise were raised in any portion of the King's dominions.
>
> Cheerful under all circumstances, self-respecting, steadfast in their bearing, most gallant in attack, Ulstermen in France and Belgium have earned a high reputation, even amongst the magnificent soldiers of the Empire, of which Ulster may legitimately be proud.

The morning of the 1st of July will be one of the glories of the Province as long as men love to think of gallant deeds.

Will there be an element of shame to the memory amongst the thousands of lusty young Ulstermen at home?

They have no part as yet in the honour of the real manhood of Ulster. They will have no part in the future when the Ulster Division comes home to enjoy the respect and esteem earned by those who have seen the path of duty and have followed it even to the end.

But if they have no part now, they need not be without it. Every man can still redeem his birthright and take a man's share in the work of the deliverance of mankind from Prussian barbarism.

He need not fear being asked why he tarried so long upon the road. He will be welcomed as an Ulsterman, and he will find himself a better and happier man from the knowledge that he has done his duty.

Christmas is a time of memories, when families are reunited and friends meet again. Years hence Ulster will still be keeping green the memory of those whose work out here is not nearly finished yet.

Young men at home still have their chance. Do they not want to be able to look their countrymen in the face, here and at home?

Do they not realise that there will be tens of thousands of men throughout the Empire who have answered the call of duty, and that the terms on which all able-bodied young men will associate together after the war will largely turn on the answer which can be given to the question, 'What did you do in the war?'

For Ireland's sake, all who love her must hope that the community at large will insist that the stain upon her national pride and self-respect shall be removed, and that the contempt which Ireland is heaping up for herself shall give place to the mutual esteem which is creating a daily stronger bond of fellowship between the soldiers of the

Empire in France and Belgium. There is only one way to gain membership, and that is not by the road upon which Ireland is drifting leaderless today.

The Ulster Division is growing stronger day by day, but its ranks are being filled by Englishmen and Scotchmen – men who have not shirked duty, and who have done for Ulster what she has, as yet, failed to do for herself.

The young men of Ulster are capable of great achievements. The whole of the history of the Province is one of achievements. It is in the earnest hope that its young men will make yet another advance on the road of honour and duty that this message is written.

Belfast Newsletter

118
Brigadier-General A. Ricardo to Nugent

[Holograph]

37 Division
29 December 1916

Thank you very much for your letter and for all you say. I am so glad that the C in C spoke to you so warmly about the Division; I have no doubt at all that it is the best Division in France!

For the matter of work – I find here that there is not the most elementary knowledge of how best to organise a system of work in the line – from companies upwards!

I hope to sustain the reputation of the 36th for thoroughness, that Hessey has evidently impressed upon them all.[26]

I send you some literature which may interest you. Gough's army were very keen on this French training – which is nothing new. It is making the platoon the little fighting self dependent unit – with its own quota of specialists.

Genl Greenly's notes helped me – especially those on consolidation. Would you please return enclosed when finished with.

May I congratulate you on your message to the Ulster men – and for the hard truths you put before them.

If only our politicians had the same courage and power of calling a spade a spade in simple language.

FC, D/3835/E/10/8

119
Nugent to his wife

[Holograph] [St Jans Cappel]
30 December 1916

I enclose the Belfast News Letter with my message to the Ulster loafers and a leading article on it. They have done me the honour of great prominence. Don't you think it is rather a good message, just some plain speaking. I have had 2 letters of protest already which shows that it left a sting.

FC, D/3835/E/2/11

120
Nugent to his wife

[Holograph] [St Jans Cappel]
1 January 1917

I had rather a horrible walk through the trenches today. We got into the middle of a rather severe shelling and 2 poor men were blown to pieces almost beside me almost [*sic*], one killed outright and I had to step over him, avoiding the pieces, the other much mangled and probably dying. Personally I don't see enough of the gruesome parts of the war to be callous to these things. Somerset was with me, the first time he has been in a strafe and he did not like the sights either.

FC, D/3835/E/2/12

121
Nugent to [Adjutant General] GHQ

[Typescript copy] [St Jans Cappel]
n.d. but *c.* 1 February 1917

Establishment of Division	12,536	Infantry
Present strength (1.2.17)	9557	"
Deficiency	3679	"

The Division has been continually in the trenches for 12 months, except 1 Brigade which has been in the trenches for 15 months.

For the last 6½ months it has been holding a Divisional front with a shortage of strength varying from 4,500 to 3679.

Whatever the actual strength of a Division may be, the obligatory deductions remain constant.

These include Regimental Transport, other employments, men on courses, furlough etc.

The balance represents the fighting strength available for manning trenches and working parties.

Result of continued shortage of men:

(a) Increased and constant strain on Officers and Men while in the trenches.
(b) Continual working parties from Battalions supposed to be resting between tours of trench duty.
(c) Practical impossibility of training specialists such as Bombers, Lewis gun men, Signallers, which are essential to the organisation of Battalions for offensive.

The men are getting insufficient rest and the Division as a body so far as the infantry is concerned is a tired Division.

The sick rate is high and increasing.

It would be inaccurate and misleading to assert that the Division as a fighting machine is as good as it was before the 1st July of last year.

Tired men, continually overworked and underrested, too weak numerically to spare sufficient men for specialist training or to organise them into special squads when trained cannot be as efficient an instrument as a Division at full strength, fully organised.

The starvation of the Division as regards men is disheartening and demoralising. The material is of the best. The mixture of Englishmen and Irishmen in the same unit would make an ideal fighting machine.

The policy which has been pursued for months past as to reinforcements for the ULSTER Division is neither fair to the State nor the Division.

It causes a constant lowering of moral[e] which must in time seriously affect the value of the Division.

This is unwise from the point of view of the State and it is unfair to the material of which the majority of the Division is still composed.

FC, D/3835/E/10/8

122

Nugent to his wife

[Holograph] [St Jans Cappel]
4 February 1917

A curious incident happened today. I have not known of a similar case. Last night they tried a raid on our lines and we drove them back and this morning 2 badly wounded Boches were seen lying in no man's land. During the morning the Germans put up a notice 'Will you let us go out and bring in our Kamerads'. Our men made no reply and presently 2 German officers and 5 men got up on to their parapet with their hands up. The officers remained on the parapet and the men walked out into no man's land, picked up one of the wounded men who now appeared to be dead and carried him in. Of course our men did not fire though they would have been quite justified in doing so. I never knew the like. One would almost think the wounded man must have been of some importance. I am sorry to say the report says he was a fat man which is quite disappointing. The other man is lying closer to our line and we are going to try and get him in this evening after dark. I expect he will be dead. No badly wounded man could have survived the cold for nearly 24 hours.[27]

FC, D/3835/E/2/12

123
Nugent to General Sir Herbert Plumer

[Typescript copy] [St Jans Cappel]
10 February 1917

I am very much interested in Harington's report of his conversation with COs.

I understand their points of view, which are frequently narrow and not always intelligent. One of the things mentioned I have made a point of – that is, getting to know COs and giving them a chance of knowing the Divisional Staff. Until the weather got too cold, I always had a weekend party of a couple of COs. They seemed to like it, and anyhow I think they appreciate being asked. It is a good thing to ask COs from different Brigades as they scarcely ever meet each other.

I have found it most beneficial in mitigating the repugnance with which the Divisional Commander is usually regarded by the Battalion CO.

As to not knowing what is going on, they are not much behind the Divisional Commander in that respect.

The average CO of the present time is a rather leaky receptacle for confidential information. He is too fond of writing it home.

I quite agree there is too much writing and too many reports. There again COs suffer from inefficient Battalion Staffs who do not read orders and send in inaccurate returns which have to go back for correction.

The Army Staff, which only gets the finished results, possibly does not realise the amount of digging required to get accurate information from battalions.

I am sure they are often right in saying they do not get all the help they ought from Staff Officers, especially the junior grades. It is a point I have constantly enquired into. I will go into it again.

I do not sympathise in any way with the attitude taken by many COs towards classes of instruction.

They are essential and we could not carry on without them. COs should have the sense and breadth of view to realise this and that their best officers and men should be sent. I have had cases of men being sent to a Signalling Course who could not read or write.

I have found men reported as first-rate Lewis Gun Instructors at the Lewis Gun School, employed as company cooks on return to their battalions, sanitary orderlies – anything but the work they have specialised in.

I do think that battalions are sometimes asked to find an undue number of Officers or NCOs at one time for various Schools, and that when they are going into the trenches it is seriously inconvenient.

It should be possible to order matters so that battalions would not be required to send Officers to Army Classes if by so doing their numbers drop below three per company.

It would be all to the good to establish better relations between the Heavy Artillery and battalions. The former never visit the trenches and are altogether unknown to battalion COs and Officers.

I quite agree that most battalions need assistance in musketry instruction.

To an even greater extent does the Division need a Divisional Machine Gun Officer. It is a grave flaw in the organisation. The average Machine Gun Officer is incapable of command and entirely ignorant of the elements of the tactical employment of his guns.

Many months ago I instituted weekly conferences between Staff Captains and the 'Q' Branch. It is a very useful practice.

It is not necessary as far as 'G' is concerned as the 'G' Officers are over the line daily and constantly see Brigadiers, Brigade Majors and Battalion Commanders.

As to the articles turned out of Second Army Workshops, we should all like to know more. Would it not be possible to circulate illustrated, or at any rate descriptive catalogues?

FC, D/3835/E/10/8

124
Nugent to his wife

[Holograph]

[St Jans Cappel]
5 March 1917

I had a strange adventure today. I was apparently chased twice by a German aeroplane.

There was a bombardment of part of the German lines opposite my front and I went into the trenches to observe. In the middle of it a German aeroplane came over flying very low and came straight for the place where I was standing firing a machine gun.

Every machine gun in our lines that could be brought to bear opened fire on it and there must have been a lot bullets flying around. It turned before it reached the trench I was in. About ½ hour afterwards as I was walking along the trench it came back and again every machine gun in the area got to work. Just as he got over our trenches, he dived right down on them firing his machine gun. I thought he was hit until he straightened out and calmly turned back over his own lines. He was a most gallant fellow and he quite frightened me. I thought he was going to empty a belt at me.

FC, D/3835/E/2/12

125
Nugent to his wife

[Holograph]

[St Jans Cappel]
17 March 1917

What a stupendous affair the Russian Revolution is.[28] I hope it is all for good so far as the progress of the war is concerned. It seems to be a genuine upheaval in Russia against German influences. What interests me more than anything else is the effect it may have on the ruling class in Germany . . . Above all I count on the effect of the Revolution amongst the people. If Russia can force the Czar to abdicate, the German people may well begin to consider whether they wouldn't have been a happier and wiser people today if the Hohenzollerns had never existed.

I see good prospects. Anyhow it will make the Kaiser and the ruling class in Prussia very uncomfortable and may appreciably affect the war.

I had no shamrock today and no one had any. The supplies either were not sent off or they have failed to get here in time.

FC, D/3835/E/2/12

126
Nugent to his wife

[Holograph] [St Jans Cappel]
19 March 1917

The advance is very satisfactory isn't it, in so far as falling back from positions they have held for over 2 years is at any rate not a sign of strength on the part of the Germans.[29] I see they are burning and pillaging each village they are retreating from. No doubt they will leave the country an absolute desert. What savages they are but of course they are entitled by the laws of war to do that. What fills me with a sort of dry rage is that we shall never get the chance of burning German villages in retaliation.

They are digging hard and strengthening their line in front of us and digging fresh lines behind the present ones . . .

I had 2 narrow escapes today going round part of the new line I have taken over. I was going up a communication trench towards the front line which I could see as I thought on a rise in front of me. The communication trench had been mostly blown away by shell fire and was no real cover. When I got within 200 yards or so, it suddenly dawned on me that the wire was on the wrong side for our trenches and I realised I was walking in full view of the

German trenches. It had just dawned on me when crack came a rifle bullet within a few inches of my head. I lost no time I can tell you in turning round and disappearing as unobtrusively as possible. Then on the way back, I took a short cut over a field to a road which I thought was out of sight. About half way across a shell came along and burst on the path I had come about 150 yds behind me. A minute afterwards another this time within much closer distance of me. After I had got on to the road I stopped to get my breath as I was rather blown and then moved on. I hadn't gone 60 yards when 3 shells landed within 10 yards of where I had been standing and 2 more followed me up the road. The Boche must have spotted me and seen my red band through their telescope and thought a general was worth trying to bag. Anyhow I was fortunate. If I had waited they would probably have got me.

FC, D/3835/E/2/12

127
Nugent to his wife

[Holograph] [St Jans Cappel]
21 March 1917

I wonder when the Belfast papers will cease to remove me from command of this Division. They still do it. Ricardo told me that James Craig said to him in London that he would have nothing to do with the Division while I was in command of it because I had said I was going to have no politics in it and because I had refused to work with the politicians. The latter I certainly did not do because it was never suggested I should work with them so I got no opportunity of refusing, but I certainly should have refused to work with them if I had been asked. I wonder how Craig supposed I could have worked with them even if I had wished to. How I hate the sordid outlook of the politician. I think the Irish brand is worse than any other. I am glad to think that they can none of them say I meddled in their tricks when in command of this Division.

I do wish we were not the 'Ulster' Division but just the 36th.

FC, D/3835/E/2/12

128
Nugent to his wife

[Holograph] [St Jans Cappel]
6 April 1917

The entry of America is a great moral affair even if she is not able to add much at present to the effective fighting strength of the Allies.[30] In any case her money will be useful. I hope she will have sufficient pride not be content with a purely passive role. At the end of this year if the war is still going on a big American Army of 500,000 men would be a very decisive factor. I am afraid that Germany may ask for terms of peace before the bitterness of the war has bitten into the Americans and that they may want to be sentimental and make things easy for the Germans. If ever there was an occasion when vengeance would be righteous it is now . . .

The Germans are very busy in front of me digging new trenches and putting up new works. They don't mean to retire from here till they are turned out. That seems evident.

FC, D/3835/E/2/12

129
Nugent to his wife

[Holograph] [St Jans Cappel]
8 April 1917

It has been a beautifully bright sunny Easter Day, though not entirely peaceful. A division of Prussians has come in hereabouts in place of some quiet sleepy Saxons and they are very much more unpleasant neighbours. They have taken to the games they used to play, that is of firing shells at individuals seen walking across a field or anywhere in the open behind the front line. They amuse themselves by firing a small piece which throws a shell known as a 'pip squeak' and as this reaches anywhere up to 2 miles behind our front trenches it is very inconvenient as we had got into the habit of using various short cuts across the open. Now I suppose we shall have to take to the old place [*sic*] of following the trenches . . .

Now is the time to make an effort to settle the Irish question. I am sure the relations between Ireland and England have a bad effect on our relations with America.

Personally I think the North of Ireland should be compelled to submit to a settlement in the interests of the Empire. I believe an Irish Home rule government would probably be the worst in the world but in the interests of the Empire and of civilisation against the Huns we should put up with it if it is necessary.

As a minor episode to show the venom of the people of the north of Ireland type, I think the letter signed by Lady Carson and others disclaiming any connection with Lady MacDonnell's Committee was deplorable, though Lady MacD's offence this time was merely that she was first in the field with a flag day for the Irish soldiers and sailors without respect of party or creed.

FC, D/3835/E/2/12

130
Nugent to his wife

[Holograph] [St Jans Cappel]
21 April 1917

I am really beginning to think the Boche is losing his moral[e] and nerve. Yesterday a Prussian calmly walked across from his own lines and gave himself up. When he was questioned he said he came over because life was absolutely insupportable, that the German Army had long given up any hope of winning the war, that they were only kept fighting by the ruling class in Germany because they were afraid to make peace, that the food even of the soldiers was so bad now that there had been cases of men refusing to go to the trenches unless they were better fed. He said he would be prepared to go back to his lines and bring in the whole of his platoon if we gave him a written assurance that they would be properly treated.

Well, we thought it worthwhile to try and so he got a written promise and was re-conducted to the front line and told to go back to his own lines and fetch his companions. Unfortunately the arrangements made by the CO of the battalion to whom this man urrendered had not taken into account our own men and they had ot been told of the arrangements so when the Prussian got out nto No man's land and was seen going towards his own line, the entries on our line opened fire on him and he ran back to shelter gain and then he lost his nerve and would not face it and so we ad to be content with one Prussian instead of a little bag of them s we hoped. A little incident but very significant of the state of eeling and discipline and he was a Prussian too. He did seem to ate and despise his officers too. Said they never came near the renches and were cowards.

C, D/3835/E/2/12

131
Nugent to his wife

Holograph] | [St Jans Cappel]
29 April 1917

am very much upset at some verbal information given me by an fficer from GHQ who was really sent over to tell it me. pparently they wouldn't put it in writing. The gist of it was that he C in Ch out here won't use us for any purpose but holding the ne so long as we call ourselves the Ulster Division, because he onsiders that it is unfair to Englishmen who have compulsory ervice that they should be sent to fill up a Division supposed be omposed of volunteers from Ulster, but who won't volunteer, that f we want to be called Ulster we must fill up our own ranks, but hat if we are prepared to drop the title of Ulster we shall be reated as any other Division and get men and be used in omething more glorious than Trench drudges.

Now the whole difficulty is this, that GHQ won't put this in vriting, but they want me to start the correspondence by offering n behalf of the Division to drop the title of Ulster. What would appen? The politicians at home would at once kick up a row, call t an insult to Ulster and so on. The War Office would then say we never suggested it. The GOC the Ulster Divn suggested it of is own initiative'.

Can't you imagine the outcry amongst the cats round Lad Carson's Committee table and the stayathomes of Belfast. The would never rest till they got me hounded out and we have to liv in Ireland after the war.

I would do it all the same tomorrow if it is the only way, but it i so unfair to try and throw the onus of taking the first step upo me that I am trying to get GHQ to say it in writing. Why should be made the scapegoat for the wrath of the dirty politicians of th Craig type.

I have felt for months how inglorious a role this Division i playing ever since the 1st July. Every other Division in the Arm except the 2 Irish Divisions has been in and out of the fighting 2, or 4 times since then.

We have done nothing but sit in the trenches. The men feel it We all feel it. There is not an officer or man who would not vote t drop 'Ulster' and be just a fighting Division. We owe nothing t Ulstermen who have done nothing to keep us up, but brag in th local papers about their glorious Division and how magnificentl Ulster has done. I am not surprised that GHQ or the WO whichever is the bottom of it to [*sic*] say 'Let the Ulstermen kee their own Division up since they brag so loudly of it, but the can't have Englishmen and still call themselves Ulster'.

Why did I ever see them. Not that I have a word to say agains the men out here. They are always good, but I wish I had neve seen a political Division and the people who thought they wer going to run it can never forgive me because I would not allow an politics in it.

You can imagine how humiliating it is to sit here month afte month, seeing Divisions come up from the real fighting, fit ou and fill up and go away again while we remain on for ever 2 Divisions from either side of us who have been several time down south since last July have just gone away again to take thei share in the honour and losses.

Well, I have lamented enough.

FC, D/3835/E/2/12

132
Nugent to his wife

-Iolograph] [St Jans Cappel]
2 May 1917

saw Sir H Plumer, 2nd Army Comdr yesterday and discussed the uestion of the title. He agreed at once that it would be most nfair to ask me to raise the question in view of all the rcumstances, but said he would do so himself and suggest the tle should be discontinued.

At the present time only half the numbers in the whole Division e Irish so that there would be no grievance except amongst the oliticians at home. My own opinion is that the WO are afraid to aise the question themselves and want someone else to do it so iat they can say if necessary that they didn't suggest it.

These Irish politicians are awful, Unionists or Nationalist, there no difference . . .

Smiley has just gone off to London to the secret session, a great onvenience having a member on the Corps staff as we shall hear l that took place. As a matter of fact the Govt don't tell the Iouse much more at a secret session than they do in public . . .

We had a little raid day before yesterday into a part of the ierman trenches which are within a few yards of ours. It was in ie middle of the day and we thought they would not be expecting s, but there must have been someone who gave it away on the lephone. The Germans have listening apparatus and can verhear our telephone conversations over a mile behind our lines. 'here are strict orders against talking on the telephone in the ont line, but it is almost impossible to check it. Anyhow the party ound the Germans all ready and waiting for them, not in the front ench but in another trench about 40 yds back and so they came ack and though the Boches fired heavily on them they did not get ny of them, which was good fortune.

C, D/3835/E/2/12

133
General Sir Herbert Plumer to Adjutant General GHQ

[Typescript] 2nd Arm

3 May 191

There has been, and there is likely to always be under preser conditions, difficulty in maintaining the 36th (Ulster) Division u to its establishment both of Officers and men if reinforcements ar restricted to Ulstermen.

On the other hand there may possibly be a natural reluctance o the part of Officers and men who are not Ulstermen to be drafte into a Division which bears a distinctive title.

It seems for consideration whether it would not now b generally advantageous to omit the title 'Ulster' and let th Division be styled the 36th simply. If desired I could ascertai through the General Officer Commanding the Division whethe there would be any objection to this course on the part of th Officers, NCOs and men who formed part of the Ulster Divisio as originally constituted.

At present there are in the Division about 64% of the Infantr and 50% of all arms who are Ulstermen.

FC, D/3835/E/10/8

134
Nugent to his wife

[Holograph] [St Jans Cappel

9 May 191

I have just finished drafting a letter to be sent to all COs askin them to consider the question and giving them the reasons. I knov what the answers will be but anyhow the politicians will not b able to say I proposed it. What a lot of hot air there will be when i gets home. I'd like to see the faces of the sweet little tolerant an charitable committee the first time they get together to spit over it Do go up to London to attend the meetings. I am sure it woul brace you up.

Also we are <u>not</u> going to vegetate. That is settled. The simultaneous bombardments of the German lines on Monday night was most exhilarating. I went up to the top of a hill near here to see it. I don't know how many hundreds of guns were in action but the noise and the fireworks were terrific and must have given the Boche some anxious moments. He must have thought we were all coming over after it.

FC, D/3835/E/2/12

135
Nugent to his wife

[Holograph] [St Jans Cappel]
13 May 1917

I went to a Horse Show of a neighbouring Division in Alick Godley's Corps this afternoon. They couldn't touch our turnouts either in polish or quality.

I gather from Bob Maxwell that there is a strong feeling amongst Ulstermen out here against any alteration, but my point is that as the military authorities have asked us a certain question on military grounds, it is our business to answer it as soldiers and not as politicians. What action the politicians at home will take is no concern of ours.

I hope they will take the right view. I am to have a conference with all the COs early next week to find out what their views are.

FC, D/3835/E/2/12

136
Nugent to IX Corps

[Typescript copy] [Ulster Camp, Dranoutre]
16 May 1917

I have discussed the question raised in attached correspondence with all Commanding Officers of units originally raised in Ulster.

The title of 'Ulster' is very highly valued not alone by Ulstermen in the Division by the majority of Englishmen in the Division. The loss of the title would be deeply felt.[31]

It is felt that inasmuch as the Division is not responsible for the circumstances which have raised the question of its future claim to the title of 'Ulster', it is hard on the Officers and other ranks of the original Division that they should be asked to voluntarily express their readiness to surrender the designation . . .

The unanimous feeling expressed was that the question is one which should be decided by higher authority and, so far as the Division is concerned, it will loyally accept whatever decision may be arrived at as to its future designation.

I may add with absolute confidence that the reluctance expressed to voluntarily renouncing the title of 'Ulster' is based on sentiment and association only and is in no way political.

FC, D/3835/E/10/8

137
Nugent to his wife

[Holograph] [Ulster Camp]
17 May 1917

I am much nearer the front where I am now and the noise of shelling is much more persistent. There was very heavy gunning last night.

We had a meeting of all COs yesterday and discussed the question of dropping the title. The general opinion was that everyone would very much feel it if the title were taken away but we had no desire to claim a distinction if we were not entitled to it, that if there was any doubt about it, it was a question to be decided not by us but by higher authority. Whatever decision was come to by higher authority the Division would loyally accept. Our attachment to the title was from association and sentiment and in no way political. The dominant consideration amongst all ranks in the Division was that the Division should be first and last a fighting unit and nothing else.

I think this was a fair way of putting it. We said in effect that it was for higher authority to settle the question and not for us to do, but we would accept whatever decision was made.

I further warned officers that they must remember they were soldiers and must not start work behind the backs of higher authority by writing to their political friends.

FC, D/3835/E/2/12

138
Nugent to his wife

[Holograph] [Ulster Camp]
20 May 1917

I have had an 'at home' this afternoon. The band played at Div Hdqrs and I asked various people who live in the vicinity to come to tea, only the best people of course, I am very exclusive. Audley Pratt came and COs.

It has been a steaming hot day. The C in C comes on Wednesday and is coming here. I don't look forward to it. Alas for my prospects, I never got on with him and we have always been anti sympatica or antipathetic or mutually antagonistic or whatever one may call it.

However, he is C in C now so I am but a humble bottle-washer in his eyes no doubt . . .

Our artillery hardly ever ceases now and at times it is a row. Especially when the Germans join in. There was a tremendous set to last night about 1 am, both sides going for all they were worth. My hut rattled. The Germans tried to raid my trenches but were beaten off leaving some dead in front.[32] We will get them in tonight to see who they were.

It must be rather heavenly at home just now. I should like to be out on the lake.

I don't believe the Govt's proposals will have the slightest effect. The North won't accept a convention and the other side won't take H[ome] R[ule] unless all Ireland is in it. However it ought to have a good effect in America as it is a clear offer to give Irishmen the option of settling the form of Govt they want and if they can't agree who else can.

FC, D/3835/E/2/12

139
Nugent to his wife

[Holograph] Ulster Camp
21 May 1917

I sent 2 of my Staff Officers and 1 Brigadier down to Arras today to get the latest tips and information from their experience which is of the latest. They went to a Canadian Division one of those which did so well in the taking of the Vimy Ridge. They came back however saying they found the Canadian Staff rather sketchy as to details which were what we most wanted to know . . .

Our camp is much admired by everyone and it is really most excellently planned and built and it is the first time since I have commanded a Division that I have had the whole of the Division Hdqrs together. Generally they are scattered about in all sorts of odd places and even in different villages according as there is accommodation for them. We have even started a flower bed of geraniums and daisies . . .

I got a parcel of socks from Mrs Blackley in Cavan for the Division, 100 pairs. But it is such a waste to send them. They are not wanted and the men can get all the socks they want by asking for them, but the scream of the matter is that Mrs Blackley sent them out through Lady MacDonnell's Comttee instead of the Ulster one. The dear ones of Ulster will become purple with indignation. The socks of course are contaminated and infected and unfit for an Ulsterman to wear so I must give them to the Englishmen who compose nearly half of the 'Ulster' Divn! I sometimes feel that I should like to attend one of the meetings and just tell the Comttee my most inward views of them.

FC, D/3835/E/2/12

140
Nugent to his wife

[Holograph] [Ulster Camp]
23 May 1917

The Com-in-Ch has been here for some time and has just gone away. For him he was quite genial but he always makes me feel like a small boy saying his lessons. Prickles rise along my backbone. I believe he means to be genial but his nature is dour and does not lend itself to the lighter moods. Anyhow he meant well . . .

We had a successful raid last night and brought back prisoners and slew some Boche, and we had no casualties ourselves except 1 officer wounded.[33]

The 2nd Army told me yesterday that the work of this Division was further advanced and better done than any Division in the 2nd Army, also that we did more and better work with fewer men than any other Division.

Very pleasant hearing.

Generally the situation seems to be improving. Russia looks like turning up again. Apparently we have been more successful in dealing with the submarines. We have got minor successes further south and the French and Italians have had some successes and at any rate the Boche has had none. Another 2 or 3 years ought to see it finished, by that time there will only be an American Army left on our side and they may decide that we have too large an Empire and wish to take some of it away. We shouldn't be able to fight them as we should have no men by then.

FC, D/3835/E/2/12

141
Nugent to his wife

[Holograph] [Ulster Camp]
25 May 1917

The C in C was really most genial for him when he was here on Wednesday. He even got so far as to call me by my Christian name and take my arm. I felt quite uncomfortable and hedge hogging. I think perhaps he meant to convey that he had heard well of me and that he didn't think me as impossible or incompetent, or whatever he may have thought me, as he used to do.

Anyhow it was a pleasant contrast to former recollections.

FC, D/3835/E/2/12

142
Nugent to his wife

[Holograph] [Ulster Camp]
26 May 1917

By the way I heard yesterday that the 'leaders' of Ulster opinion are simply furious with me over my letter to Ulster last Xmas, because they took it as a reflection on their province which never under any circumstances can do anything wrong. People out here who have learned to see things in true perspective were delighted with it but you couldn't teach the people at home anything beyond their keyhole outlook.

They were all quite delighted too with my letter about the title. It exactly represented their views.

FC, D/3835/E/2/12

143
Nugent to his wife

[Holograph] [Ulster Camp]
27 May 1917

I . . . had William Redmond to lunch and after lunch we had a long talk in my hut on the prospects of a settlement in Ireland. He is very hopeful though he recognises that the people of NE Ulster and Belfast will be the obstacle. He said all the respectable Nationalist classes in Ireland sincerely desire a settlement and would make any concession almost to the extreme party in Ulster in order to gain a settlement by consent but short of partition to which no Nationalist will agree. He also told me of the proceedings at the secret session. I can't remember if I told you. Anyhow the 2 principal things were that we were doing very well against the submarines and that we had enough food in Gt Britain to carry us over the next year. Both pieces of good news.

FC, D/3835/E/2/12

144
Nugent to his wife

[Holograph] [Ulster Camp]
28 May 1917

We had a bad night last night and have had to clear out of our camp. Just after dinner the Germans began to shell the camp. Almost the first shell landed on one of the staff huts, office hut and killed 1 of the clerks and wounded 4 and of course wrecked the hut. Then they began to put them into the camp steadily. Naturally everyone scattered, there was nothing else to do. We lay under such banks or in any hollows we could find. Henry my ADC was slightly wounded by a splinter but nothing to speak of, but my C[ommander] R[oyal] E[ngineers] Colonel King[34] was killed. He is a terrible loss to me at this juncture. He was such a nice fellow and he appealed especially to me because he was absolutely first-rate at organisation and I liked him so much. The Germans shelled us all night. No one could go to bed, because we could not get into the camp, or at least it didn't seem worth trying as you couldn't tell whether the next shell mightn't land on your hut. I lay under a hedge in a ploughed field until I thought it was over and people began to gravitate towards the camp. Then they began again and we had to bolt.

We spent the night dodging from one place to another to avoid the parts he was specially shelling. One shell covered me with earth but that was the nearest I was to one, but that was unpleasantly close.

When morning came we found there had been a good many casualties, 70 horses killed and 60 to 70 men wounded, but very few killed I am thankful to say.

Anyhow we felt pretty certain that the position of my Hdqrs had been given away and that we should have no peace or security as long as we stayed there, so this morning we separated into various small camps.

I and my fighting staff have moved to another spot previously prepared from which I can overlook the German lines but where I have had a deep tunnel in a hill prepared to shelter in in case of shelling.

FC, D/3835/E/2/12

145
Nugent to his wife

[Holograph] [Kemmel Hill]
29 May 1917

We didn't get much rest last night either as the Germans started shelling my new HQ about 12 o'clock at night and kept it up most of the night. They couldn't actually hit us because I am at present tucked away in a ravine in a wood with a hill top just above us about 100 feet, but their shells came over just skimming the top and bursting below us. One brought a tree down just above us with a terrific crack. Then our heavy artillery behind us joined in and the roar and crack of our guns and German shells made sleep out of the question. This went on till daylight and then the place grew quiet. However I am going to sleep in a deep tunnelled dugout tonight which burrows into the hill and which we had made for this many weeks ago and in there you can hear nothing. I would have slept in there last night but it was very hot last night and some idiotic engineer had painted the gallery of the tunnel white to lighten it up and the smell of paint was overpowering.

It smells pretty strong still, but one must try and get some sleep. However I am not too badly off. I had a good sleep after the racket stopped at daylight.

The noise of our own big guns is rather trying. We are in front of them and the crashing of them goes on hour after hour. It makes the air shake and one's inside seems to give a rumble in sympathy each time so it becomes monotonous. However I am glad I am not the Boche in the front line or behind it. He must be having a rotten time.

I am just going to write to Mrs King, the wife of my late CRE. I am told she is a very charming woman. She lost her only son at the beginning of the war and now she has lost her husband, poor woman.

I am in such a pretty place if it wasn't for the war on the slopes of a hill covered with beech and undergrowth. We spoil its picturesqueness and the nightingales have not had a chance so far.

FC, D/3835/E/2/12

146
Nugent to his wife

[Holograph] [Kemmel Hill]
4 June 1917

We have had 2 very successful daylight raids, yesterday and today.[35] Yesterday a party of Bob Maxwell's battalion went in, surprised the Germans in their dugouts, brought back 19 prisoners and killed several more.

Today a party from another battalion did a raid and brought back an Officer, 30 men and a machine gun and killed quite a number of Germans. I watched both raids from my hill top, but I really could hardly bear to watch them. It looked such a little lonely party going out from our trenches into the awful country beyond the German lines. The men however thoroughly enjoyed themselves. We covered them well, I need hardly say, with a tremendous bombardment first and then put what is known as a box barrage all round the area to be raided. The Germans were driven into their dugouts by the bombardment and no one could come to their assistance through the box.

Some of them put up a fight but most of them were only too thankful to be safe.

I must say it was horribly thrilling to watch through the telescope, our men bombing the dugouts and dragging out

Germans, some of whom had to be bayonetted because they wouldn't come along. In each case we had very few casualties. The men are delighted and it has given them great confidence both in themselves and in the Artillery.

I was probably the most anxious person in the Division. As I watched them wandering about and searching the ground, they appeared to be absolutely standing up on the skyline and every moment I dreaded to see a big German shell land in the middle of them, but I don't think the Germans behind could know what was going on from smoke and dust of our barrage and I am perfectly certain every telephone wire behind the German lines had been cut long ago.

FC, D/3835/E/2/13

147
Nugent to his wife

[Holograph] [Kemmel Hill]
5 June 1917

We have got great kudos so far from the Army. The Army Commander was so struck with our daylight raids yesterday and day before that he ordered the whole Army to do the same today, but we don't do things that everyone else does so we didn't. Sweet! He sent the Division a telegram of congratulations last night so we are good boys up to now.

I did the heavy General out of the book yesterday to the German Officer when he was brought in. I expressed my sympathy on the fortunes of war in his case and told him he would have peace and quiet for the rest of the war anyhow and then I ordered the beast to be fed and led away.

I don't think he was sorry to be safe, but he said they been told that we kept black troops behind the front line to kill the prisoners because our men wouldn't do it. He honestly believed it himself which shows the kind of barbarians the Germans are. He was a Saxon.

FC, D/3835/E/2/13

148
Nugent to his wife

[Holograph] [Kemmel Hill]
6 June 1917

I have just been round the Division this afternoon. While I was away the Germans put a shell plumb on the top of my observation post on the hill above the camp and blew it to pieces.

Most fortunately no one was in it at the time, but it is finished so far as my use is concerned. Well, I might have been in it with a lot of my staff.

It was we thought carefully concealed during building and was built of thick concrete but it wasn't good enough to keep out the German shells.

FC, D/3835/E/2/13

149
Nugent to his wife

[Holograph] [Kemmel Hill]
7 June 1917

6.45 a.m. We have been deep in the great adventure since 3.10 am this morning.[36] Up to now reports are all good. We are well into the German lines and our casualties are slight.

I went up to my observation post to see the start. It was of course quite dark then. The signal for the attack was the sending up of great mines at various points along the front. These had been dug and charged many months ago. They were a wonderful sight to see in the early dawn when they went up in a lurid gigantic sheet of flame. At the same moment something like 3000 guns opened fire along the 2nd Army front and the whole country beyond the German front line became a sheet of flame and smoke. It might have been literally the end of a world. There was no wind and the dense pall of smoke and dust from the mines and shells hung like a black pall over the ground, lit up continually by the flash of bursting shells and as for the noise no words could describe that. It absolutely cowed one, because the roar prevented one from hearing anyone speak and the continual concussion became painful. We all retired to the trench and we just sit by the telephone for the reports sent back by the people in front.

12.30. Up to now, thank God, all seems to have gone well. We have captured Wytschaete side by side with the 16th Irish Division. The Anzacs on our right have got Messines and the 36th Divn have got all the ridge between the two places. For over 2½ years the Germans have looked down from Wytschaete and the ridge and Messines on us at the bottom of the hill. I hope they will never get it back now. The aeroplanes report that the Germans are massing behind and we may be sure that their counter attack will come before long.

So far as we can learn our casualties have been slight in the attack, about 600 which is small nowadays but there is a long day and several tomorrows before then.

The heat is very great and already reports from the front speak of the exhaustion of the men.

The Corps Commander has just been in to congratulate me on the success of the Divn but all the Divns seem to have done equally well. We mustn't be too optimistic at once. The Germans won't give up the ridge after 2½ years without a fight. It is his main look out along the Flanders front. Meanwhile there is a lull but we renew the attack with fresh troops this afternoon. I think that this offensive is going to be the biggest we have undertaken yet since the war began. How long it will last I cannot tell, but I am pretty sure there will be no pause for many weeks.

The Division has so far sent in 750 prisoners, but the totals are not all in yet and there may be more.

They report the ground strewn with dead Germans.

2.30. Have just heard the Germans have counter attacked on our right but have been beaten back. They won't be satisfied with one beating, I am sure.

The bag of prisoners is 855 by latest tally. These are all ours. I don't know what other prisoners have been taken by other Divisions.

The cry from the front is for water. I am sending it up in petrol tins on mules and horses, as fast as I can but it would be impossible to supply the demand.

It is a terrible hot day. Tanks have taken part in today's operations, but so far as we are concerned they never caught us up till we had reached our objective.

The total of prisoners taken by the 36th Division is well over 1000 and in addition we have captured 2 batteries of Artillery.

The battle has only begun, but I think there is no doubt that so far as the fortunes of the day are concerned, it has been the most successful the British Army has had in this war.

I am very happy over the share in it of this Division and the splendid way they fought today.

I feel I have done some share of good work.[37]

FC, D/3835/E/2/13

150
Nugent to his wife

[Holograph] [Kemmel Hill]
8 June 1917

The Division had a quiet night. The Germans counter attacked on our right against Messines but got no good out of it. They have since made another this evening but also no use.

This morning I went over the battlefield to our advanced lines. It is a terrible scene. Most of the dead and all the wounded have been removed, but there are a goodish number of German dead and some of our own still scattered about and other gruesome sights. The contorted attitudes of most are horrible. The most pathetic sight of all I think, is to see where a man's little belongings have been scattered on the ground, private letters, photos of wives and children, all sorts of little things which the poor miserable Boche had evidently treasured. I even pitied the Boche. He had such an appalling ordeal to go through. To see the ground is to realise how awful our shelling must have been.

The whole of the way back from the German front line to the top of the ridge and beyond it is one waste of shell craters where there isn't one living blade of grass even. It is really the most appalling desolation and waste I have ever seen. It makes me long more than ever to smash the people who are responsible for loosing this awful war on humanity.

Our men are in great heart. They say they have got their own back at last. They did most extraordinarily well. I have learned that this Division took all its objectives with less loss than any other Division in the Army and we took more prisoners. This may be accounted for by the fact that our men are kinder hearted.

The Army Comdr was here today to congratulate the Division and he brought the C in C's congratulations as well. In fact we have had congratulations all round and we will feel happy to think that the long weeks of preparation are crowned with success

The Germans are making another counter attack south of us at this moment. I can hear the guns going for all they are worth, but it is beyond us.

FC, D/3835/E/2/13

151
Nugent to his wife

[Holograph]

[St Jans Cappel]
10 June 1917

I had no time yesterday to write. The Germans made a heavy counter attack on Friday night (8th) preceded by very heavy bombardment, but they got no good out of it and next morning we could see hundreds of them lying dead or badly wounded in front of our line. I was anxious for a while as the shelling was very heavy.

All yesterday he shelled our new lines and once or twice I thought he was coming on again but he didn't.

He is shelling hard today but I have my doubts whether he will make another serious bid to get back his front line on the ridge. He must have lost a lot of men in the last 10 days.

We have been relieved by another Division now and we went back into reserve last night. It is a welcome rest. We have had a pretty strenuous time for the last fortnight, but the men are in tremendous spirits and would ask nothing better than to have another go. They say hunting Boche is the finest sport in the world.

I am back at my former Chateau where I spent the winter near Bailleul, but I do not expect we shall be there for long. There is more work to do.

When we left here to move up, the Mayor of the Commune sent a letter on behalf of the inhabitants thanking the Division for their considerate behaviour and for the courtesy and kindness they had shown all the time they were here and saying there had not been the least damage done the whole time. Very unusual and very gratifying.

The C in C came yesterday to my advanced Hdqrs and thanked me for the work we had done in preparation and for the splendid performance of the Division. That also was gratifying. What pleases me more than anything is that the 16th Division did equally well and there was nothing to choose between them so neither side can make any capital out of the performance of its own Division in Ireland. As a matter of fact we were first on top of the ridge, because the 16th were hung up by wire in a wood, but there was nothing to choose between the Divisions, nor in fact any Division so far as I can hear. It was a great success.

FC, D/3835/E/2/13

152
Nugent to his wife

[Holograph] [St Jans Cappel]
13 June 1917

Today has been a peaceful day. The Germans are either going to resign themselves to the loss of the ridge or they are preparing something striking. I think they will resign themselves, because every day makes us stronger now in the new line.

One hears so many interesting stories of Company Officers' experiences every day now. One officer, a great big burly subaltern, told me of how his company had come across a nest of German machineguns and had had a little fight of his own with them eventually getting round them and driving them into a big dugout where they eventually put up the white flag. When our men closed round it and ordered the Germans to come out, a lot of men came out first, blubbering with terror and in a state of absolute collapse. They thought they were all going to be murdered and couldn't believe it when they found they were only going to be prisoners.

Then someone went into the dugout and found no less than 30 Hun officers in it including a battalion commander. They were all pulled out, some very white and shaky, others trying to swagger but not succeeding very well. One Boche officer by way I suppose of currying favour, seized hold of the hand of the officer who told me and kissed it whereupon the Ulsterman hit him a clap on the jaw, because he said he didn't want to be kissed by any dirty Boche.

After the battle, various kindly disposed friends sent me souvenirs to take home. Among other things which came to Div Hdqrs there was a cannon, a large trench mortar, a rifle, 2 machine guns and an oxygen breathing apparatus. I was duly grateful but did not see my way to carrying them home, besides which it is strictly forbidden for officers or other ranks to acquire any loot.

FC, D/3835/E/2/13

153
Nugent to his wife

[Holograph] [St Jans Cappel]
17 June 1917

We are leaving here tomorrow or next day and going to another Corps and Army. I understand we have been specially asked for. Anyhow our Corps Hdqrs are almost in tears at losing us. We are quite the bright, particular boys or stars of this Army. I shall be sorry to leave our present Army Commander. He is such a delightful, loyal person to soldier with and one feels all the time that he has no ax [*sic*] to grind. He is always accessible and friendly and I like him immensely.

FC, D/3835/E/2/13

154
Nugent to his wife

[Holograph] [St Jans Cappel]
17 June 1917

The official cinema photographer has been sent out to take photos of the Division.[38] He arrived today and among other pictures he wants the Divisional Headquarters so I shall be displayed all over the United Kingdom shortly in studiously unconscious attitudes before the camera.

FC, D/3835/E/2/13

155
Nugent to his wife

[Holograph] [Merris, nr Kemmel]
4 July 1917

The Divisional Commanders with their Brigadiers met [the King] today in a field near Kemmel and he passed along making a few remarks to each. Great jealousy all round as he stayed more than half the time he was in the field talking to me! He was most gracious, said he was very pleased to meet me again and congratulated me on the work of the Division. The other Divisional Comdrs had not talked to him and mostly had merely grinned nervously and made things very stiff so I thought a little bit of buck wouldn't do us any harm and immediately waded in with anecdotes. He was delighted and became quite childish. I told him of the 2nd Lieut who captured 30 German officers in a dugout and then knocked down the one who kissed him on the hand. The K roared over that and chortled for a long time.

He then asked after the Division and whether we were getting any Ulstermen. I said 'None' and he said, but you still call yourself the Ulster Division. I said I expected we should always be the Ulster Division and that we found that the Englishmen coming to us were as keen to belong to us as any Ulsterman and were quite proud of being in the 'Ulsters'. Hamilton Gordon the Corps Comdr said they like coming to a Division with such a distinguished record and the K said 'Yes I suppose thats it'. I said 'Oh no, they like coming because they know they will be properly looked after in this Division'. Whereupon old Plumer who had listened with a humorous smile to my buck, went off into silent guffaws behind the King's back and made a fearful face at me.

The King asked what the Division was going to do and when I told him we were leaving the 2nd Army and going behind for some brushing up he said he supposed I should like some leave. I said I was always ready for leave but had recently had some, whereupon old Plumer broke in with 'Yes he only came back this morning I believe' (more laughter). Altogether we were all very childish and merry and bright.

I am just going off to my Corps Comdr now to have tea and say goodbye to him and staff.

FC, D/3835/E/2/13

156
Nugent to his wife

[Holograph] | [Wizernes]
20 July 1917

By the way I had to inform 2 of my COs the other day that I did not think they were up to the mark and must try some other job.[39] One of them came to me today and calmly informed me that unless he was given a better job there could be a row made at home as his father in law was a very influential politician in Belfast and would be sure to have a try to raise a row in Parliament I suppose. I don't think he meant that he himself would do anything to down me but that his father in law would. I am very curious to know who his father in l[aw] is. I forgot to ask him. We do have our trials out here.

Needless to say I told him that his father in l might do what he pleases.

FC, D/3835/E/2/13

157
Nugent to his wife

[Holograph] [Poperinghe]
31 July 1917

The battle has begun, this morning at dawn.[40] We have not been in yet, but are waiting just behind and expect to be sent in within 2 or 3 days.

There has been heavy fighting all day and the artillery fire has been absolutely terrific. The results are not too satisfactory as far as we can tell at present.

It is always hard to get information from the fighting line and it has been a dull dark day with rain about and this evening looks like being a wet night, bad for the fighters and wounded alike.

I have somewhat come down in the world as regards accommodation. My Hdqrs have been a good deal damaged by shellfire at different times. Nearly all the windows are broken, but it doesn't so much matter while the weather keeps warm . . .

The whole of the traffic for the front passes this house and its pavé road and the din never ceases. Endless streams of motor lorries night and day keep passing and the house trembles the whole time as I have felt a bungalow in India tremble in an earthquake. My bedroom is at the back of the house fortunately, otherwise I could get no sleep. Those who slept in rooms facing the street could not sleep at all last night, but they will get accustomed to it after a couple of nights. All the same it is not restful.

FC, D/3835/E/2/13

158
Nugent to his wife

[Holograph]

[Poperinghe]
1 August 1917

It has been raining continuously for nearly 24 hrs. The whole of this country is a vast bog and it is impossible to move men or guns or stores, so the day has been quiet. Neither the Germans nor ourselves have been able to do anything and there has been very little shelling. All over the country guns and wagons are stuck in the mud and there is no prospect of moving them till the ground dries. It looks like raining for days.

As I write I have just got a wire that the Germans have attacked on our right and broken into our lines in one place. We shall probably counter attack immediately, but it is awful weather for active operations.

We thought we were going in at once this evening, having got orders to be ready, but these were afterwards cancelled. I suspect we shall move very soon . . .

My Hdqrs is rather miserable in this weather. It is very damp and the rain comes through the holes and broken windows . . .

Arthur returned with his squadron from the front last night. He will probably be sent back altogether now. Cavalry are not wanted.

FC, D/3835/E/2/14

159
Nugent to his wife

[Holograph]

[Mersey Camp, Ypres]
4 August 1917

We have all moved up and taken the place of the Division which was in front of us, so we are now in front and the next move falls to us.[41] The weather conditions are simply indescribable.

My Hdqrs are in a grove of trees about ¾ mile off the main road, and there is only one track to it.

It is knee-deep in some places and the mud in camp is only surpassed by the mud in front.

I went up this morning to the front, not right up to the new line as that is unapproachable by day and it was really pitiful to see the conditions in which these unlucky men were living. The whole country has been ploughed up by shellfire, all drains stopped and there is nothing but water and mud everywhere.

I passed various old Hdqrs in which I had lived in 1915 and I came back through Ypres. It is no longer imposing in its [indecipherable] but squalid and miserable beyond words. It is very little more than heaps of rubble now. The Cloth Hall has gone and there is nothing left of the great Cathedral but part of the tower . . .

I met Audley Pratt looking rather curious up in front. He had not had a wash or his clothes off for 3 days nor shaved and was caked in mud but still cheerful.

I do not think there is any chance of a move until the ground dries up and that may take a week or more from the time it stops raining.

FC, D/3835/E/2/14

160
Nugent to his wife

[Holograph] [Mersey Camp, Ypres]
6 August 1917

It looks like more rain I am afraid. There was heavy artillery fighting yesterday and we are having a number of casualties I am sorry to say.

It is always the most unsatisfactory way of all that one can lose men, because it goes on day after day gradually frittering the men away and shaking their morale with no tangible results in the shape of ground gained or visible dead Boche. We are I daresay inflicting a lot of loss on him but we don't see it.

Another aeroplane came our way last night and there was a very hurried exodus from huts and tents into the dugouts. No harm done but it is very unpleasant. There was another in the middle of the night but I slept through that. There is a pretty solid row going on all day and twice yesterday it rose to the dimensions of a battle.

Where our front line is now is very much overlooked, in fact no one can show a nose on it by day and we shall continue to be overlooked until we gain more ground . . .

I can't go up to the front line partly because I can't get there and partly because there is constant heavy shelling and it isn't my business to get knocked over if I can avoid it, also I can't go far away lest the Germans should take it into their heads to start an attack so I find time hangs rather heavy on my hands just now.

FC, D/3835/E/2/14

161
Nugent to his wife

[Holograph] [Mersey Camp, Ypres]
8 August 1917

The rain has begun again and it looks very bad. Nature is surely fighting for the Boche this time. Meanwhile we are living under continual shell fire overlooked at every point. It is a matter of absolute vital need to get forward as soon as possible and there is no prospect of it that I can see as yet.

One day's rain in this country means 4 or 5 days' delay because there is no drainage and the water simply lies . . .

Gough, the 5th Army Commander came to see me yesterday and stayed quite a long time. I liked him as far as one can judge from a first impression.

FC, D/3835/E/2/14

162
Nugent to his wife

[Holograph] [Mersey Camp, Ypres]
10 August 1917

The weather has cleared up and it looks like remaining nice. I counted 19 balloons of ours up today along the front and later there were 25. The aeroplanes in the air look like flocks of vultures. I have never seen so many up at once before. There is constant fighting going on between our and the Boche machines, but so high that it is hardly possible to see them with the naked eye.

It must be horrible being shot down from such a height, fortunately most of the victims don't know much about.

The shelling is extremely heavy, far heavier than anything we have had to endure before and it is all over the front, not alone on the front line. Even at my Hdqrs shells are continually dropping around. However that is a trifle compared to what battns are getting up in the line and our casualties are getting very heavy. It is a horrible wearing form of fighting having to sit still and be shelled night and day . . .

I had a long letter from Anna today giving me a regular wigging for abusing Tom and repeating all the stale old arguments that the Irish are traitors and murderers and only the Ulster people are holy and ending up that she hoped I would always remain on the right side![42]

I must write and tell her that I have secretly joined the Sinn Feiners. The fact is Anna cannot realise that there is all the difference in the world between her family and ours.

She is not Irish and has not a drop of Irish blood in her veins. She is the descendant of Scotch settlers who have never intermarried with the Irish.

We are Irish because we have intermarried with the Irish who owned the country before us. The country people look upon us as Irish. There never has been any disagreement between us and the country folk except the excitement caused by my organisation of the Cavan Volunteers: the excitement that caused is really proof of how much the country people look upon Nugents as their natural leaders, because they considered I had deserted the side I ought by heredity to be in sympathy with. Well, I hope it won't be long before we are back amongst them, though I fear it will be at least 2 years.

FC, D/3835/E/2/14

163
Nugent to his wife

[Holograph] [Mersey Camp, Ypres]
16 August 1917

It has been a truly terrible day. Worse than the 1st July I am afraid. Our losses have been very heavy indeed and we have failed all along the line, so far as this Division is concerned and the whole Division has been driven back with terrible losses.[43]

Audley Pratt is gone, Somerville another of my Colonels also gone, Bob Maxwell I grieve to say was last seen wounded and lying out in front and we have been driven in since then and he was not brought back. Blair Oliphant another of my Colonels has not been heard of for several hours.

Peacocke another Commanding Officer has not been seen or heard of since early morning and his whole battalion has disappeared. We don't know where they are but we hope they may be holding out in shell holes in front and will get back after dark.[44]

Tomorrow we have to make another attack at dawn and I have no men to do it with. It is a ghastly business. Our failure has involved the failure of the Divisions on both sides of us and that is so bitter a pill. In July of last year, we did our work but failed because the Divisions on either flank failed us. This time it is the Ulster Division which has failed the Army.

I am heartbroken over it and I fear we shall be absolutely wiped out tomorrow. We have not enough men left to do the attack or to hold the line we are to hold, even if we get it.

My poor men.

Now I mustn't go on like this. It isn't fair to you . . .

I have no time for more. Bless you all my dearest. How I wish I could have given you a more cheering letter.

PS Just heard Bob Maxwell has been got in and is in the Field Ambulance, shot through thigh but nothing serious.

FC, D/3835/E/2/14

164
Nugent to his wife

[Holograph] [Winnezeele]
17 August 1917

My Division did not make any further attack. When we went into numbers available it was realised how serious the losses had been and I pointed out that it was out of the question. Other Divisions on my right and left all agreed as to their own men. The losses had been so heavy that there was nothing more to be done.

I thought my Division was the only one to fail but it isn't so. On the left the Guards and French and 2 other Divisions got where they were supposed to go, but it was recognised that they had a comparatively easy job and that they are not in touch yet with the German main position. On the right we are right up against it and no one got on. It was not only the Ulster Divn which failed but nearly all. A poor satisfaction certainly but still some. It was Machine guns which did us.

We had Bavarians against us and they were magnificent fighters. We hardly saw any of them. They were snug in concrete emplacements so strong that our Artillery failed to smash them in and they just mowed down our attack.

We are coming out tonight and go back into rest to reorganise and receive reinforcements.

If they have more to give us we shall probably be sent off to the old trench drudgery somewhere down the line.

Bob Maxwell was shot by a machine gun through the thigh and he managed to hobble back to our line and was brought in.

P Coote[45] came up yesterday evening to tell me and as it happened Arthur was in camp too and it was a great relief to us both. It is probably not serious.

FC, D/3835/E/2/14

165
Nugent to his wife

[Holograph] [Winnezeele]
19 August 1917

We are back in the area from which we moved up. On the 22nd we move away down south to a quiet part of the line to lick our sores. We are going to the part where we were on the 1st July of last year from which the Germans retired this Spring. It is quiet enough, I believe, as the Germans are not even in sight, but there isn't a house or a tree left standing so I suppose we shall be in huts and tents.

I feel sore enough about it. I don't want see my men knocked out of course, but I do feel I want to get back on the Germans.

I gather that everyone's experience was the same as ours, at any rate all the right of the Army. It was the MGs that stopped the whole attack. They were everywhere, that and wire which the Germans had put up between the first and second attacks.

I do not think we could have done more than we did. At any rate we could not have got through. I am not quite satisfied all the same that we couldn't have done a little more than we did do, but it is easy for us behind to criticise those in front.

FC, D/3835/E/2/14

166
Nugent to his wife

[Holograph] [Winnezeele]
21 August 1917

I went to see Gough this afternoon. He was very pleasant and is a charming person as he always is, but my dearest, no one can talk to him and come away thinking that he is mentally or intellectually fit o command a big Army. He isn't and it is wrong that the lives of housands of good men should be sacrificed through want of orethought and higher leading. Being a good cavalry soldier and a ;ood fellow are not the only qualifications for the command of ;reat armies in which cavalry takes no part . . .

I dread the long dreary time which I fear lies in front of us vithout men and trying to do with insufficient numbers the work of a Division at full strength.

'C, D/3835/E/2/14

167
Nugent to his wife

Holograph]

[Winnezeele]
21 August 1917

: fresh Divisions attacked the same ground that we and the 16th ttacked over. They attacked yesterday and before I left for 3oulogne I heard the attack was a complete failure. They could do no more than we could. If this is so it means that 6 Divisions have now been wasted over the same piece of ground and so far as I can ee the Corps have learned nothing from our experiences nor from he experiences of the Divisions that attacked before us. Neither pparently has the 5th Army.[46]

We can't go on losing men like this. We haven't got them. As it s the whole summer is being wasted in useless loss of life and we ave gained nothing of value, except the Messines Ridge, the ttack on which was a very different show than anything the 5th Army have ever done.

Yes. Audley Pratt was killed just as he came out of the dug out vhere he had been to see his Brigadier.

The one shell fell about 10 paces from him and a big piece went hrough him. He would have known nothing about it, poor old Audley.

Yes, weather, and machine guns are what defeated us and it was nachine-guns that defeated the attack yesterday.

'C, D/3835/E/2/14

3
Cambrai and St Quentin, September 1917 to June 1918

Introduction

During the final eight months of Nugent's period in command politics featured less prominently than before: the Irish Convention ground its way to stalemate between July 1917 and April 1918 without impinging greatly on his consciousness, though he did host a visit by Sir Edward Carson to the Somme battlefield that autumn [170–2].

From early September the Division was back in the line near Havrincourt, and the cycle of raid and counter-raid resumed [168, 169, 174, 175]. Manpower continued to be a problem: a further round of battalion amalgamations that autumn (during which Nugent met a former adversary from Talana Hill, Deneys Reitz [173]) brought temporary relief but after Cambrai numbers were again low. The reorganisation in early 1918 of the BEF's infantry, which saw the number of battalions in divisions reduce from 12 to nine, led to disbandment of six of the Division's 10 remaining original battalions. Nugent resisted considerable lobbying on behalf of particular units and went to some lengths to justify retaining his best units while losing the weaker [191, 206]. The disbanding units were replaced by regular battalions and by February 1918 Nugent had five under his command. (Several had been reluctant to come – an officer of the 1st Irish Rifles wrote 'Definitely settled that the Battalion will leave that fine Division the 8th and go to the 36th – the political division as we know it'[1] – but their protests were overruled.)

The reshuffling of units and the casualties at Langemarck exacerbated one of Nugent's perennial problems, the supply of suitable commanders for his infantry battalions. In all some 50 infantry COs served under him. Of these three were killed (a surprisingly low figure), five wounded and evacuated, and four captured; six were promoted to brigadier, two of whom later returned to the Division; and six left as a result of the disbandment of their battalions.[2] Excluding the nine in post at the time of Nugent's departure, therefore, 17 COs left the Division because of sickness, exhaustion or other causes; of these around half appear to have been removed as incompetent. There was a seasonal pattern to the turnover of COs, clustered around winter reorganisations and summer operations. Six left, from all causes, during the winter of 1915–16; six between June and August 1916; seven during the winter of 1916–17, including the last two COs who had gone to France in 1915; and eight between June and August 1917. In the Ulster Division the average tenure of a CO was just under a year but the turnover was significantly higher in the weaker units: the war diary of the 14th Rifles, for example, complained in January 1917, when their recently joined CO was evacuated sick: 'Usual luck of this Bn, cannot keep a CO, this is number seven since we came on service.'[3] As Captain Whitfeld, adjutant of the 1st Irish Rifles which joined the Ulster Division early in 1918, later wrote: 'There is nothing worse for a battalion than frequent changes of Commanding Officers. Efficiency, discipline, esprit de corps all suffer.'[4] Like all divisional commanders Nugent was heavily dependent on his better COs – who included, at different times, Hessey, Ricardo, Blacker, Peacocke, Perceval-Maxwell and Cheape – to set the standard for the rest of the Division. The loss of such men through death, wounds or exhaustion had a disproportionate impact.[5]

Nugent's last two battles, Cambrai and St Quentin, differed from their predecessors in both duration and complexity. For the Ulster Division the assault phases of the Somme, Messines and Langemarck had each lasted less than 36 hours. At Cambrai, by contrast, it was in action continuously for seven days during the British attack and a further 10 days during the German counter-attack, and during the March 1918 retreat the Division was engaged in eight consecutive days of desperate fighting. The physical and mental strain on the troops, and on Nugent himself, was the most sustained of the war.

The Cambrai offensive opened at dawn on 20 November.[6] The Ulster Division's task was to protect the British left flank by advancing on a narrow front up the Hindenburg line, which here ran along the Canal du Nord. As the main British attack began Nugent broke into the enemy trenches using Farnham's 10th Inniskillings and began a leapfrog advance northwards. Gains of 4,000 yards were achieved that day and over 500 prisoners taken [177]. For the next three days, however, the Division became stuck in heavy fighting for the village of Moeuvres, twice taking it before being forced out. This fight formed part of the larger struggle for Bourlon village and wood, 3,000 yards to the east. Nugent's problem was that he lacked the firepower to suppress the defences opposite him, the Germans were reinforcing heavily and nearly all available British artillery was committed to supporting the troops at Bourlon [178–80]. On the 22nd Haig called on him, and noted in his diary:

> At Ytres I saw Nugent Commanding 36th Division (Ulster). On the 20th he only used one brigade and their casualties had been very small. Enemy fell back quickly or surrendered. Today had been hard fighting at Moeuvres. He thought that Enemy had no infantry on their front only machine gun companies. Several of these machine gunners fought like fanatics and instead of surrendering blew out their brains.[7]

On the 24th, never afraid to speak out, Nugent told his Corps commander that he was not prepared to attack again without adequate artillery and tank support: Woollcombe,[8] to his credit, accepted this [180–1]. On the night of 26/27th the Division, tired out by both the fighting and the winter weather, was withdrawn.

After scarcely a day's rest, however – it took almost two days to get to billets through the congestion behind the British lines – the Division was rushed back into action, this time on the right flank at Welsh Ridge, near La Vacquerie, to help stem the German counter-attack which began on 30 November. For 10 days from 4 December it held the ridge, for several days experiencing strenuous fighting in cold weather as the Germans tried to break through [188–190]. By the time the Division was pulled out the men were exhausted and sickness levels high. Nugent, who had had reservations about the offensive from the outset, made no bones about the indifferent performance of some British units during the German attack [187, 192].

The cumulative strain was now affecting many of the remaining officers and men who had come out with the Division in 1915. Brigadier-General Ricardo broke down during the fighting and had to be relieved: other long-serving officers followed over the next few months, including two of Nugent's most experienced COs, Peacocke and Perceval-Maxwell [190, 218, 219]. Nugent himself was very tired:[9] but though disappointed not to have been recognised in the honours list he remained ready for the fight. He was dismayed, therefore, in early 1918 to see that the high ommand had begun a policy of bringing in younger officers as divisional ommanders. The changes were substantial. Of the BEF's 38 New Army nd Territorial divisional commanders in January 1918, 18 had been noved by May, along with eight of 18 corps commanders. Not all were acked: for example, two divisional commanders (Harper and Shute) ere promoted, another (Feetham) was killed and at least three others ere wounded or taken ill during the fighting in March and April. But 14 f these generals, along with at least three of their successors, had been ansferred to non-operational posts by the beginning of June. The BEF ould fight its Hundred Days campaign in 1918 under considerably evamped senior and middle management, since comparable changes ere taking place at brigade level also.[10] When in early March Lawrence, Iaig's new chief of staff, pointedly refused to give him any assurance bout his future Nugent knew his days in France were numbered [203, 07, 209].

In January the Division had taken over a 6,000-yard sector of front rom the French immediately south-west of St Quentin. It was already lear that, following Russia's collapse, a major enemy offensive in the est was coming as Germany tried to win the war before the Americans rrived in strength [200, 207]. Nugent and his men, hampered by bad eather, worked frantically to strengthen their inadequate defences efore the blow fell, but with limited results.

The German offensive opened on 21 March 1918, and the Ulster Division spent the next eight days fighting for its life.[11] For Nugent and is men it was an ordeal in which one day merged with another, but in etrospect the battle can be divided into three phases: the fight for the British frontline positions on 21 March; the fight for the Somme rossings, a few miles to the rear, on 23/24 March; and the fighting at rches, some distance to the rear, on 26/27 March. The scale of the ffensive was unprecedented. During each stage of the battle the Ulster Division was significantly outnumbered – it fought eight different German divisions in eight days – and by the end had been forced to etreat over 30 miles, lost more than 6,000 men and twice only narrowly scaped annihilation. It was the severest test Nugent faced during the var, and his letters convey vividly the confusion and strain as he truggled to hold the Division together during a succession of fighting vithdrawals [209–15, 218].

Nugent, like his soldiers, was completely drained by the battle. He lamed Gough, perhaps unfairly on this occasion, for the defeat, and eard of his removal with relief [214, 221]. He also passed on to Maxse what he felt were the main tactical lessons of the fighting [222]. Hi immediate task, however, was to rebuild his shattered Division and following a large influx of replacements and with the extraordinar resilience of First World War formations, the Ulster Division was i action again in the battle of the Lys, near Ypres, just eight days later Only one brigade (108) was directly engaged in this fighting, sufferin heavy losses, but for several days the rest of the Division expecte imminent attack [220–1, 223–5]. By late April the German offensive ha run out of steam.

Nugent's war ended where it began, on the outskirts of Ypres. On May his fears were realised and he was replaced by Major-Genera Clifford Coffin VC,[12] ten years his junior, who commanded the Divisio for the rest of the war. Griffith and Withycombe, his infantry brigadier since 1915, also left. The change happened so quickly that Nugent ha no time to visit his units, sending letters to the COs instead [226]. Ther was genuine sadness at his departure. At the time of the handover he wa one of only two New Army divisional generals who had come out t France in 1915 still with their original commands.[13]

168
Nugent to his wife

[Holograph] [Ytres]
2 September 1917

I am afraid I have missed 2 days post owing to unforeseen emergencies. The night before last the Germans took it into their heads to suddenly attack one of our advanced posts and we had to take it back which we did in the early hours of yesterday morning, but I had to go over there to inquire into things and last night they attacked again and took it and we had to retake it early this morning. So I again missed the post owing to having to go down and inquire into why the garrison allowed it to be taken by the Germans a 2nd time and to see that better arrangements were made for tonight because I am sure they will try again tonight and we can't go on being turned out and having to retake places.[1]

I presented French decorations this morning on a church parade to a number of officers, having been deputed to represent the President of the French Republic! . . .

Arthur was as sorry as any of us at losing Audley Pratt, but my child all our feelings in that way are blunted out here. It is too much the occurrence of every day to stir one over much. I find that however much I really liked a man who gets knocked out, my first thought always is 'Who shall I put in to replace him'.

FC, D/3835/E/2/14

169
Nugent to his wife

[Holograph] [Ytres]
5 September 1917

I am waiting for the 3rd Army Commander, Julian Byng by name, to come.[2] He wants to take a walk round my sector or part of it this morning. I wish he would come earlier as he is not due till 11 am and it will be roasting hot. Trenches are fearfully hot places when the weather is really hot as there is no air in them.

The Germans made a 4th attack on a particular piece of my line last night, a bit they are very annoyed at having had taken from them. They were met by bombs and rifle fire and beaten off and the report says the cries and groans could be heard a long distance so I hope they got it in the neck and that they will now make up their mind that they can't have their ground back.

Barring this piece of ground it is a quiet part of the line where we are. Neither the Germans nor ourselves have much artillery on this front and we are spread out over a wide area so there are not many men in any part of the line. I want peace and quiet at present as we have a tremendous lot of work to do to make the line safe for the winter rain and frost. As it is at present it would fall in the first heavy rains or frost.

Then we have to build shelters and huts for the men to live in, using such walls as are left standing in the villages and fixing roofs and digging dugouts for shelter in case the Germans amuse themselves by shelling the villages as they are almost sure to do . . .

I sent £100 from Divisional Canteen Funds as a contribution from the Ulster Divn to the W Redmond Memorial fund. Most of the Division favoured the idea but some of the Belfast lot objected. However they were in a minority so I overruled them. Another black mark against me though.

FC, D/3835/E/2/14

170
Nugent to his wife

[Holograph] [Ytres]

16 September 1917

I got a telephone message yesterday afternoon from the Army HQ that Sir E Carson was staying with them and wanted to meet me and see the battleground of the 1st July of last year with me so

I am meeting him this afternoon and taking him to Thiepval. I don't think he will be able to go over half or quarter of the ground. It would take all day and would finish him off. It is difficult walking.

The Germans have started their old trick of shelling the back areas with long-range guns. Yesterday they did it off and on all afternoon and hunted the men out of our camp close by us here. They put a shell into the middle of one hut and it went up in fragments after which we saw the whole battalion firmly but quietly walking off into the surrounding wilds. The worst of these long range bombardments is that one never knows when the next shell will come and in any case there is no where to go and one place is as likely to be shelled as another. You just have to sit tight and hope someone else will be shifted . . .

I have just had to speak seriously to the parson who took service at Div Hdqrs this morning for having no hassock [*sic*] on and only a short surplice over his uniform looking exactly as if he had put on his day shirt and forgot to tuck it in. Also for not having any accompaniment for the hymns and for starting them flat and in the wrong key. I have to do Archbishop at times.

C, D/3835/E/2/14

171

Nugent to his wife

[Holograph] [Ytres]
16 September 1917

I met Sir E Carson this afternoon and had quite a long drive with him over the battle ground of last year ending up at Thiepval. We did not attempt to walk over the ground as he could not have done it and anyhow there was no time. We just drove along and I showed him the Ulster Division's attack from different places. Afterwards we went to tea with Sir J Byng, the Army Commander.

He did not produce much news (Sir E C[arson]) and I asked him no questions that ought not to be asked. I gathered that the

Government were not happy over the submarine war, that the Germans were sinking ships faster than we could build them. He seemed to doubt if the Americans would really be able to get or maintain a large Army over here owing to shortage of ships. Altogether he is not what you would have called a cheery man. He had R McNeill[3] with him, principally known I believe as the man who threw a book at W Churchill in the H of Commons and hit him in the neck. We came across the skeleton of a German today in a shell hole, so he has not taken long to return to brother earth as he can't have been dead for more than a year.

It was a beautiful day and quite warm.

FC, D/3835/E/2/14

172
Nugent to his wife

[Holograph] [Ytres]
20 September 1917

The weather continues well. In fact it is as warm as it was in July. A great thing for us as we are able to get on with winter preparations, house building, trenches and dugouts which we could not do at all if it was bad weather. I see the 2nd and 5th Armies up north have started again. We have heard that the 2nd Army has made a good start including the 9th Corps, our late Corps in 2nd Army.[4]

We have not heard how the 5th Army have done, but I doubt they will do as well as the 2nd Army.[5] That is the Army I shall always swear by. They know how to get things done, and what is far more important they know and understand the British Infantryman. At any rate Sir H Plumer does . . .

I was rather amused at a remark of E Carson's when I was driving with him and were passing through Albert. The troops in it were very slack about saluting us or me as we drove through and I said 'I wonder who this rabble is. If they were the Ulster Division they would hear about it.' Carson laughed and said 'Yes, I imagine they would. I have heard many things about you, but failure to say what you think or being slack in matters of discipline have not been mentioned as failings of yours'. I said 'I suppose you have heard lots of things, but I can assure you I do not care a d— what you hear. I know what I expect and I take no less and you may also believe that popularity hunting isn't one of my failings either'. He said 'No, I know it isn't and no one respects you the less for it and they know now that you know your business' or words to that effect.

FC, D/3835/E/2/14

173
Nugent to his wife

[Holograph] [Ytres]
23 September 1917

I met a major called Reitz today, a Boer, and found that he had fought against us at Talana.[6] We both agreed that that was a gentleman's war compared with this one and he is coming to dine with me tonight. I am quite sure it will be a long time before I ask a German to dine with me after the war is over.

FC, D/3835/E/2/14

174
Nugent to his wife

[Holograph] [Ytres]
4 November 1917

We had a very good raid last night into the German lines. Killed over 40 and blew in dugouts which we know contained men.

It was a complete surprise carried out without any preliminary bombardment. The whole party 64 of them crawled on their bellies for over an hour until they got up to the German wire where there was a gap. Then they rushed in and first met a party of 16 men coming out of their trenches. They had a lively fight with them and eventually bayonetted the whole lot. Another party of Germans were hunted out of the trenches up against their own wire and they were either bayonetted or shot. The squealing of the Germans could be heard back in our lines. Our men were rather excited and saw red and they took no prisoners. They did take some at first but got bored with them and killed them. The Germans fought quite well apparently when they were cornered. We had about 17 casualties, three killed, remainder light wounds except 1 officer who was rather badly wounded. The men are very pleased. They are men of the North Irish Horse recently sent to us and have never yet had a chance of killing a German and they got excited and killed everyone instead of taking some prisoners as proof of success and also because we want some prisoners [as] often as possible for examination.[7]

Yesterday afternoon I went to a tank demonstration which was quite interesting. It is really rather wonderful to see how they can get over fences and flatten out wire. They are a great improvement on what they were last year. There were about 12 of them and they made nothing of crossing trenches.

FC, D/3835/E/2/15

175
Nugent to his wife

[Holograph] [Ytres]

18 November 1917

I am so furious, the Germans raided me last night and walked off with a Sergeant and 5 men, belonging to the 1st Battn R Irish Fusiliers, one of the regular battalions that has been recently sent to me. It was most important that the Germans should get no prisoners to question. I should like to shoot the whole party. Goodness knows how much the men taken prisoners knew, but the Germans will get everything out of them they do know, I am quite certain.

We have not lost more than 3 or 4 men as a result of German raids since we came to France and this wretched regular battalion which ought to be an example has let us down.

Well, it is no use howling over it. The mischief is probably done. All I hope is it will be too late for the Germans to do anything.[8]

FC, D/3835/E/2/15

176
Nugent to his wife

[Holograph] [Ytres]
19 November 1917

Just a line before I go to bed. No harm in telling you we begin a big attack tomorrow morning and the results will be known long before you get this. The feature will be Tanks of which there are over 400 and we hope the attack will come as a complete surprise to the Germans.

Well, it is on the knees of the Gods. We have been very fortunate in weather during the period of preparation but it is late November and I fear the men will suffer greatly. They can carry nothing but what they stand in and it may be an operation of some days. The days are so very dark for operations. The hours of daylight are too limited.

I hope all will go well and that my men will not throw any discredit on their country. I am sure they won't.

FC, D/3835/E/2/15

177
Nugent to his wife

[Holograph] [Ytres]
20 November 1917

So far all goes well, at any rate up to the latest information, but information is hard to get when fighting is on and it is a dull misty day with no visibility.

Arthur led off for the Ulster Division by a well executed attack on a Mound which the Germans have always had strongly held and which was our gateway into the German lines. His battalion did their job brilliantly.[9] He only had 4 casualties and killed a number of Germans and took over 100 prisoners and then pushed on up the German trenches to cover the crossing of the rest the brigade. His job is finished for the day and the other battalions have passed through his battalion and are getting on well.

The other Divisions are I hear getting on well too. It is early to speak of results yet and the Boche will kick back soon but he may not be able to do it before tomorrow. The hours of daylight are too short for all we have to do and the long nights help the Boche. If all goes well tomorrow, I may be moving forward tomorrow into reconquered territory and have to pitch my shack in another ruined village. This time it will be us who have done the damage as the Germans won't have had time I hope. However he is pretty sure to burn the villages before he leaves. If he leaves them standing, I shall be very cautious about going into them or into any house in them until they have been examined.

I don't like booby-traps of the kind the Boche sets.

FC, D/3835/E/2/15

178
Nugent to his wife

[Holograph] [Ytres]

22 November 1917

We had a hard day's fighting yesterday and made very little progress. On my left I have been hung up by machine guns and uncut wire round the village of Mouevres which we have been trying to take all day, but we could not get on. The Division on my right also failed to get very far. The Division on their right got some ground.[10] We are fighting for the high ground around the village of Bourlon in front of us and the Germans are getting over the first surprise and their resistance is stiffening. Today we attack again. I have relieved the Brigade that has had the most of the fighting during the last 2 days.[11] My other 2 Brigades are comparatively fresh but as seems always to happen when we fight the weather has changed. It rained hard all the night of the 20th and most of yesterday there was a soft drizzle. The mud is awful and there are no roads into the recaptured area. The men have neither greatcoats nor blankets and no shelter and they have been out in the open since the 20th without a chance of sleep except what they can get lying in the mud.

All the same I have had warm thanks from the Army and the Corps for our work. We did very well and much better than the Army or Corps thought we could do as we were given no Tanks which the other Divisions had. Our total advance the first day was well over 4000 yards and we took quite a number of prisoners. I got the enclosed [congratulatory note] this morning from Alick Godley who is in this neighbourhood I believe, I don't know where.

I am rather afraid that we have got to the end of our effort. The success of the operation depended on our being able to exploit the surprise of the first day's attack. This is the 3rd day and we may be sure the Germans are rushing up reinforcements. The fact is it is too late in the year. Fortunately it is not cold for the latter end of November, but that is only comparatively speaking. It is cold and utterly wretched for men lying out all day and night.

I went round our front or as near as I could reasonably safely go yesterday and into Havrincourt village which I have been looking at for months. It is pretty badly shattered.

There were not a great many horrible sights, but I was not looking for them and possibly the most of the dead have been buried.[12]

2 of my Brigades are fighting now and I am just waiting for news. This is a funny sort of war, because once the orders have been given there is nothing more one can do but wait for results.

FC, D/3835/E/2/15

179
Nugent to his wife

[Holograph] [Ytres]
23 November 1917

There was much fighting yesterday and we are at it hard today.[13] Yesterday one of my brigades got the village of Mouevres on the left of our line after hard fighting and I thought all was well then and to my consternation the Germans counterattacked in the late afternoon and retook it. Too late in these short days to do anything to retake it. This morning I have pounded it with heavy artillery and I am attacking it again but have had no reports as yet. Another brigade is attacking on the right of my Division up the Canal which divides my front and the latest reports are that it is going well but unless we get Mouevres we shall be hung up. The Division on my right is attacking Bourlon Hill and village. If we get that we shall have the high ground and it will greatly facilitate our work on the left.

I can't get information as quick as I should like. We are using Tanks again today. I have some of them working with my right brigade but none with my left brigade where I most want them. They can't get over the Canal without going so far round that it would take a whole day as the Germans have destroyed all the bridges. We know the Germans have brought up large reinforcements and in my opinion what we don't get today we shan't get at all, unless we get Bourlon Hill. After 4 days' continuous fighting we are all rather 'out' and the situation is not clear.

No news in this sort of fighting is often bad news.

FC, D/3835/E/2/15

180
Nugent to his wife

[Holograph] [Ytres]
24 November 1917

I am tired and no mistake. We did no attacks today with this Division but our Artillery was very busy. All the fighting was round Bourlon. We took Bourlon yesterday afternoon, another Division, and the 36th Division took Mouevres for the 2nd time and both Divisions were driven out again by a counter attack.[14] Tomorrow the other Division is to retake Bourlon and we sit tight till we can get enough Artillery and I hope Tanks to help us. We have suffered all through by being the left Division of the attack and with a canal between us and the main objective which is Bourlon. We have had no Tanks and not enough artillery and we have had to attack continuously strong defences with heavy wire in front of them. I spoke strongly to Corps today about it and told them it was not fair to ask us to go on losing men and spoiling the men's morale by asking them to do what they know to be impossibilities. The Corps Comdr agreed and said he would not ask us to do any more attacks until he could give us artillery and Tanks, so tomorrow at any rate we shall be able to sit tight, always unless the Boche attacks which I am certain he will do. He attacked my front today but it was rather a half-hearted effort and died away but I am certain it was only to test our defences and when he next attacks he will do it in force. The men are terribly tired. I saw Arthur in a captured German trench today. He looked terribly tired.

I went round our front as near as I could today but the Germans were shelling heavily and there was a good deal of dodging to do. I was passing behind some of my Artillery today which were in action and were being rather badly shelled. I saw a German shell land on one of my guns and demolish it, blew up all the ammunition that was beside it and knocked out 13 men. I saw one German attack which was beaten off.

I don't think there is any chance of our being able to be relieved till 4 or 5 days more at least. There is no one to relieve us.

For once the weather has been good to us. It is dry and for the time of year not cold and today there has been a high wind which has dried the ground considerably. You have no conception what the mess of transport and wagons behind the line is like. It is almost impossible to get anywhere.

The Boche corpses are turning black and look horrid. Most of our men have been buried by now.

FC, D/3835/E/2/15

181
Nugent to his wife

[Holograph] [Ytres]
25 November 1917.

I do not know why the papers are so hysterical. I think it is a great pity. The battle is by no means over and much may happen between now and the end . . . We are holding on on our side and won't do anything very desperate until other operations of more immediate importance are finished and guns and Tanks can be spared.

I am more anxious about the men than anything else. They are absolutely worn out from cold and lack of sleep and above all want of hot food. It rained very hard last night and there is a cold north wind today. It is great experience and I am more rejoiced than anything that we have had a share in it. I wish we could have held on to Mouevres but it was too strongly defended and in the absence of Tanks or sufficient artillery preparation we could not do more than we did. I have told the Corps Comdr that I won't attack it again till it is properly prepared. Our share was only a minor one or was meant to be as the real attack was further to our right. As a matter of fact we bumped up against a very strong point indeed and have been hung up by it. However the best news this morning is that Bourlon village has been retaken by us, was in fact retaken last night, good work.

I shall be very glad all the same when it is our turn to be relieved. It is really dreadful going round to see the white drawn faces and red eyes of overtired men and their clothes poor beggars. They have no time to wash nor much water to wash with.

FC, D/3835/E/2/15

182
Nugent to his wife

[Holograph] [Ytres]
27 November 1917

We are being relieved tonight by another Division and are going out of the battle to have a few days rest before returning. It was time too. We have been 9 days without rest or a change of cleaning, the men have not had their clothes off and have lain out night after night without even a blanket, continually fighting, constantly shelled, no hot food and the weather has changed to wintry cold. It was bitter last night and today. The men are absolutely beat.

The only thing which has kept the operation going is that we have had no rain. If the weather breaks we shall be done.

I was never enthusiastic over this venture and I am very sorry the papers chose to become hysterical over it.

Everything was a success up to a certain point, so long as the Tanks kept going, but once they had got to the limits of their power of moving we stopped. We have really gained no ground since Thursday. Bourlon village has been lost again and must be retaken tomorrow morning.

If successful we shall have a narrow salient sticking into the German lines, a very bad position for us. Mouevres has still to be taken and every day's delay makes it stronger. The Division which relieves us has to take it and they don't like the job. I have been with their General this evening telling him all I could about it.[15]

The fact is we were surprisingly successful owing to the Tanks, but they have a very limited life, half of them have been knocked out and are lying all over the country and there has been severe casualties among the Tank crews and the remaining Tanks are short of men to work them.

As soon as the Germans recovered from the surprise they rushed up machine-guns and the whole country in front of us is bristling with them. There is no possibility of advancing against machine-guns. They must be dealt with by Artillery, that means long delay, communications, getting up masses of ammunition and we have not got the guns here nor even roads to bring them by. The papers are full of what the Cavalry have done. It is a fact that the Cavalry have done absolutely nothing except block the roads and follow the Infantry. It makes us all so furious to read the frantic efforts made to boost the Cavalry which is as much out of date in this war as a naked man with a stone axe. I am very sorry we could not stay in long enough to capture Mouevres, but as it can't be attacked for 2 or 3 days yet, I do not think we could have done it. The men could not have stood the constant exposure.

FC, D/3835/E/2/15

183
Nugent to his wife

[Holograph] [Ytres]
29 November 1917

We are off to another area tomorrow, near Arras in the XVII Corps, commanded by Sir Charles Fergusson,[16] a very nice man. I am glad to get the Division out with comparatively few casualties, not many over 1000 which in these days is light.

Bourlon was attacked again by us yesterday (not by this Division) and Fontaine was attacked by the Guards Division. Both failed and we were not a yard to the good by the end of the day.

Mouevres is not going to be attacked again for the present anyhow. It is too strong to try without Artillery or Tanks or both. I always thought we were premature in joybells and promotions and cheering. Not that we have not gained some ground. We have and we did capture the Hindenburg Line but we have failed to get complete success and it would have been so much more dignified if we hadn't lost our heads. It will make the Boche scoff. However

I am very glad we were in it and did well. The Times of 27th has quite an appreciative article from its special correspondent and the Belfast papers can be trusted to do all that is needed in blowing our trumpet.

You can tell Lady Carson if you like that our casualties were very light, a little over 1000 and most of them light wounds. I do not think we have more than 200 killed.

Arthur is all right. I don't think you need worry about Bill and Jim.[17] The Cavalry never got as far as the Infantry and did nothing.

No time for more my child. I hope we shall have a few days rest for reorganisation before we go into the line again somewhere else, probably in the Lens area.

FC, D/3835/E/2/15

184
Nugent to his wife

[Holograph] [Lechelle]
1 December 1917

There has not been much rest for this Division. We left the fighting area on the 29th and we were told we should have 3 weeks rest before we were asked to do anything more. On the morning of the 30th we were ordered to get back as quickly as we could. We marched all day and got into billets of sorts late at night and tomorrow we go on again. We left the zone of operations by train and lorries but we had to march back, 2 days long marching.

The news was rather serious yesterday. The Germans counter attacked very heavily on both sides of the bulge we made in our attack.[18] On the left the Division which relieved us lost some ground which we had taken and are some way back. On the right the Germans broke in some considerable distance, how much I don't know. It is all rather obscure, but it is reported that one of our Divisions has been very badly smashed. There was very heavy fighting yesterday and I don't know how the matter stands, but it is pretty sure that we shall be back in the line again tomorrow or next day. Oh dear, those misplaced joy bells when everyone ought to have been touching wood!

The Germans are not a beaten enemy. They are stronger now than a year ago because they can draw on all the troops they had in Russia and they have all the guns they took from the Italians.

I don't know how long we can continue fighting. It is winter and today is bitterly cold. Once it begins to rain we simply can't go on. We are not in a good position now and we must either improve it or fall back.

I met the C in C yesterday on my way back and he stopped me to talk. He again said some complimentary things about the Division, but he looked rather worried.

FC, D/3835/E/2/15

185
Nugent to his wife

[Holograph] [Lechelle]
2 December 1917

Well we are back again in our former area, not in the line as yet except our Divisional Artillery but I expect we shall go in tomorrow.

It is very hard to get accurate information as to what happened the day before yesterday. The Germans seem to have attacked all along our new front and on the extreme right they broke through and got some 2 miles behind our old front line. 2 Brigades with the Brigadiers and Brigade staffs are said to be gone and some of the Divisional staff were it is said captured or killed. The Divisional Commander had been wounded and apparently had just gone back to the Ambulance so he escaped, but it is all very obscure. We counter attacked at once and a lot of the ground has been recovered on that flank.

On our front we seem to have lost the top of Bourlon Hill and to have been pressed back along the front this Division handed over to the Division which relieved us. We seem to have killed a great many Germans but to have lost very heavily ourselves. We must get back the top of Bourlon Hill because unless we do our position will be untenable. The Germans can overlook us in every direction.

We may be thrown in tomorrow but in any case by tomorrow night.

FC, D/3835/E/2/15

186
Nugent to his wife

[Holograph] [Lechelle]
3 December 1917

We have gone in again, 1 Brigade is in, the others go in tomorrow.[19] The situation is very serious but I hope we will retrieve it without losing all our gains of the 20th of November. The Germans are attacking very heavily and we have lost a great deal of ground south of where we made our advance. That advance made a big bulge outwards and the Germans as is their normal custom, attacked very heavily at the places in our old line where the bulge began as by breaking in there we should be compelled to give up all the bulge or risk the loss of all the men who are holding it. Reinforcements are arriving but the Germans have got in a long way and the situation is a very serious one. I go forward tomorrow with my Hdqrs so as to be nearer but the place I was going to is being heavily shelled this afternoon so I must try and find another. I think it will probably have to be in tents, not a cheerful prospect in December and it is freezing and there is a most bitter wind. I am sorry for the unfortunate men, but how much more for the wounded lying out. It will mean hundreds of them dying who might otherwise have a chance if they could be got in.

FC, D/3835/E/2/15

187
Nugent to his wife

[Holograph] [Sorel-le-Grand]
5 December 1917

We have had to give up all idea of holding on to Bourlon Hill and we have come back, not to where we started from but to the Hindenburg Line which was immediately in front of us before. It is a great disappointment after a fortnight of hard fighting but it was better to recognise the necessity before something worse happened to us. I am holding a part of the Hindenburg Line but it is a bad line.[20] It projects into the German lines and is overlooked from behind from Marcoing which we have given up and from the hills south of us that the Germans captured from us on the 30th. I have grave doubts about it. The Germans made an attack here this morning while I was up there but it was easily repulsed but the shelling and machine gun fire was unpleasant and persistent.

The German attack on the 30th took us completely by surprise. Thousands of men were captured in the dugouts asleep or at breakfast. They got into Gouzeancourt before anyone knew they were coming and captured officers in bed.

One Divisional Commander, De Lisle,[21] with his staff had to run for their lives leaving everything behind them and the Germans firing at them. One of his staff was wounded, they could not carry him and had to leave him, but when the Guards recovered Gouzeancourt a few hours later they found him in a dugout none the worse. There were large parties of Labour battalions on work in the roads in Gouzeancourt many of whom were bayonetted by the Germans before the old men and conchies realised Germans were there at all.

Naturally the papers try and put a camouflage over the business, but it was a bad business and reflects no credit on anyone on our side. The upshot of it was that we have lost probably at least 6000 prisoners, 80 to 100 guns, numerous machine guns and stores of all kinds and we have had one of the worst rebuffs we have had in the whole war. It is no use trying to conceal facts which must come out. We were not prepared for a counterattack just where it was most likely to come but the poor show the men put up was not entirely due to fewness of numbers. They were absolutely worn out from cold and exposure and hard fighting and want of sleep. Men are not machines and they should never have been asked to do what they failed to do at this season of the year.

FC, D/3835/E/2/15

188
Nugent to his wife

[Holograph] [Sorel-le-Grand]
6 December 1917

I could not write yesterday as I was taking over a sector of the line.[22] As a matter of fact I could not get into it as when I went up there was a battle going on on that very front. The Germans got into our lines and when I assumed command they were still there and, in consequence we were fighting all night, mostly bombing in the trenches. The 9th Inniskillings finally drove the Germans out but in their zeal they followed them too far and the Germans got in behind them and they had to fight their way back and had many casualties, all the Company Commanders were either killed or wounded and in the confusion the men came back and the Germans have again got into our trenches.

When I went up this morning I saw from the ridge behind the one where our trenches are that there was a fight going on and I saw a number of men running about, so I carried on to General Ricardo's Hdqrs in the Hindenburg Line and found considerable excitement. The men were on the parapet and he himself was rather excited and thought the Germans were coming on in strength. However I knew that was not likely as we had plenty of men and machine guns ready for that. They were just bombing their way up the trench we were in and the obvious answer was to organise a bombing party back again. I had to be rather sharp and terse in my remarks so as to get things calm again and the necessary steps taken to stop them coming any further. Tomorrow morning we attack them again with I hope a proper system which there does not seem to have been before and I hope we shall finally eject them and keep them out. There was a great deal of fighting today along the front and the general expectation is that the Germans are massing for a big attack to throw us out of the Hindenburg line back into our original line.

I am not too confident. The men are absolutely tired out. Every Division says the same. This offensive was started in a light-hearted way without forethought or preparation for a possible heavy counter attack and now that that has come we are not prepared.

This battle is the hardest of the war and there are a number of fresh Divisions come from Russia for which we have to thank Lenin and the Bolshevists

I am very tired but I see no prospect of rest and if I am tired what must the officers and men of battalions be.

Arthur's battalion is in the line but has had a quiet 2 days. He is not with it this time as I never allow the CO and 2nd in command to be in together, so that each in turn gets a rest.

He is here, looks very well and is coming to dine with me tomorrow night. He came to tea this afternoon and I gave him Aileen's letter to read. Last night the Germans were bombing the back areas from aeroplanes half the night. They dropped a lot of bombs close by here. I lay in bed and quavered.

FC, D/3835/E/2/15

189
Nugent to his wife

[Holograph] [Sorel-le-Grand]
7 December 1917

Well, we did our job last night or rather early this morning and drove the Germans out of all the places he had got into, so that is satisfactory. It is a great relief to us all including the Corps and the Army. However the Germans are pretty sure to attack again. We are holding the key position on this part of the front. It is the highest ground, as long as we hold it, the Germans cannot overlook us behind and we can move in some security and above all we overlook his communications for miles and he cannot form up for attack unknown to us. Therefore he will fight for the ground until he is taught that it is no use trying. Anyhow we have won the first round, but as I have mentioned before the men are terribly weary. The frost has gone but it is even colder, with a keen wind that bites through all one can wear . . .

Our present Corps Comdr is Pulteney, once a Guardsman. He seems a cheery good fellow.

FC, D/3835/E/2/15

190
Nugent to his wife

[Holograph] [Sorel-le-Grand]
10 December 1917

The shelling is increasing in weight and volume. The impression is that a big attack is coming. There are a lot of Germans round us now and their Artillery is increasing very much. It is a question of physical endurance. My men are completely exhausted and I don't feel confident about their powers of resistance in case of a big attack.

The class of pilot we have got nowadays or at present anyhow is not good enough. He has not got the nerve nor the courage.

I do not think the Germans will rest till they have got back the Hindenburg Line or had to admit it can't be done, but at present they are superior to us and in greater numbers. It is a very anxious time and the 36th Division ought to be withdrawn. Unfortunately we are very hard up for fresh Divisions, what with those we used up in the Ypres offensive and in this.

I have had to send General Ricardo home to my very great regret but in this recent fighting I saw he had lost his nerve and looked so old. One can't afford to run risks in this war and I sent for him and told him he must go home for a long rest. He was quite glad really and owned to being perished.

I am very sorry to lose him.

FC, D/3835/E/2/15

191
Nugent to Adjutant General GHQ

[Typescript copy] [Sorel-le-Grand]
11 December 1917

Is there any prospect of anything being done to make up the three battalions of Inniskilling Fusiliers in the 109th Brigade of this Division? Their average strength is now under 660, giving a trench strength of about 350. They are first-rate fighting battalions and it is a pity to see them dwindling. Would the following suggestions meet with approval:–

1. To give the Division two Inniskilling Fusilier battalions, one of which would be a regular battalion, and the other to be broken up to make up the other four battalions of the Inniskilling Fusiliers.
   The 109th Brigade would then be a homogeneous Brigade of Inniskillings.
2. The 14th Royal Irish Rifles, now in 109th Brigade, to be broken up and used to make up casualties in the Royal Irish Rifles battalions in the Division. This battalion should in my opinion be broken up in any case.

About a year ago, I reported them as totally wanting in military spirit and asked for a CO and a large draft of Englishmen to try to create a fighting spirit in them. You gave me both, and while Cheape[23] was in command they certainly improved, but since he left they have been tried and found wanting. It is significant that the present CO told me two days ago that most of the English draft sent to them a year ago have become casualties.

The Brigadier says he cannot trust them and I know that he is right. They are poor stuff, either as workers or fighters, and have been a constant source of anxiety during the past three weeks.[24]

I can put all this officially if necessary but I would sooner not if it can be done otherwise.

FC, D/3835/E/10/8

192
Nugent to his wife

[Holograph] [Sorel-le-Grand]
13 December 1917

We are going to do nothing to relieve matters. The question is rather whether the Boche is going to kick us out of what bit of his line we have still got. The improvement of the line affected by this Division the other day was a small matter. The fact is you must in war as in other things count the cost before you begin. We didn't. The result has been a bad set back. We began shouting 'Victory' after the first round instead of waiting till the battle was over. You must admit I wasn't over-excited in my letters even in the first 3 or 4 days. The fact is we had failed in the first 48 hours. We effected a surprise the first day and we profited to that extent but we couldn't use it and the reason why we couldn't was partly that the German machine gunners were better men than ours and held out with splendid courage. It was they who saved the situation for the Germans. There were other reasons too but they had better be left unwritten, but I don't wonder that Bill[25] described himself as broken-hearted.

As to the German attack on the 30th, the less written about it the better too. It isn't a story to be proud of, notwithstanding the silly rubbish written by the war correspondents of feats performed by supermen against hundreds of thousands of Boches who existed solely in their imaginations.

The Ulster Division did well but they aren't supermen either and they didn't do better than other people.

The slippers arrived but my old thing I'm not a char woman, I couldn't wear such awful things.

FC, D/3835/E/2/15

193
Nugent to his wife

[Holograph] [Sorel-le-Grand]
15 December 1917

We are really going out to rest this time, always of course if the Boche permits.[26] We are going right back into civilisation behind the Somme battlefields into real villages and houses. It will be everything to the men to get into comfortable surroundings where there are estaminets where they can meet and talk and feel warm and we shall be able to start our Follies[27] and cinema again. I hope nothing will intervene to prevent us moving out of this sordid waste of mud and ruins.

My next trouble will be how to make up the Division. There are no recruits to be had and we have got to the end of absorbing Irish battalions from other Divisions because there are no more. It is really time to drop all pretence of being an 'Ulster' Division and become just the 36th. I am going to raise the question as soon as we get out of here and can count our losses. They are not so heavy in fact. Considering we shall have been practically a month in the fighting, longer than any other Division, they have been very light, but the point is there are no men to replace them.

We have certainly done our share in this adventure. Though we have not had spectacular fighting every day, we have had a lot of small scrapping, bombing fights and such like and never ending shelling, while the hardship has been worse than we have had any previous experience of, though I don't suppose it has been anything like as bad as on the Somme last winter and in 1914.

I have asked for Hessey to take Ricardo's place and the Mil Sec has wired home to know if he can come out at once. He used to command a Brigade after commanding a battalion in this Division but broke down after the Somme and had to go home, but I hear he is fit and anxious to get out again. He is a good man and I should be glad to get him.

I have sent Campbell[28] and another of the Staff off to the area we go to today to allot billets and to choose a suitable Div HQ. I told Campbell not to choose Chateaux unless they were really capable of being kept warm but to try and find an ordinary comfortable house where one would not be frozen into an Aspic. The French are extraordinarily uncomfortable people in their country houses.

I did not know Allenby had lost a son. I am very sorry. It is better to wait before rejoicing over Jerusalem. We are not at the end of the war yet.

C, D/3835/E/2/15

194
Nugent to his wife

Holograph] [Lucheux]
29 December 1917

There is no promotion for anyone. No one has been promoted to command a Corps for over a year now. I think if I had had the opportunity of coming out in the first months of the war I should have got a Corps when so many new ones were formed but it was natural that Corps Commanders should have been selected from those who had borne the burden of the fighting at the beginning. I can't help thinking that a good many of the Corps Commanders would be better at home. There are a good many duds among them, but they did good work at a critical time as Divisional Commanders.[29]

C, D/3835/E/2/15

195
Nugent to his wife

Holograph] [Corbie]
2 January 1917 [*sic* – 1918]

I have to confess to feeling a little bit flat after seeing the Honours List. I couldn't help looking forward to it and I wondered if there would be anything for me in it. I admit being very disappointed but it is really quite fair and I have nothing to feel aggrieved about. The only thing I could get now is a KCB and they have been given this time entirely to Generals who have been out since the beginning of the war and who have had their CBs for 2 or 3 years. I came out late and have had my CB for only a year so I am not really entitled to a KCB. So I am not going to be disappointed or feel that I have a grievance. The only thing I do feel is that I know the Division will think I ought to have got a KCB and they may think the less of me for not having one. They are built that way.

FC, D/3835/E/2/16

196
Lt Gen A. H. Hamilton Gordon to Nugent

[Holograph] IX Corps
2 January 1918

The omission of your name from the list received this morning has caused me real distress, from which I shall take long to recover.

I can think of no explanation but I can at least tell you how sorry I am and offer my sympathy.

I think it is only fair to myself to tell you that it was due to no omission on my part. I suppose I am not at liberty to say exactly what I recommended, but I may say that I gave the fullest expression to my appreciation of the good work and valuable services of yourself and your Division while under my command, and that this expression of my opinion was in its terms in no way inferior to those used for any other Division.

I deeply regret that my recommendation was not acted on.

FC, D/3835/E/2/20

197
Nugent to his wife

[Holograph] [Ollezy]
14 January 1918

I have now taken over line again, this time from the French.[30] I must say nothing could have been nicer than the way they helped us to knowing [*sic*] all about the line. Never were people so helpful. They have not all cleared off yet but those who are left are now under my orders.

The drawback to this sector is that the Germans overlook us very much and in consequence we can't drive anywhere near as close to the trenches as in other sectors I have been in and we have very long distances to walk in consequence.

C, D/3835/E/2/16

198
Nugent to his wife

Holograph] [Ollezy]
20 January 1918

All the trenches have disappeared. The combined effect of frost nd rain has brought them down entirely. The result is we can't use them and no more can the Germans and so all movement in he front line is being carried out in broad daylight over the top. In act there is a sort of informal truce on which will last I daresay until one side has got its trenches habitable first and then they will nipe the others who are not ready. The trouble is you can't shovel he earth, because it won't come off the spades. Certainly the French have only dug for fine weather and have made little preparation for wet. There is no place on this front that I can drive o that is less than 4 miles from the front line.

The Boche chose his ground well and has us all under view. The result is I have a very long walk every time I try and get to the renches and it means being out the whole day. Even then as he trenches are entirely impassable we have to walk over the top nd always in full view, but the Boche is quiet and doesn't shoot nd so we are not going to do so either at present.

C, D/3835/E/2/16

199
Nugent to his wife

[Holograph] [Ollezy]

27 January 1918

Arthur has come back and he told me the [Irish] Convention had really failed to come to any agreement on the points which really mattered. I expect Carson and Craig have resigned because they knew the Govt mean to insist upon a settlement at once on lines which the north of Ireland won't approve. My own point of view is that at the present time, a bad govt which the majority of Irishmen want is better than a good govt which they don't want. The interests of the Empire must come before those of a corner of Ireland.

I am afraid it will certainly be a bad govt but I doubt if it can possibly be worse than the govts we have had for the 12 years that the Radicals have been in power.

At any rate a settlement is an urgent necessity. There have been some very violent attacks on the higher command lately in Parliament by some obscure members and I don't think the govt have shown any undue zeal in defending Sir W R[obertson] or Sir D H[aig].

FC, D/3835/E/2/16

200
Nugent to his wife

[Holograph] [Ollezy]

1 February 1918

Ivor Maxse, who is the Corps Comdr, came round some of my trenches. He was most tiring because he would not walk out. He dawdled along, stopping to talk every other minute until I felt inclined to seize him and shake him. I like him. He has sound ideas on training.

Poor Arthur's battalion is one of those to be broken up. I don't know where he will go and he is very miserable at the notion of leaving the Division. I would gladly have kept his battalion but I ıad to be strictly impartial and he [*sic*] was one of the junior ›attalions and so had to be marked for disbandment . . .

The time is drawing near when the Boche may be expected to nake his great effort if he makes it at all.

If he does he will probably begin early in March. He has not nuch time to waste. He will fight this year as much to save the nilitary system of Germany as to give him the final victory of the var. If he thinks the German people and the army are no longer to ›e relied on for a great sustained offensive, he will probably emain on the defensive so that he can at any rate be able to say hat the German military system had broken every allied offensive. f he attacks and fails, the effect will probably be to cause a evolution which will sweep the military party into the limbo of hings that are passed. Which it is to be, we ought to know very oon.

C, D/3835/E/2/16

201
Nugent to his wife

Holograph] [Ollezy]
15 February 1918

delivered an address this morning to the officers and sergeants of ›ne of the Brigades and have to repeat it to the other Brigades in urn. Warning them of the possibilities of the future and what is xpected of us.

I see an announcement in the M[orning] Post that Sir W Robertson may be leaving the War Office for another position ›f high influence. In other words he may be shunted. I wonder if his is true but the Morning Post is rather wild in its statements of ate. There is I am afraid a good deal of friction in high circles.

Lloyd George is a very quick witted Celt with intuition and flair ılmost if not quite amounting to genius and Sir WR and DH[aig] ıre slow, cautious brains who have to see the whole road before they start along it. They are the very opposite poles in methods to men like LG and Henry Wilson who think in a flash.

It does not follow that the latter think right but when you have people at the top of the tree who should think in harmony and who don't, it is almost inevitable that one or other must go.

I hear anti-aircraft guns firing hard so the Boche aeroplanes must be overhead and in broad daylight too, most insolent. He is not too fond of coming over in daylight as a rule. It is a cloudless afternoon and just the day for photography.

FC, D/3835/E/2/16

202

Nugent to his wife

[Holograph] [Ollezy]
18 February 1918

So the Government have got rid of Sir 'Wullie'.[31] I thought it was looming. The Times and Daily Mail evidently were foreshadowing it. It is a personal triumph for Henry Wilson. I hope it may be for the good of the State. The Government and the State will never have a more loyal and devoted servant than Willie Robertson.

Henry is of course a far more quick witted man but he couldn't be more thorough. I hope Henry at the WO will be able to work purely for the good of the State and that no personal feelings may enter in . . .

The weather here keeps wonderfully bright and clear and we are all very busy. The Germans are [as] busy as us. It is rather an anxious time, this waiting and wondering when the storm will burst. It may come at any moment or not for another month. When and if it does it will be a hurricane . . .

I hear Congreve's Hdqrs were bombed last night and 4 of his staff were damaged. I think we shall have to go underground soon. These night bombing expeditions are becoming a regular feature now.

I must quit as I have to go into a conference.

FC, D/3835/E/2/16

203
Nugent to his wife

Holograph] [Ollezy]
19 February 1918

have just come back from a conference on training to get some unch and have to go in again directly after so I have only time for scribble.[32] Days keep very bright and sunny and suitable for eroplane enterprises at night. We were not bombed last night for wonder and I did not hear any dropping round . . .

What worries me is that we are entirely dependent on being ble to keep 2 establishments going in England and Ireland on my ay. I may lose my job out here, you never can tell. I am, I fear, oked upon as rather old to command a Division in France at the resent time. The tendency is to send home the older ones and ut younger men in command of Divisions. I do not feel my osition is secure at all nowadays. I have not said anything about his before but I know it is so. I see every month some older Divisional Commander is sent home and a man who would have een commanding a battalion before the war is put in command. o dearest we may be short of £1500 a year at any moment. It is ot a question of merit or demerit so far as I am concerned.

C, D/3835/E/2/16

204
Nugent to his wife

Holograph] [Ollezy]
20 February 1918

The recent military changes are very interesting and are almost ertain to lead to more. Henry Rawlinson who takes Henry Vilson's place at Versailles is as clever as they make 'em but I do ot think he has the brains that Henry Wilson has and he has not a race of the thoroughness and caution of D H[aig] or Robertson. I ave usually looked upon him as rather a superficial person with nore regard for his personal advancement than anything else.

What we would all like to know is, who is going to dictate to th other, Henry Wilson to Harry Rawlinson or vice versa. Henry W one can imagine did not leave Versailles to be put in a lowe position at the WO, nor would Rawly have left command of a Army to take a position at Versailles which would not give hin increased authority.

What one hopes naturally is that neither of these eminen soldiers thought of personal advancement at all, but only of usin their brains to the best advantage in beating the Boche. I wonder.

FC, D/3835/E/2/16

205
Nugent to his wife

[Holograph] [Ollezy
24 February 191

I do not think the Germans are likely to postpone operations late than the middle of next month unless there is a break up in th weather . . .

We had a narrow squeak yesterday. I had met the Corp Commander at a village in the forward area to ride over some nev lines we are digging. There were about 12 of us all in a cluster or our horses when we heard a shell coming. We could hear it comin for so long getting louder and louder and suddenly it fell almost ir the middle of us in the midst of a pile of bricks where there hac been a house. It was a dud! If it had burst there would have beer vacancies as we were all round within a few yards of it. We lost nc time in moving off and then another arrived which wasn't a duc and looking back at the explosion we were able to realise what we had escaped with the first one.

FC, D/3835/E/2/16

206

Nugent to James Johnston, Lord Mayor of Belfast

[Typescript copy] [Ollezy]

28 February 1918

In reply to your letter of 9th instant, I regret to say the break-up of the 36th Division in respect of the greater number of its original battalions is already accomplished.[33]

The Division now consists of 5 Regular North Irish battalions, and of 5 battalions of the original Division.

As General Officer Commanding the Division, I had the most unpleasant duty of selecting 2 battalions of Inniskilling Fusiliers and 4 battalions of Royal Irish Rifles for disbandment.

I decided that the battalions to remain in the Division should be those which were composed of the men who first came forward to form the Ulster Division.

I therefore selected the senior of the three battalions of Inniskilling Fusiliers to remain.

In the case of the Royal Irish Rifles, I selected the senior battalion to remain. This was the 15th Battalion, a Belfast Battalion originally raised as the 7th Battalion.

The next senior of the original battalions of the Ulster Division would been the 10th Royal Irish Rifles.

This was also a Belfast Battalion and I decided that it would be unfair to the Counties of Down and Antrim that they should have no representation amongst the original units of the Division. I therefore selected the 12th Royal Irish Rifles as the other battalion to remain.

The remaining third battalion of Royal Irish Rifles, the Pioneer Battalion, which [*sic*] was not affected by the reorganisation of the Division.

I have gone into the matter at this length because there is no reason why you should not know the principle on which I acted in naming the battalions which I considered should be disbanded.

I need hardly say how deeply I regret the disappearance of so many fine battalions from the Division.

The claims of the 14th Royal Irish Rifles to remain in the Division were put before me by the OC, the battalion, but in view of the principle of selection I had decided upon I felt I could not accept his views.

As to the point of the reconstitution of the 14th Royal Irish Rifles after the war, I do not think you need anticipate that there would be any difficulty in doing so if it were considered desirable.

I greatly regret that I am not able to meet your wishes, and those of the Citizens of Belfast, in respect of the retention of the battalion.

FC, D/3835/E/10/8

207
Nugent to his wife

[Holograph] [Ollezy]
8 March 1918

The indications and the reports of prisoners look like an imminent German attack somewhere on this particular front, but the exact place we cannot tell. There seems to be no doubt that the Germans have tanks, how many we don't know and being Germans they are going to have them fitted with flame projectors.

The C in C was round here today and saw some of my works and heard my proposals and in the end complimented me on my arrangements and on the work done by the Division. I have a suspicion that he meant it as a farewell and that my days in command of a Division out here are numbered. The new chief of the staff was with him, Lawrence, I spoke to him and said I hoped I should not be one of the officers to have to go home. He did not say I was going to be one of them, but said it was necessary to give promotion to younger men and that it was decided that a number of the older Division commanders were to go home to command Divisions at home to make way. I feel I am to be one of them.

It is a very bitter draught to have to swallow and if I am kicked out it will not be treating me with fairness nor with any recognition of the work I have done.

Well, there is no redress and one must only bear it.

FC, D/3835/E/2/17

208
Nugent to his wife

[Holograph] [Ollezy]
18 March 1918

Still an uncanny silence and quiet all along our front. 2 deserters have just come in to our lines, I hear over the telephone and report my Division is to be attacked tonight! If any truth in it, it will be a raid I expect. So I don't worry myself. In fact I shouldn't worry anyhow as it does no good. The sun is as hot as in June. I have no memory of a March like this. I suppose if I get home soon, it will rain all the time.

Bob Maxwell is still staying with me. I am trying to get him a job. It is rather bad luck for him if he has to go and command a battalion entirely strange to him and in which he can't take any interest.

He has been twice wounded and has 3 sons out in France of whom 2 have been wounded so I think he ought to have a chance of a less risky life than that of a CO . . .

I had a long letter from Neills today asking if he should send my guns to Curran, the police Sergt in Mount Nugent to keep, as he felt sure they would be raided by the Sinn Feiners. The silly old man. No Sinn Feiner from round about us would raiding [*sic*] anything belonging to us and they are really rather harmless lunatics.

The Boche did a bombing expedition about here last night, but did not drop anything very close to my Hdqrs.

FC, D/3835/E/2/17

209
Nugent to his wife

[Holograph] [Ollezy]
20 March 1918

2 Alsatian deserters came in last night and from their statements which are confirmed from other sources there seems no doubt that

the day is very near. We expect to be attacked tonight or tomorrow and it is going to be a very big attack and will last for weeks. It is very grim sitting still and waiting. Arthur's battalion is in the front line. I wish it wasn't with all my heart. He will never spare risk I fear if he thinks it is his duty to go to any part of his line and we know the Germans have an enormous amount of Artillery and are going to use gas very heavily.

Well we shall know all about it very soon now. The weather has broken and it is raining and thick. On the whole more to our advantage than the Germans. They may postpone their attack in consequence, but from all accounts, they have such large forces close up that they can't keep them crowded for long.

I have heard no more at present of my being one of the Div Comdrs to go home. 4 have already gone I know and several of the old Corps Comdrs.[34] If I don't go this time I am bound to go with the next batch.

Bless you all my dearest. I wonder if I shall be able to write you tomorrow.

FC, D/3835/E/2/17

210

Nugent to his wife

[Holograph] [Ollezy]
21 March 1918

The long expected has come at last. The German bombardment began at ¼ to 5 this morning and is still going on. In all my experience out here I have never known anything more terrific. It isn't a series of reports, but it is just one long roar. It seems as if there were some strange devil who watches over the Germans. This morning dawned with so thick a fog that we can't see 200 yards. All we can hear are the shells, we can see nothing and all the lines to the front are already cut and we have to depend on runners and byke [*sic*] orderlies, a very slow process when as in this case the Germans are shelling all the roads.[35]

It is the first real fog there has been for months and it is disastrous that it should have come today. We are the people who suffer from it. This time it is the Germans who are attacking. They know where they want to go and we don't so it is all against us. It is now 8.15 am and the roar has never ceased since ¼ to 5. We don't know whether the German Infantry has come over or not. I cannot hope after this terrible bombardment that many of the front line troops can be left alive or at least unwounded.

I am so anxious about Arthur. I feel the responsibility of having given him a battalion, though if I hadn't someone else would have in some other Division. Well, dearest, we can only endure and fight on and try and live up to the watchword of the French at Verdun 'Ils ne passeront pas'.

From reports from the Corps, it appears that the heaviest bombardment is up in the Cambrai sector, where we were last November.

10.30 am. Still without news. The bombardment is as heavy as ever and reports from as near the front as we have communications still going say that there has been heavy gas shelling.

The Germans are shelling all these back areas too with heavy guns. There is no doubt they have a tremendous mass of Artillery, far more than we have.

So far as this Corps is concerned, the weight of the shelling is nearly all on my Division front and then away to the right on the next Corps front. The 14th Division [*sic*] on my right but we can get no communication with them. Their wires are also all cut.

12.30. The latest is the Germans have got all our forward lines along the whole front of attack as far as I can make out.[36] From our 2nd position we can see the Germans on the ridge in front, where our front line was. There is no doubt it is all captured and Kitty dearest, Arthur was in front. He must be either dead or a prisoner. Poor Arthur and poor Aileen. It is terrible. I am afraid there is no hope that he got away. He would not have left his men and all his line is gone. We know that.

Things have gone badly for us. I am heartbroken about Arthur. Don't breathe a word yet to anyone.

Goodbye dearest. It is a very anxious time.

FC, D/3835/E/2/17

211
Nugent to his wife

[Holograph] [Ollezy/Freniches/Beaulieu]
22/24 March 1918

I had no time to write in time for post this evening so I must tell you how things went since 12.30 pm yesterday. First, I have heard about Arthur. A German Officer sent a pigeon message by one of our pigeons captured in the redoubt Arthur's battalion or part of it was holding. He wrote 'Have captured the redoubt and have got the battalion commander a prisoner'. That would not have been much help as there were 3 redoubts and there were 3 battalion commanders in front, but I sent to our pigeon loft to ask the pigeoneer if he remembered which battalion the pigeon was sent to and he was able to say it went to Arthur's battalion. There is therefore no reason to doubt that Arthur is safe though a prisoner and if he had been wounded I expect the German would have mentioned it. At any rate it is something for Aileen to know and will take some of the load off her mind. I got Bob Maxwell to write to her telling her of the message.

All yesterday and late into the night we were fighting hard. The fog lifted about 1 pm but it had done its foul work by hiding the Boches until they were close up to our main battle line.

Then the Division on our right, I regret to say the 14th and my old Brigade the 41st too, gave way and let the Germans in behind me. I had to move up a battalion and made a line at right angles to my front to keep them off and we fought all day like that.[37]

The Germans were in greatly superior numbers and had a terrific superiority in Artillery and here and there and bit by bit they got the front line of the main battle line all along the front of somewhere about 50 miles. At nightfall the Germans were in our front line in various places and we were holding it in others and the situation was very obscure. Then we were ordered to withdraw our right and a Brigade of another Division was given me as reinforcement.[38] It was a most anxious night. There is nothing so difficult as to withdraw troops in close contact with the enemy without letting the enemy know. It was 4 am before I could lie down. As it was, one of the battalions withdrawing ran into an ambush of the Germans who had got behind them and they lost a lot of men, I am sorry to say.[39] In the middle of the night too I had to shift my Hdqrs as it was getting dangerous and disturbing owing to the shelling.

Today we have had hard fighting and we are again withdrawing to a fresh line in rear all along the whole Army front and I have had to move Hdqrs again, a rather exciting move too as the Germans were shelling a bridge we had to cross with a big gun. We had to get as close as we could to it, wait behind a house till the shell came and then gallop to get a safe distance before the next arrived. I think there is no doubt we have killed a large number of Germans, but on the other hand we have had very heavy losses. We began by losing 3 battalions who could not be got away and we have lost a great many men. I have not got the figures yet but they are very heavy indeed.

The 1st Battn Inniskilling Fusiliers are the heroes of this Division. They are one of the regular battalions. Their duty was to hold a redoubt in the main line and they held it to the end. No man came back from it. They beat back 12 different attacks made we believe by the 1st Guard Division of the Prussians and at the last those who were watching from other places said the Germans just poured over in a wave, but none of the Inniskillings came away. They were ordered to hold their line and they held it to the end. All the officers and all the men died where they stood. It is a great and gallant story.[40]

March 23. I do not known when I shall be able to send you a letter. Everything is too disorganised at present and posts neither come nor go. Early this morning we got news that a Division on our right [*sic* – left] had given way and let the Boche across a river and marshes into Ham, a most serious disaster. We were holding the line of the river next to Ham and we are still holding it but it is a very precarious hold and the Germans have made a big dent in the line and may break in on us at any moment. It is very critical as we are certain the Germans will pour in reinforcements which may enable them to turn the whole of the river line.[41]

The French are coming up in support and some have already arrived but it will be touch and go. My hope is the Germans may not be ready yet to try and smash through at this point.

I can hardly believe it is only the 3rd day since the battle began. It seems a month. I am moving my Hdqrs further back this evening.

I doubt if the whole Division could now produce more than the equivalent of a full Battalion. It has been far the worst battle of the war as far as we are concerned, but if in the end we beat the Germans, it will be worth it. At present he has had matters rather his own way, but then he attack[ed] us in terrific force and with a terrible weight of Artillery.

I should say we will have to be withdrawn, not only us but the whole Corps to refit and to be made up again and if we are I may be able to get my leave.

The net result of today's operations is that we are holding our own. We have been pressed back here and there, but the Germans have not tried us very highly. They are evidently making ready their next bound and getting Artillery up before making a big effort to force the line of the Somme. They have only a few crossings near Ham so far as I know and it is not possible to pass a big Army across at one point. The risks of being caught in a bottleneck are too great. Tonight is the risk as they may pass large enough forces through at the bridge at Ham to attack us in force tomorrow morning.

March 24. I have sent my last men up to support the defence. I have collected even the Officers' Servants and all sorts of odds and ends of men. Freddie Drummond has gone with them at his urgent request and I sent them off in lorries at 2 am this morning.

The morning's news is not so good. The Germans have gained more ground during the night, but it is still only in small parties. There is not up to the present 11 am any sign of a big attack though some prisoners captured last night say 2 German Divisions were in Ham which were to cross during the night and were to attack us this morning. I hear a post will go out at 3.30

pm today and so I will finish this now and leave it to go out as I must now go up and see my Brigadiers.

Bless you all my dearest.

PS Have had no letters either for the last 3 days.

FC, D/3835/E/2/17

212
Nugent to his wife

[Holograph] [Auricourt/Guerbigny]
25 March 1918

It is all a ghastly nightmare. I cannot credit that it is only 5 days ago that we were holding the trenches just in front of St Quentin. Yesterday was a bad day for the French and British Armies. We lost much ground, a great deal of guns and ammunition have been captured. The French have been rushing up Divisions to try and stop the rot, but there is a great deal of confusion and the Germans are giving us no rest. What is left of my Division had terribly heavy fighting yesterday and we had to fall back again in common with French and British.

Last night I passed through the French who have now formed a line in front of me and other Divisions of the 5th Army. We are reorganising just behind them. A very heavy fight is going on just in front of us. I pray the French will be able to hold the Germans. My men have had no food, some of them for 2 and 3 days. They have had no sleep for 5 nights.

They are absolutely beat. We are in support of the French but if they call on us before I am reorganised and before the men have had at any rate one good night's sleep, we shall be no help to them.

This is truly Armageddon. Unless we can finally stop the German attack soon, I fear it will be the end.

I am now under the orders of the French Divisional Commander who has taken over the front of this Division. He is a man called Margot. I have just been to see him.

It is a funny situation as I am now part of the French Army. I hope we shall not fail them. At any rate yesterday evening, the French retired before we did. They and my Division were all in the battle together. I had to go up to the front and it was a horrible scene of confusion. French and British retiring, guns, wagons, horses and men in most inexplicable confusion, a roar of shelling and machine guns and the very heaviest kind of German shells bursting all round us. At one time when we got into a narrow road and hopelessly wedged in, I really thought I might have to abandon my car.

I am leaving my Hdqrs again today, as the battle is very close and we expect this village to be shelled at any minute.

I feel more than anything the attitude of the French towards us. They hardly pretend to be civil and I can hardly wonder. We have let them in disastrously. There is sure to be the devil of a row at home over our debacle. I think it may cause the downfall of the present Government and of either Henry Wilson or DH[aig]. Certainly no one could have even in their worst moments anticipated so complete a catastrophe.

I do not think there will be any leave for me yet awhile. There can be no rest for anyone while every man, young or old, fresh or tired is wanted. FD[rummond] is all right, but I have not seen him. Goodbye my dearest and love to you all.

FC, D/3835/E/2/17

213
Nugent to his wife

[Holograph] [Sourdon]
28 March 1918

I wrote the other letter on 25th but it never went on so I am putting this in too as there is a post going out in 20 minutes.

All is most critical as the papers will have told you. The French have taken over our Divisional front since last night and the remnants of the Division have been withdrawn from the fighting line last night. It does not amount to much as there are hardly any left, just a few hundred men.

When I last wrote we were at Beaulieu, fighting just S of Ham. The French had by way [*sic*] of relieved us and we were ordered back to Guerbigny to reorganise. What I feared happened. The French failed to stop the Germans and in the early morning of 26th, we were ordered to form a line to fill a gap and to hold it to the end to give time to the French to get up behind. Some of the men had been marching all night but we had to turn about and take up a position on the left of a French Division. We have had desperate fighting on 26th and 27th and I hope we have done what was required. At any rate the Division has fought almost to the last man. As far as I can make out there not more than 500 men, exclusive of clerks and transport men, left.[42]

It was certainly an exciting 2 days. I had just time to ride round our position on the morning of 26th and give orders how it was to be occupied, before the attack began. I then went back to my Hdqrs in Guerbigny just behind. We held on during the day but in the evening the trouble began. Part of the line was driven back and made a gap. After dark a number of Germans got in behind us and amongst them a lot of cavalry. It seems that our people thought they were our men or French troops pulling back, as the Germans marched absolutely without concealment and disappeared behind our line. In the evening I sent my GSO(1) Col Place out to see one of the Brigadiers who was close by, but told him to return from there. He took one of the cars, saw the Brigadier, but instead of coming back, he took 2 COs of battns with him and went off to see General Griffith, another of my Brigadiers who was on the left near a village called Erches.

It seems he drove straight into a cavalry party of Germans and was captured with both COs.[43] One of our men saw the thing happen, he was captured too but managed to escape and brought the news. Meanwhile I heard nothing and about 9 pm I had just sat down to eat something when an orderly ran in to say the Germans were in the village. I had kept my car ready for emergency use and so I and the 2 staff officers with me rushed out, jumped into the car and started off down the road. As we came out of the gate on to the road, a German machine gun fired I suppose at us from a rise in the ground just within 200 yards of us.

It was very bright moonlight. I went about 1½ miles along the road to where there was a French Brigade Hdqrs, told the Brigadier and asked him to send a party to clear the village as all my men were in front and I had no reserves of any sort. He went to telephone, came back and assured me it was all a mistake, that the party who had fired was one of his own, who had lost their way, saw our men and thought they were Germans. I returned to the village then and again tried to get something to eat. I had just cut a slice of bread when the man who had seen Place captured came in and told us and at the same time a German prisoner who was actually captured in the village, one of the German party [*sic*]. This time there was no mistake, so again we bolted, the Germans actually close to us. I went back to [*sic*] same village as French Brigadier and insisted on his sending some men to guard the approaches through Guerbigny and clear the village. Eventually he sent 2 parties to hold the roads, but would do no more. I sat up all night sending out warnings, but all the despatch riders I sent out have disappeared and must have been taken. During the night General Griffith's Hdqrs was surrounded, some of his Staff Officers killed or taken. He himself and others scattered and got away and he managed to escape and turned up in the morning having had a very exciting night.

In the morning the Germans began to shell the village I was in. I was hit by pieces of a shell, but fortunately only frightened.

1230. No time for more. The Germans have broken through again at Montdidier. I have to collect the fragments of the Division to help the French.

FC, D/3835/E/2/17

214
Nugent to his wife

[Holograph] [Essertaux]

29 March 1918

Dearest, I had to break off in a hurry yesterday as the Commander of 1st French Army, General Debeney came to see me and to tell me the Germans had broken in his line, west of Mont Didier and to ask for every man I had. I gave them of course and the poor devils who have been fighting for 7 days without rest had to drag themselves out to a village called Coullemelle where we took up a position. Fortunately the Germans did not come on and the French drove them back where they had broken in. I spent the night on a mattress on the floor of a deserted house and Guy C tried his hand at cooking an old hen he found, but it defeated me.

The night passed quietly on this front. I have not heard any news from other fronts. My judgment is that it is only the pause before the worst blow of any yet falls and I think tomorrow will be the beginning of the decisive battle. The Germans are close round Amiens now and if they take it, it will threaten our communications with the Channel Ports. It is a very serious moment.

Gough has gone home or at any rate has been relieved from command of 5th Army.[44] If it had only been done 6 months earlier. The sad part of it is that we have not inflicted a tithe of the losses, in the 5th Army at any rate, that the Germans inflicted on us.

Yesterday after being shelled out of Becquigny, I raced back to Fignieres, then while I was away to speak to the Corps, we were shelled out of that and moved to Hargicourt and in the evening the advance of the Germans compelled us to come back to Sourdon. This morning that was filled up with French troops and we have come back to Flers sur Noye.

My Corps has ceased to function as I am working under the French and the other Divisions of the Corps are also acting under their orders, but they have no troops and I want to go right back out of the fighting zone, else I shall never be able to reorganise. As it is, it is I fear too late as all my instructors and most of my battalion staffs have gone, there is nothing to build on, but I doubt if even our broken fragments can be spared now.

I think another week will decide the war.

FC, D/3835/E/2/17

215
Nugent to his wife

[Holograph] [Gamaches]
31 March 1918

We are out of the battle now. Most of the Divisions which have borne the first onslaught have been replaced and we are back at a place called Gamaches, west of Abbeville, close to the sea to reorganise and refit and I hope to fill up, though I do not known where the men will come from.

We came back yesterday afternoon, being relieved by the French. The Germans I hear got into the village where my Hdqrs were yesterday shortly after I left, a place called Sourdon, but I hear the French drove them out again. It has been raining pretty hard off and on yesterday and today and there was very heavy rain last night.

Reinforcements are coming over in adequate numbers from England I hear, but for the last 36 hours I am out of all news. It is most trying. There must be heavy fighting somewhere, because the Germans cannot afford to lose a moment. It is probable that they have outstripped their guns and that they must pause to let them get up. Then I believe there will be such a smashing blow at us and the French as will dwarf even the first. The rain will not have helped the Germans as they cannot move off the roads in the old Somme battlefield. Unfortunately they are well in front of that now in many places. It is most maddening not to have news. You probably know more than we do as the papers and posts are very erratic now. I got 3 letters from you the day before yesterday, 2 dated 22nd and one without a date, but probably 23rd.

Please address enclosed to Aileen. It is just a letter of sympathy and telling her I am sure Arthur will be well treated. The Germans are such snobs, they will treat Arthur all the better for being a peer.

I hope the situation will enable us to remain here long enough to get reorganised. At present we are very disjointed and we had to burn a lot of baggage and office papers to prevent the Germans getting them. I don't know yet how much of my kit is lost.

Fortunately having a closed car, I am able to carry a bag and bedding on the roof but many officers and some of the Hdqrs messes have lost everything.

FC, D/3835/E/2/17

216
Nugent to his wife

[Holograph] [Gamaches]
1 April 1918

I am in a most delightful old 13th Century house in the village of Gamaches, a few miles from the sea. The Division is now collected around the area and I hope we may be given time to reorganise and get some men and specialists trained. There is no news as far as we are concerned, except reports that we are holding the Germans. I hear from my French interpreter that the French are very much discouraged at the success so far of the Germans and that if the Germans get Amiens, the French won't go on fighting. I can hardly believe that it is true and hope it isn't. The French are so mercurial that they are always either in the heights of optimism or the depths of despair. There is no need for despair, but every need to set our teeth and fight.

I do not expect to be long out as we shall need every man that can be raised, but on the other hand I don't know where our reserves and reinforcements are to come from as the Irish regiments are exhausted and there are no reserves left in Ireland.

One can hardly realise the 9 days of nightmare really existed. I seem to want to do nothing but sleep. Everything passed so quickly and the strain was so great and one was so strung up that now the tension suddenly has relaxed, it seems as if I had never really gone through the time.

I think it is very hard on the Division that the C in C has made no mention of them. I am afraid that the Divisions of the 5th Army will get very little acknowledgement. It was not their fault, but that of the dispositions which were made and which caused the sacrifice of so many battalions and so much loss of ground.

I think the Germans are probably having great difficulty in getting guns and supplies forward and that is the reason of [*sic*] the pause.

I expect a terrific fresh attack very soon and I am only surprised it has not come sooner. If the Daily Mail man, Pyke, is correct it is Germany's last effort. It would be unthinkable that the French should desert us now and I do not believe they will do so. I do not believe the stories told by correspondents of the prodigious slaughter of Germans. I know it can't be true for the whole battlefront. Here and there of course the Germans have had the heaviest losses in attacking points in our line, but in many places and especially on the 5th Army front, I know they have not had heavy losses.

FC, D/3835/E/2/17

217
Nugent to his wife

[Holograph] [Montreuil]
5 April 1918

I am by way of staying with John Fowler.[45] In reality I am staying at an inn here and using his mess. I got a new temporary plate yesterday at Boulogne and today I am merely resting and go on to Ypres tomorrow, where I expect to find the Division assembled again. We are to be made up to strength at once, but of course the difficulty of making them into a good fighting force within reasonable time is greater this time than any previous time because I have lost so many COs and Officers and NCOs. I should think it possible we may go back to fight as soon as we are made up if the Germans continue to attack.

The pause in their attack is baffling and creates a very great strain on everybody here as it is difficult to know where the next blow will fall. I believe we shall stop them now on our front. I wish I was as confident of the French, but there are plenty of troops available now I think, unless the Germans do something unexpected. I think their losses have been very heavy. One hopes they are heavier than they can well support.

I have spent 2 interesting days here going round various offices and meeting old friends at GHQ. Tomorrow I shall call in on the 2nd Army Hdqrs and renew acquaintances with them. I hope I may see General Plumer.

I find everyone is very pleased with the Division and the way they fought, and I find we are considered to have had the heaviest fighting almost of anyone and the most difficult as we had so often to move owing to the Germans breaking in on the front of Divisions to the right or left of us and because we did not get all the support from the French that we were supposed to get.

I wish the C in C had given us the satisfaction of recognising this by mentioning us as among the Divisions which had done well.

FC, D/3835/E/2/17

218
Nugent to his wife

[Holograph] [Poperinghe]
7 April 1918

I returned to this delectable place, not so far from Poperinghe yesterday evening. We are in a camp at present but tomorrow I go forward and take over a Hdqrs consisting of huts and dugouts. My own residence consists of two dugouts, one as office and the other as bedroom, dugouts with a steep bank with the fetid canal on one side and a more fetid stream immediately in front and the surrounding mud for miles. The only communications are duckboard tracks laid over the surface of the mud.

However I am getting reinforcements rapidly and we shall be shortly up to nearly full strength again. It is somewhat interesting and very significant that the 2 Divisions which were on either side of mine are not to be made up and may be broken up. There are a list of 5 or 6 in all to whom this may happen and they are notoriously Divisions which failed to do their duty.[46] No Division I think suffered more than the 36th by the failure of the Divisions on either side to stick it out. I am thankful that my Divn never gave way and never retired until they were ordered to do so.

I spent the morning questioning various men of battalions who were all through the fighting and they all agree that they did really kill a very large number of Germans.

All leave is suspended at present so I shall not be able to get home yet. Arthur would be shown as Missing because the pigeon message was not official and prisoners are always 'missing' until officially notified through neutral agencies in Berlin as 'prisoners of war', that may be a very long time now as, I fear, there are many prisoners and if they are wounded as well, it takes still longer as they are not usually reported till they have left the German hospital.

I got an official letter of thanks from the French Army I was with today, thanking me for my valuable assistance and complimenting the men on their steadiness and courage.

The situation in front of Amiens is still very critical and the Germans have gained a little ground there again. In any case they are within Artillery range of the railways through there and they are very vital to us.

You couldn't hear from me more often than you did while the fighting was going on because, either I had no opportunity to write or there were no posts out. As a rule when I realised we should have to retreat soon, I sent everything and everybody of the Hdqrs back several miles so as to get them out of the way and I stayed on with just 2 or 3 staff officers, a couple of cars, a lunch basket and kettle and remained until I had given every order that appeared possible to give and until we had actually begun to move back.

John Peacocke has had a nervous breakdown and I am replacing him in command of his battn and he will probably go home at once for rest. He did most excellent work but was not really very fit when it began. One day 2 officers he was walking with were both killed by the same shell, one on either side of him, he was untouched but greatly shaken. He was standing talking to Audley Pratt the time Audley was killed.

General Hessey and his Brigade Major, George Bruce, were both magnificent. I can't describe adequately how splendid they were on a very critical occasion, the day the French first came up to reinforce us and then broke and the Division on my right also broke and some of our Cavalry who were in front of us also came streaming back and it looked like a debacle. Hessey and Bruce rode right up into the line, threatening to shoot any waverers and cheering and encouraging our men. Then our cavalry turned about and charged and the 36th Division rallied and charged after them and the situation so far as the Division was concerned was saved. That was the time when I had to dash off to the French Divn Comdr to ask him what the d—l his men were about.[47]

Anyhow so far as we were concerned Hessey and Bruce saved the situation. You can quote this to Mrs Hessey if you like. It will surely please her and there will be no harm in its being said.

You can assure Aileen that Arthur's battalion did all that men could do. The proof being that I have not been able to find a single man who came back from them.

To think that so much of the losses and not only of men and material but of the ground it cost us 6 months and countless lives to win in 1916 should have been lost because of the incompetence of an individual.

FC, D/3835/E/2/17

219
Nugent to his wife

[Holograph] [Ypres]
9 April 1918

Here I am back in this filthy Ypres sector in the very place where I had my Hdqrs at the time I left to command this Division. Somewhat altered and enlarged and there are huts now, but I still live and work in the dugouts in the canal bank. The Germans are further away, that is all, but the country to the front and rear is an indescribable waste of mud, shellholes and water, bleak and desolate beyond words . . .

I had to send Bob Maxwell to command a battalion owing to the shortage of COs, but he doesn't want to go and says quite frankly his nerves are not equal to taking the strain with a new battn of men from all parts, all strangers to him, so I told him to write to me officially and say so and I would try and get him a home job.

After all, he isn't a soldier, he has been twice wounded and has 2 sons out here who have each been wounded and I don't blame him for wanting to get home. I am sorry he was ever sent out again.

There are strong indications that the Germans are preparing a heavy attack on another part of our front. Heavy artillery fire and so forth.

I am going to a conference this afternoon at which I hope the general situation will be made a bit clearer.

Gough is still out here, I hear, but I can not believe that he will be employed again. I don't think public opinion would stand it and I am sure the French wouldn't.

I have just been reading the official report of one Brigade of the 10 days fighting. Bald as it is, it reads like an epic.

FC, D/3835/E/2/17

220
Nugent to his wife

[Holograph] [Ypres]
10 April 1918

There was bad news this morning when I woke to find that the Germans had taken Messines which we took from them almost 10 months ago to a day. How they managed to do it I can't think. We had 10 months to make it impregnable, but as always I suppose we thought he would never come back. It is not on my front but very close and I have had to send one of my brigades along in motor lorries down there to help, but I am afraid it is too strong a position to be easily taken without a stronger force than we have available and more artillery than we have got here. Unless we get it back it will I am afraid make our position here rather difficult.[48]

Then further south the Germans attacked the Portuguese and what happened I don't know but apparently 2 of our Divisions had to be rushed up and have been fighting hard so I expect the Portuguese bravos legged it. What between them on one side and les braves Belges next door to me I feel very anxious.

The unpleasant feature of it all is that the Germans seem able to attack with success in so many places.

The general idea seems to be that he is going to attack until he gets a dominant position, possibly till he has Amiens and so controls the railways of Northern France and that he will then offer us peace on his own terms. I fear if that happens that the French may give in. They seem to have given up hope of getting back Alsace and Lorraine. The prospects are not brilliant just now, yet if we can only held on for another 6 weeks or 2 months, I believe the Germans will crack, if we can only do it. The want of men may defeat us at the last hour.

FC, D/3835/E/2/17

221
Nugent to his wife

[Holograph] [Ypres]
13/14 April 1918

The situation on this front is rather better today. The Germans have not made much progress anywhere and there are reinforcements arriving on our side now . . .

So far only one of my Brigades has been engaged and they had a quiet day on Kemmel, except for shelling which was very severe indeed. We captured a Colonel at Neuve Eglise today who said that if the attack on Neuve Eglise succeeded, Kemmel would be attacked next day. Neuve Eglise has stood firm all day so far.

The Germans shelled us heavily last night and cut all the electric light wires, in consequence of which we were in darkness all night . . .

It is extraordinary the change of spirit and tone in the 2nd Army, compared with the 5th Army. Here everybody has such absolute confidence in Plumer. In the other, the mere fact of going to the 5th Army was like a death blow. It used to take all the heart out of troops. Service in the 5th Army was hated by Generals, regimental officers and men alike. The 5th Army never had a success and was responsible for the loss of more lives uselessly than all the other Armies put together. Gough had no qualification for commanding an Army, neither intellectual nor by training.

He is a most gallant and dashing Cavalry soldier whose proper place would be in leading a cavalry charge. Please God for the sake of the British Army and the cause for which we are fighting he will never be employed out here again.

I hear that Repington, the late 'Times' correspondent is now at work preparing an indictment of Henry Wilson with a view to trying to prove that HW is responsible and not Gough. Repington's hatred of HW is an obsession and he would be absolutely unscrupulous in trying to prove by any means fair or the reverse that HW is the man who should be hanged.[49]

April 14. Last night was a quiet night and such a relief. We had a hard day's fighting on the right of this Army but only one of my brigades was involved and we have not budged. It is at Kemmel, a very important locality . . .

I have this moment had a telephone message from my Corps, which is the 2nd, commanded by Jacob,[50] a good man I believe, that all the Divisional Commanders are to meet him at my HQ at ¼ to 1, that is in about ½ an hour. So I suppose there is something brewing, but I shan't in any case be able to tell you what it is, even if it would be proper to tell you because the post goes out directly.

FC, D/3835/E/2/17

222
Nugent to Lt Gen Maxse

[Holograph]

[Ypres]
14 April 1918

I was sorry not to have had an opportunity of saying goodbye to you and your Staff. I would have written sooner to thank you for your remarks on the work of the Division during the retreat, but since we came up here we have had little time for writing. So far only one (108th) Brigade has been in the fighting up here, but it has been very severe and the German Artillery fire has been worse than anything we have known.

I should have sent you some notes if I had been able to collect them myself, but I have not had time to put them down in tabulated form.

They are mainly tactical and show the necessity of Brigadiers being close up to the fighting line and of the Div. Comdr being within view or at least within 15 minutes reach by D[espatch] R[ider] from Brigadiers.

Certain points are obscure. I am told that on 26th March when we were between Guerbigny and Andechy and the 30th Divn and one of my brigades (107th) had been driven back to a line between Erches and Brouchy leaving a gap of 1200 yards from Andechy to Erches which I was unable to fill, that 61st and 20th Divisions had unemployed troops behind the 30th and though asked by 30th Division to move them up to close the gap, the Div Comdrs of 61st and 20th would not move. Possibly there is an explanation and equally possibly I have been misinformed. I have not repeated this to anyone else as I might make mischief on incorrect information. I am more than ever convinced that in the present state of training of our Armies, it is absolutely necessary that platoons should be kept together and that they should <u>see</u> their own troops on either flank. The new Army is obsessed with the dread of being what they call 'in the air'. So long as they can see each other they are happy.

For communication in moving fighting, wireless from the Brigades to the Division and reports every 10 minutes are the only sure way until the wireless gets smashed and that wants a direct hit on the instrument. Aerials are easily repaired. This means adv. DHQ must be within 5,000 yards of BHQ.

I must thank you and your Staff for your and their unfailing readiness to help us at all times while we were in the XVIIIth Corps. We found your staff [indecipherable] of the pleasantest to deal with.

I expect we shall all be in the thickest of the soup up here before long. We are doing something tonight which goes to my heart.[51] You can probably guess.

IWM, Maxse Papers

223
Nugent to his wife

[Holograph]

[Ypres]
16 April 1918

The news is not good. This morning Bailleul was captured and Wytschaete and the Germans gained some very important heights. They are close to my old Hdqrs at Jans Capelle now and very close to Kemmel. The Brigade I have had in the fighting at Kemmel was withdrawn last night for rest but I fear it may have to be used again.

It is still I believe considered that the blow here is not the main one and so we are not getting many reinforcements. Last night we withdrew from practically all the ground we captured with such heavy loss last summer in this part of Belgium. We are now back very close to where we were in 1915. I got all my Division back in safety and the Germans did not make any move to follow us until this afternoon. They are now shelling us, but that is not a new thing. We saw them this afternoon feeling their way forwards over the desolate plain in front of us. I do not believe they will come very far after us on this particular front. They will get all the gains they want if they can extend their front towards Hazebrouck and Cassel . . .

I think we shall probably be relieved soon and go back to reorganise. We got no opportunity after the retreat and we are not really properly equipped. Neither Officers nor men in the battns know each other by sight. My 108th Brigade has had a lot of casualties during the past week. They have been in the fighting about Messines, Wytschaete and Kemmel.

Bad luck on them to have to see the loss of the places they helped to take last time . . .

We are in a grave position but not desperate. We are still on the defensive for the time has not yet come for our counterstroke. We have just to endure and fight. We may have to fight for months, but I think this will be the last year of it.

FC, D/3835/E/2/17

224
Nugent to his wife

[Holograph] [Ypres]
19 April 1918

I suppose Mrs Hessey felt one good turn deserves another. I am surprised to hear so much devotion is felt towards me. I wonder if it is really so.

Poor Hessey, I have had to send him home yesterday to my great regret. He has an old rupture and has to wear a truss and 2 days ago he slipped, fell down and displaced his inside.

It is a case of operation to get a permanent cure and in any case he will be laid up for some time so I have had to ask for another Brigadier, who I believe arrives today, one Vaughan.

I am so thankful about Arthur. We all are. I have his horses here and am going to ride Forester, his special favourite.

My 108th Brigade has been withdrawn to rest behind the remainder of the Division, I am glad to say. They have had a lot of casualties. We are having constant scrapping with the Germans in front.

I have a number of posts out in front of my real line to deceive the Boche as to where we really are and the Boche constantly bumps up against them and gets biffed. Yesterday evening having located a post, we sent a party out to stalk it and they did so with complete success, killing 3 and capturing 4, also a machine gun and another party bagged 2 Boches. I am doing the same again tonight. It is snowing heavily now and the ground is particularly slushy and horrible and it is very cold and clammy.

I can't write more as the postman is standing outside in the snowstorm looking martyred.

FC, D/3835/E/2/17

225
Nugent to his wife

[Holograph] [Dragon Camp, Ypres]
27 April 1918

We are at it all along the Divisional front again. The Germans followed us up pretty smartly when we retired last night and this morning we were in touch with them along the whole front.

There was very heavy shelling last night on all the roads and dugouts along the Canal and there have been various minor encounters along the front between our advanced troops and the Germans. So far they have not tried to attack us but are no doubt just feeling our strength. They shelled the back areas heavily again this morning and blew up a big Ammunition dump behind my Hdqrs.

It was a terrific explosion and shook the ground like an earthquake. It killed or wounded over 70 men I hear and for hours afterwards the cordite in the dump was going up in gigantic flares. At night it would have been an impressive spectacle.

I do not like my new Hdqrs at all. They are in a wood along a road. There is a sort of railway terminus of light railways along one side and engineers are everlastingly blowing off steam or whistling or filling the air with smoke from the foulest of coal. The wood is full of troops of all sorts and there are big guns immediately in front and behind. What that means when you are trying to work or sleep has to be endured to be realised . . .

Freddie seems to have settled down again. He does not mention going back to the 14th Division anymore and Guy says he does not want to now that they have been practically broken up and reduced to a training Division for Americans.

These Americans don't seem to be coming along yet. I wish they would. We could do very well with some of them even if they are green and raw.

FC, D/3835/E/2/17

226

Nugent to 36th Division Commanding Officers

Typescript copy] [Dragon Camp, Ypres]
6 May 1918

As I cannot come round and see all the Units of the Division to wish them good-bye, I must say what I can on paper.

I want you to tell them how much I appreciate the splendid work they have done during the 2½ years that I have had the honour and pleasure of commanding the Division.

They have never failed to reach a high standard of performance. They have shewn at all times a high sense of duty and conscientious thoroughness in the discharge of it.

I know they will do their duty as thoroughly in the future as they have done in the past.

I should like to have had the opportunity to thank all your Officers personally for their work and to have told them how I appreciate it but I can only ask you to do it for me.

I wish you all good luck in the future. I know you and your men will not fail.

PC, D/3835/E/2/20

227

Brigadier-General W. F. Hessey to Nugent

Holograph] Winkenhurst, Hellingly, Sussex
12 May 1918

I cannot thank you enough for your kind letter and all that you have done for me. I will of course try and do my best should I be called upon to take on much greater responsibilities – but I know my limitations only too well.

I am most awfully sorry you are leaving the Ulster Division: but I think from your point as to future prospects it is for the best as everyone in the division felt very keenly that you had been deliberately left out in the awards and honours lists for a long time past.

I am sure I wish you the very best of good luck in India. And all of us who have been privileged to serve under you will always remember the devotion you gave to the division and the care you took of the interests of all in it.

FC, D/3835/E/2/20

228
General Sir Charles [Tim] Harington to Nugent

[Holograph] War Office
2 June 1918

Forgive me for not having written before. I am very distressed to find that your name was never sent in from France for a K. I think it is a most damnable shame. I'm sure had anyone known or thought that it wd not have been that I could have got Sir Herbert [Plumer] to write irrespective of your not being in his Army as I know what he thinks about it. You can rely on me to see that it is put right next time and I am telling Sir C Monro about it.[52] Write to me before the end of the year. Its got to be done. All good luck.

FC, D/3835/E/2/20

Postscript
India and Ireland, July 1918 to June 1926

Introduction

Nugent left England for India in late July 1918 to assume command of the Meerut Division, where he remained until he retired from the Army in 1920. The Division was now an administrative rather than an operational formation [229, 230]; Nugent provided troops for, but was not personally engaged in, the Third Afghan War, and his units were involved in quelling the widespread civil disorder which spread across northern India in early 1919 (and which in April culminated in the Amritsar massacre, fortunately in a different area).[1] He was joined by Kitty for part of the period, and also by St George, newly commissioned into the KRRC.

In the autumn of 1920 he returned to Cavan. Ireland was again in turmoil, and it was not clear what reception he and his family would receive. In July 1920 he had written to his daughter Alison:

> I wonder what it will be like at home. I do not expect the people will be allowed to show any civility and I think everything is likely to be very unpleasant but I do not think they will shoot at us when we appear out of doors. I hope they won't. It would be such a nuisance to have to go out for a walk crawling on one's tummy.[2]

In fact they were left unmolested, other than losing their car to raiders in 1921: the family's roots in the area and the regard in which Nugent himself was held locally were certainly crucial. But he was fortunate that the revolutionary struggle in south Cavan was never as bitter as it was in, say, west Cork – where one of his former COs, John Peacocke, was shot dead at his home in 1920 – or local affection might not have been enough to safeguard him or his property. He disapproved of much of the behaviour of the police and Army during this period, particularly the policy of reprisals, official and unofficial, both because he thought it wrong and counter-productive and because the sight of uniformed personnel running out of control was anathema to him: on one occasion he intervened to secure the release of a local youth seized by the Black and Tans.[3]

After the creation of the Irish Free State in 1922 he threw himself into managing his estate: unlike some other Cavan landed families he had no thought of leaving, though the early 1920s were difficult times for former Unionists in the new state. (Plumer wrote to him in 1925: 'You do not give a very cheerful account of your life in Ireland just now, nor of the prospects for the future. We can only hope things may improve. You are setting a fine example by staying on in your home and I am sure exercising influence for good on other people around you.')[4]

In January 1922, 11 months after Haig stepped down from active command, Nugent was at last knighted for his war services (Henry Wilson, the CIGS, told General Hutton 'I was really and truly glad to be able to help Oliver to get his well-deserved honour and I hope it will be some comfort to a gallant soldier'.)[5] The letters of congratulation that flooded in [231–4] deplored the delay, but only one correspondent referred explicitly to the reason: 'You should have had it long ago, if – as I have always understood – Haig is responsible for the omission – it doesn't enhance his reputation for fair play.'[6]

Unlike his fellow Irish divisional commanders, Mahon and Hickie, Nugent was not – unsurprisingly, in view of the formation he had commanded – given a role in the public life of the new state by being appointed to the Senate. But he played an active role in the welfare of ex-servicemen, remaining closely associated with the work of the Ulster Division Fund which he had established during the war (funded largely by receipts from the Division's canteens) to provide support for wounded or otherwise unemployable former members of the Division; by 1922 it had disbursed over £17,500 to almost 3,000 applicants. He also took a keen interest in the preparation of the Divisional history, written by Cyril Falls and published in 1922, and was a member of the committee (along, somewhat uncomfortably, with James Craig and Spender) that oversaw the building of the Ulster Tower at Thiepval.

He was also in demand to open war memorials at home. Commemoration in Ireland was a sensitive issue after the war, given the complex motivations which had impelled many Irish soldiers to enlist; as Keith Jeffery was pointed out, the subtlety of Nugent's language when nveiling the memorial at Virginia, Co. Cavan, in 1923 demonstrates his wareness of the fact:

> The day is not, I hope, far distant when the memory of all those of our country who gave their lives for Civilization as we interpret it and in obedience to what they believed to be their duty will be honoured and perpetuated in every town and village in Ireland.[7]

Ie also made a point, when speaking in Northern Ireland, of stressing ne need for inclusiveness. As he told his audience in Ballymena in 1924: In treasuring the memory of the gallant and devoted service of Jlstermen, do not forget that it was shared by Ulstermen of all classes nd religious denominations.'[8]

In late May 1926 Nugent caught a chill which soon developed into neumonia, and on 31 May he died at Farren Connell. He is buried in Aount Nugent, where there is a memorial to him in the parish church. A nemorial service was held in St Anne's Cathedral, Belfast, shortly after is death. Reflecting the political difficulties he wrestled with, no senior olitical member of the Northern Ireland government attended. But in ecognition of Nugent's qualities as a soldier, hundreds of former nembers of the Division did, including Wilfrid Spender.

Professionally Nugent was a highly capable officer, and the Ulster Division earned an enviable reputation under him. In his dealings with oliticians he was sometimes clumsy; he was prone to fits of bad temper, nd occasionally treated people unfairly as a result. He never courted opularity with either subordinates or superiors, and would have been ppalled by any suggestion that he should. But he also had the virtues of he pre-war regular officer: an insistence on high standards and attention o detail, and an absolute and overriding concern for his men. He was pen to new operational ideas, and earned the respect of the best British ommander on the Western Front, General Plumer. He possessed hysical and moral courage and, underneath a severe exterior, a sharp ense of humour. Had his relations with Haig been better, he could ndoubtedly have gone further.[9] A friend and former subordinate, vriting after the war, summed up his strengths and weaknesses with nblinking candour: 'I see it is a strain of intolerance that has andicapped you – but you can't have all the virtues and no failings – so vhy should you complain – you have done great things and come hrough critical times, and never with anything but honour.'[10]

229

Nugent to his son St George

[Holograph] Mussoorie, UP, Indi
14th August 191

The area I command is 350 miles by 250 and there are somethin over 70,000 troops in it. My Hdqrs are at Meerut but this is th hill station for the best weather something over 7000' high. W have not seen much view so far as though the rains are a tota failure up here we still have constant clouds. I am beginning tour about the 15th Sept and it will take me a month to go roun the Command . . . It is lovely life living in India nowadays a one might almost as well be at the poles for all the news one get from home. I have not seen a line from England since I left o 21st June.

India is the limit in the way the Indian Govt pinch officers. M travelling expenses on duty are not sufficient to pay my expenses. have to buy my own horses and even a motor car. The Govt o India won't supply cars though they know we can't do our wor without them. They allow us a certain amount of mileage when w use our cars and yet expect us to be always travelling.

The news from France is very good up to now. I think we hav at last found a great soldier in Foch.

How are you getting on at Sandhurst? I should so much like t hear. I suppose you have had a spell off by now.

There are some queer specimens of officers out here but that i to be expected.

FC, D/3835/E/6

230
Nugent to his son St George

[Holograph] Meerut
21st October 1918

Since I last wrote you I have travelled many miles by road and rail visiting the various stations in the Command. I have been travelling almost continuously since the 9th Sept spending 2 or 3 days in one place, a day in another and so forth. I don't know how many miles I have travelled but I suppose it must be nearly 1000. I have inspected almost 50,000 men and still have nearly 25,000 men to see. In Meerut alone there are nearly 15,000 men, cavalry, gunners and infantry. I have not done them yet and there are still some outstations as well. The new native Army is much like the new British Army, not as well drilled or trained as the old but still not so bad.

'C, D/3835/E/6

231
Brig Gen A. Ricardo to Nugent

Holograph] Sion Mills, Co. Tyrone
2 January 1922

There can be no one more delighted to see your name in the New Year's Honours List than I am. I have always deplored the dirty work that kept you out of a reward that everyone recognised was your due and had been earned many times over – and I hated to think of your very natural soreness at the treatment and what was behind it. I have always quoted it as the worst case of injustice in the Honours lists that I know of. Late though it is, it must be a satisfaction to you to see a wrong righted – and your many friends in your old division will rejoice. The only jar is to see Neil Malcolm's name in the same list!![1] He was answerable for a good many failures.

C, D/3835/E/13

232
Maj Gen Sir William Hickie to Nugent

[Holograph] Kildare St Club, Dublin
3 January 1922

At last I am able to write to congratulate you on the belated promotion which you should have had four years ago. I have always felt your bad treatment just as keenly as if it had been my own for we had very similar tasks and difficulties.

I am very glad to feel that there is still some sense of justice left in parts of the War Office.

Wonder what's going to happen over here?

Although I have not had the privilege of meeting Lady Nugent I take the liberty of an old friend and beg you to give her also my congratulations.

FC, D/3835/E/13

233
Gen Sir Charles Harington to Nugent

[Holograph] HQ Allied Forces of Occupation, Constantinople
8 January 1922

I was just delighted to see your KCB in the New Year Honours List just received. It was monstrous, as I have so often said, that you had not received it years ago and your many friends all thought the same. Yours was the best run Division in our old Second Army. Anyhow no one is more pleased about it than I am and send you my best congratulations and wishes for the New Year.

I am having an interesting time here but I hope they will arrive at a settlement before long. All these nations are not easy.

FC, D/3835/E/13

234

Field Marshal Sir Herbert Plumer to Nugent

Holograph] The Palace, Malta

11 January 1922

have only today seen the Times of 2nd Jany.

I am more than delighted that you have at last been given a KCB.

It should have been given you long ago. It is a case of 'better late than never' – and that is all that can be said.

Anyhow you have my very hearty congratulations.

My wife asks me to send you hers too. And she joins me in wishing you the best of luck in 1922.

C, D/3835/E/13

Appendix 1
Biographical Notes

Allenby, Edmund Henry Hynman (1861–1936). Commissioned Inniskilling Dragoons, 1882; Bechuanaland Expedition 1884–5; Zululand 1888; South Africa 1899–1902; commanded 1 Cavalry Div. 1914; Cavalry Corps, 1914–15 V Corps, 1915; 3rd Army, 1915–17; CinC Egyptian Expeditionary Force 1917–19; Field Marshal, 1919; High Commissioner for Egypt and Sudan 1919–25. In the year ahead of Nugent – who disliked him intensely – at Staff College, and his Army commander in the winter of 1915–16.

Asquith, Herbert Henry (1852–1928). Liberal MP, 1886–1918 and 1920–4 Home Secretary, 1892–5; Chancellor of the Exchequer, 1905–8; Prime Minister, 1908–16; created Earl of Oxford and Asquith, 1925. Despised a ineffective by Nugent and many other senior officers.

Brock, Henry Jenkins (1870–1933). Commissioned RA, 1889; South Africa 1899–1902 (wounded); Lt Col 1914; CRA Ulster Div. 1915–18; retired a brigadier, 1922. Younger brother of the future Admiral of the Fleet Si Osmond Brock, he was a very competent gunner officer.

Byng, Julian Hedworth George (1862–1935). Commissioned 10th Hussars, 1883 Sudan 1884; South Africa 1900–1; commanded 3rd Cavalry Div. 1914 Cavalry Corps 1915; IX Corps (Gallipoli) 1915; Canadian Corps 1916–17 Third Army 1917–19; Governor-General of Canada 1921–6; Field Marsha 1932. The Ulster Division served under him at Cambrai: Nugent wa unimpressed by the extent to which Third Army was caught unawares by th German counter-attack.

Carson, Edward Henry (1854–1935). Unionist MP, 1892–1921; Solicitor General, 1900–6; one of the main leaders of Ulster opposition to Home Rule in 1912–14; Attorney General, 1915; First Lord of the Admiralty, 1917 Member of the War Cabinet, 1917–18; Lord of Appeal in Ordinary, 1921–9 One of the few politicians Nugent admired.

Comyn, Lewis James (1878–1961). Commissioned Connaught Rangers, 1899 AA&QMG Ulster Div. 29 Oct. 1915–4 Nov 1917; retired as colonel 1934 One of the first Catholic officers to join the Division, and a capable staf officer.

Couchman, George Henry Holbeche (1859–1936). Commissioned 13th Reg 1878; served Burma 1885–7 (DSO), 1891–8. Commanded territorial infantr brigade 1910–13, retired 1913. Commander of UVF in Belfast 1914, and c

107 Bde from 14 Sept. 1914 to 20 Oct. 1915. Dismissed by Nugent within days of arriving in France.

Craig, James (1871–1940). Served in Army (Capt, R Irish Rifles); South Africa, 1899–1902 (taken prisoner at Lindley, May 1900); Unionist MP, 1906–21; with Carson, one of the leaders of Ulster resistance to Home Rule; heavily involved in raising the Ulster Volunteer Force and subsequently the Ulster Division; served SW Africa, 1914–15; Parliamentary Secretary, Ministry of Pensions, 1919–20; Financial Secretary, Admiralty, 1920–1; first Prime Minister of Northern Ireland, from June 1921 until his death; created Viscount Craigavon, 1927. Nugent's relationship with him deteriorated markedly from 1916 onwards.

Crozier, Frank Percy (1879–1937). Worked as tea-planter in Ceylon. Served in South Africa 1899–1902; Manchester Regt 1902–6, att. West African Frontier Force; left the Army, returned briefly to South Africa, rejoined but again resigned his commission in somewhat murky circumstances, 1909, and went to Canada; returned to Ireland 1912 and joined UVF; second-in-command and then CO 9th Irish Rifles, 1914–16 ; commander 119 Bde 1916–18; CO 3rd Welch Regt, 1919; adviser to Lithuanian army 1919; Auxiliary Division RIC 1919–21. A strange individual, he was a tough commander obsessed, in his later writings, with shooting his own men. He thought highly of Nugent, whose opinion of Crozier was more equivocal.

Farnham, Arthur Kenlis (Maxwell), 11th Baron (1879–1957). Commissioned 10th Hussars; South Africa 1900–2. Irish Representative Peer from 1908, and a member of the Ulster Unionist Council before and during the Great War. A major in the North Irish Horse in 1914, he served as Nugent's ADC 1915–16. He returned to the Division in late 1917 as CO of first the 10th and then the 2nd Royal Inniskilling Fusiliers, and was captured in March 1918. Two of his sons died young in 1916; the third was killed at Alamein in 1942. A major Cavan landholder, he and Nugent were close friends from before the war.

Godley, Alexander John (1867–1957). Commissioned Royal Dublin Fusiliers 1886; South Africa 1899–1902 (including siege of Mafeking); transferred to Irish Guards 1900; GOC New Zealand Forces 1910–14; divisional commander at Gallipoli and GOC II ANZAC Corps 1916–19; CinC BAOR 1922–4; Governor of Gibraltar 1928–33; retired as general 1933. Not an especially popular commander. An acquaintance of Nugent's from before the war, the Godley family seat being on the Cavan–Leitrim border.

Gough, Hubert de la Poer (1870–1963). Commissioned 16th Lancers 1889; Tirah 1897–8; South Africa 1899–1902; commander 3rd Cavalry Bde 1911–14, playing a leading role in the Curragh incident; commanded 2nd Cavalry Div. 1914–15; 7th Div. 1915; I Corps 1915–16; Fifth Army 1916–18; removed from command March 1918; retired as general 1922. The Ulster Div. served under him in the summer of 1917 and again in the spring of 1918: Nugent never forgave him for the disastrous attack at Langemarck.

Griffith, Charles Richard Jebb (1867–1948). Commissioned Bedfordshire Regt 1887; South Africa 1899–1902 (DSO); CO 1st Bedfords 1914; commanded 108 Bde Dec 1915–May 1918 (CMG 1915, CB 1918); retired as brigadier 1919. After the war was a member of the War Office Standing Committee on Prisoners of War (in which role he examined in late 1918 and early 1919 a number of returning Ulster Division officer POWs captured in March 1918). He worked for a year in the historical section of the Committee of Imperial Defence. Dependable and calm in a crisis.

Hacket Pain, George William (1855–1924). Commissioned Queen's Royal Regt 1875; Egypt and Sudan 1888–9, 1896–8; South Africa 1901–2 (CB); CO 2nd Worcestershire Regt 1900–2. Retired as colonel 1912. UVF's Chief of Staff. Commanded 108 Bde 1914–15; 15 Reserve Infantry Bde 1916; Northern District Irish Command 1916–19; Divisional Commander RIC 1919–21. MP South Londonderry 1922–4. Not medically fit for frontline service; nor did Nugent rate him highly in any event.

Haig, Douglas (1861–1928). Commissioned 7th Hussars 1885; Sudan 1898; South Africa 1899–1902; GOC I Corps 1914; 1st Army 1914–15; CinC BEF 1915–19; Field Marshal 1917. In the year ahead of Nugent at Camberley, they did not get on.

Hamilton Gordon, Alexander (1859–1939). Commissioned Royal Artillery, 1880; Afghanistan 1880; South Africa 1899–1901; GOC Aldershot 1914–16; commanded IX Corps 1916–18; retired as lieutenant-general 1920. A lugubrious man nicknamed 'Sunny Jim', he was the Corps commander under whom Nugent served longest. They got on well together, despite Nugent's reservations about 'gunner generals'.

Harington, Charles (Tim) (1872–1940). Commissioned King's Regt 1892; South Africa 1899–1900; BGGS Canadian Corps 1915–16; MGGS 2nd Army and Italian EF 1916–18; DCIGS 1918–20; commander Allied forces in Turkey 1920–3; GOC Aldershot 1931–3; Governor of Gibraltar 1933–8; retired as general 1938. From a Tipperary family (his father's surname had been Poe) he was much admired by Nugent as Plumer's chief-of-staff, a regard which was reciprocated.

Hessey, William Francis (1868–1939). Commissioned Royal Inniskilling Fusiliers 1890; South Africa 1899–1902; retired as major 1913. Rejoined 1914; CO 11th Inniskillings 1914–16; commanded 110th Bde 1916–17; returned to Ulster Div. at Nugent's request in Dec. 1917 to command 109th Bde, which he commanded for the rest of the war. An outstanding commander at both battalion and brigade level, despite being handicapped by a hernia injury; Nugent regarded him highly.

Hickie, William Bernard (1865–1950). Commissioned into the Royal Fusiliers, 1885; South Africa 1899–1901; on staff of II Corps and commander 13th Bde 1914; 53rd Bde 1915; 16th Div. 1915–18; retired as major-general 1921. He and Nugent faced similar problems (though Hickie, who was sympathetic to Home Rule, was more tactful in his dealings with politicians); they developed a friendly working relationship in 1916–17 which survived the war, with their shared interest in projects to help ex-servicemen.

Hickman, Thomas Edgecumbe (1859–1930). Commissioned Worcestershire Regt 1881; Egypt and Sudan 1884–9 and 1896–1900, including the battles of the Atbara and Omdurman; South Africa 1900–2. Unionist MP for South Wolverhampton 1918–22. Inspector General of the UVF. Commanded 109 Bde till May 1916. A competent soldier, despite believing in creature comforts (he brought his butler to France as his batman), he and Nugent got on reasonably well; but politically they were some way apart and Nugent was relieved when Hickman returned home in the spring of 1916.

Lloyd George, David (1863–1945). Liberal MP for Caernarvon 1890–1945; President of the Board of Trade 1905–8; Chancellor of the Exchequer 1908–15; Minister of Munitions 1915–16; Secretary for War 1916; Prime Minister 1916–22; created Earl 1945. Nugent's initial welcome for his supercession of Asquith soon turned to suspicion.

Macready, Cecil Frederick Nevil (1862–1946). Commissioned Gordon Highlanders 1881; Egypt 1882; South Africa 1899–1902; GOC Belfast 1914; AG BEF 1914–16; AG War Office 1916–18; Commissioner Metropolitan Police 1918–20; GOC Ireland 1920–2; retired as general 1923. The antipathy he developed towards Ireland before the war was not improved by the problems over Irish recruitment.

Maxse, Frederick Ivor (1862–1958). Commissioned Royal Fusiliers 1882; Sudan 1897–8; South Africa 1899–1902; commanded 1st (Guards) Bde 1914; GOC 18th Div. 1915–17; XVIII Corps 1917–18; IG Training 1918; GOC Northern Command 1919–23; retired as general 1923. A good commander whom Nugent liked, but of little practical assistance to him during the March retreat.

Morland, Thomas Lethbridge Napier (1865–1925). Commissioned 60th Rifles 1884; Nigeria 1897–8, 1901–3; Inspector General West African Frontier Force 1905–10; GOC 2nd London Territorial Div. 1914; X Corps 1915–18; XIII Corps 1918; GOC Aldershot 1922–3; retired as general 1923. A kindly man, his inept handling of his reserves on 1 July 1916 cost the Ulster Division dear, and nearly cost him his job.

Murray, Archibald James (1860–1945). Commissioned 27th Regt, 1879; South Africa 1899–1902 (badly wounded); chief of staff BEF, 1914–15; DCIGS 1915; CIGS 1915; commander Egyptian Expeditionary Force 1916–17; GOC Aldershot 1917–19; retired as general 1922. A friend of Nugent's from Staff College and South Africa, he was instrumental in Nugent's appointment to command the Ulster Division in 1915.

Place, Charles Otley (1875–1955). Commissioned Royal Engineers 1895; South Africa 1899–1902; GSO1 36th Div. 5 April 1916–26 March 1918; retired as colonel 1923. A very able staff officer, he was captured in the March 1918 retreat.

Plumer, Herbert Charles Onslow (1857–1932). Commissioned 65th Regt 1876; Sudan 1884; South Africa 1896, 1899–1900, 1901–2; V Corps 1915; 2nd Army 1915–17, 1918; Italian Expeditionary Force 1917–18; Army of the Rhine 1919; Field Marshal 1919; Governor of Malta 1919–24; High Commissioner for Palestine 1925–28. Nugent admired Plumer enormously, who in turn had a high opinion of him and his division.

Rawlinson, Henry Seymour (1864–1925). Commissioned 60th Rifles 1884, transferred to Coldstream Guards 1892; Burma 1884–9; Sudan 1898, including the battles of the Atbara and Omdurman; South Africa 1899–1902; IV Corps 1914–15; 1st Army 1915; 4th Army 1916–17 and 1918; CinC India 1920–5 (died in post). Nugent, who did not altogether trust him, thought him ungrateful for the Ulster Division's efforts on the Somme in July 1916.

Ricardo, Ambrose St Quintin (1866–1923). Commissioned Royal Inniskilling Fusiliers 1888; North-West Frontier 1897–8; South Africa 1899–1902 . Retired 1904. UVF officer. Rejoined Army 1914, CO 9th Inniskillings 1914–16; commanded 112 Bde 1916–17; returned to Ulster Div. and commanded 109 Bde Jan.–Dec. 1917; relieved during battle of Cambrai and commanded base at Dieppe until the end of the war. Though English, his wife came from Co. Tyrone, where he settled; he was an enthusiastic 'Ulsterist', and there was some friction between him and Nugent early on; they subsequently became quite close. Tall, talkative and a good organiser, Ricardo was one of the Division's characters. He drowned near his Sion Mills home in July 1923.

Spender, Wilfrid Bliss (1874–1960). Commissioned RA 1897. Resigned over the Home Rule issue in 1913, and became a key organiser of the UVF and subsequently of the Ulster Div. Served as GSO2 of the division in France 1915–16, and afterwards at GHQ and as GSO1 with the 31st Div. Was later Permanent Secretary of the NI Ministry of Finance and Head of the NI Civil Service (1925–44). An outstanding staff officer and later public administrator, he was both highly political and ambitious. The wariness with which he and Nugent regarded each other did not end with his departure from the Division. An intelligent and complex man, he was less bigoted than parts of his wartime correspondence might suggest.

Withycombe, William Maunder (1869–1951). Commissioned KOYLI 1888; South Africa 1899–1902; CO 2nd KOYLI 1914; commanded 107 Bde Oct. 1915–April 1918; retired as brigadier 1924. Popular with his troops as well as competent.

Appendix 2
36th Division Order of Battle

1 July 1916

GOC: Maj Gen O. S. W. Nugent

GSO1: Lt Col C. O. Place
AA&QMG: Lt Col L. J. Comyn

CRA: Brig Gen H. J. Brock
153 Bde RFA
154 Bde RFA
172 Bde RFA
173 Bde RFA

107 Bde (Brig Gen W. M. Withycombe)
8th Royal Irish Rifles (East Belfast)
9th Royal Irish Rifles (West Belfast)
10th Royal Irish Rifles (South Belfast)
15th Royal Irish Rifles (North Belfast)

108 Bde (Brig Gen C. R. J. Griffith)
11th Royal Irish Rifles (South Antrim)
12th Royal Irish Rifles (Central Antrim)
13th Royal Irish Rifles (Down)
9th Royal Irish Fusiliers (Armagh, Monaghan & Cavan)

21 March 1918

GOC: Maj Gen O. S. W. Nugent

GSO1: Lt Col C. O. Place
AA&QMG: Lt Col S. H. Green

CRA: Brig Gen H. J. Brock
153 Bde RFA
173 Bde RFA

107 Bde (Brig Gen W. M. Withycombe)
1st Royal Irish Rifles
2nd Royal Irish Rifles
15th Royal Irish Rifles

108 Bde (Brig Gen C. R. J. Griffith)
12th Royal Irish Rifles
1st Royal Irish Fusiliers
9th Royal Irish Fusiliers

1 July 1916	**21 March 1918**
109 Bde (Brig Gen R. J. Shuter) 9th Royal Inniskilling Fusiliers (Tyrone) 10th Royal Inniskilling Fusiliers (Derry) 11th Royal Inniskilling Fusiliers (Donegal & Fermanagh) 14th Royal Irish Rifles (Young Citizens Volunteers)	109 Bde (Brig Gen W. F. Hessey) 1st Royal Inniskilling Fusiliers 2nd Royal Inniskilling Fusiliers 9th Royal Inniskilling Fusiliers
Pioneers: 16th Royal Irish Rifles (2nd Co. Down)	Pioneers: 16th Royal Irish Rifles
RE: 121st, 122nd, 150th Fd Coys	RE: 121st, 122nd, 150th Fd Coys
RAMC: 108th, 109th, 110th Fd Ambulances	RAMC: 108th, 109th, 110th Fd Ambulances
MGC: 107th, 108th, 109th Bde MG Coys	MGC: 36th Bn

Notes

Introduction

1 C. Barnett, *Britain and Her Army* (London 1970), 314.

2 T. A. Heathcote, *The British Field Marshals 1726–1997* (Barnsley 1999); idem, *The British Admirals of the Fleet 1734–1995* (Barnsley 2002). (The figures exclude honorary appointments, e.g. members of the British or other royal families.)

3 *Burke's Landed Gentry of Ireland* (1958); D. Fraser, *Alanbrooke* (London 1982), 39; Adair family memorial, Parkgate parish church, Co. Antrim.

4 Further work is needed on this explanation, including on variations in the level of the gentry's military involvement in different parts of the country and the tension between the 'economic necessity' argument and the fact that many Irish military families were relatively prosperous (and necessarily so, since Army officers continued to require private incomes until well after the Great War). Some prominent gentry families, like the Nugents, predated the settlers of the seventeenth century; a not insignificant number were Catholic, such as the family of General Hickie of the 16th (Irish) Division.

5 Appendix 2 to E. Spiers, *The Army and Society 1815–1914* (London 1980).

6 See, for example, N. Robertson, *Crowned Harp* (Dublin 1960), 101.

7 Figures based on families in Cavan, Monaghan, Longford and Fermanagh who owned 1,000 acres or more in the 1870s (from de Burgh's *Landowners of Ireland* (1879)) and who still lived on their estates in the Great War period (from Walford's *County Families of the United Kingdom*, 1920 edition), with details of individuals derived where possible from *Burke's Peerage/Landed Gentry of Ireland* (various editions).

8 Obituary, *The King's Royal Rifle Corps Chronicle* (1927).

9 Ibid.

10 Ibid.

11 Quoted in T. R. Moreman, *The Army in India and the Development of Frontier Warfare, 1849–1947* (Basingstoke 1998), 51.

12 Supplement to the *Allahabad Pioneer*, 29 Sept. 1895 (FC, D/3835/F/2).

13 Letters from Lockhart to Nugent, 22 Oct. 1895, and Nugent to Lockhart, 15 Nov. 1895 (FC, D/3835/E/13).

14 Haig, Robertson and Allenby became field marshals, Murray was CIGS and commander of the EEF, Macdonagh and Fowler held senior staff

appointments, and the remainder were corps or divisional commanders, other than Dyer, of Amritsar fame, and Edmonds, the official historian.

15 Tim Travers, *The Killing Ground* (London 1987), 3–36.

16 The children were St George (1899–1929), commissioned into the KRRC in late 1918, died of tuberculosis contracted in the Middle East; Theffania [Stoney] (1903–91); and Alison [Hirschberg] (b. 1909). Kitty died at Farren Connell in 1970, aged 97.

17 T. Pakenham, *The Boer War* (London 1979), 131.

18 Murray, on Symons's staff, wrote home from Ladysmith on 2 Nov. 1899 (opening his letter with 'I do not know when this letter will be able to get through') with an account of Talana, which concluded: 'All that evening and part of the night I was preparing the telegrams, giving the names of the killed, wounded, and missing. Oliver Nugent had three bullets pass through him, I do not think you know the others' (IWM, Murray Papers).

19 CVF Scheme [1914] (FC, D/3835/E/10/1).

20 H. Strachan, *The Politics of the British Army* (Oxford 1997), 112; I. Beckett (ed.), *The Army and the Curragh Incident 1914* (London 1986), 3–29.

21 See note 7. The impact of Great War losses on the southern Irish Protestant community in particular remains a matter of debate (see, for example, P. Hart, 'The Protestant Experience of Revolution in Southern Ireland' in *The IRA at War 1916–1923* (Oxford 2003), 224–40). These figures suggest that on the gentry it was psychologically and statistically significant, e.g. 13 per cent of males aged 50 or under in these 73 families were killed during the war.

Prelude: Hooge, July to August 1915
Introduction

1 J. E. Edmonds (ed.), *Military Operations, France and Belgium* (*OH*), 1915, ii, 103–6.

2 Nugent to Kitty, 3 Aug. 1915 (FC, D/3835/E/4).

3 Hutton to Lord Stamfordham, 18 Sept. 1915 (RA, PS/Q824/1–3).

Letters 1–3

1 Nugent's official account of the action is in the 14 Div. war diary (NA, WO95/1864).

2 Hutton had written to Nugent on 9 Aug. expressing sympathy (FC, D/3835/E/2/20). It seems Hutton had Nugent's original letter typed before forwarding it to Stamfordham, and inserted the officers' details appearing in parentheses.

1
The Somme, September 1915 to July 1916
Introduction

1 Nugent corresponded regularly with Murray while in 14 Div.; on 17 Aug. Murray wrote reassuringly: 'I was so glad to get your letter of the 21st and to hear the full truth of the 14th Division's hard fight. I want to show it to Lord Kitchener for I do not think that your troops have got the credit that they should for gallant and brave work. I am sure the 41st is safe in your hands and I look forward to your getting a Division very soon' (FC, D/3835/E/13).

2 Maj Gen Sir Charles Powell (1857–1943), an Indian Army officer.

3 See T. Denman, *Ireland's Unknown Soldiers: The 16th (Irish) Division in the Great War* (Dublin 1992); C. Hughes, *Mametz: Lloyd George's 'Welsh Army' at the Battle of the Somme* (2nd edn, Guildford 1982).

4 T. Bowman, 'The Ulster Volunteer Force and the Formation of the 36th (Ulster) Division', *Irish Historical Studies*, 32, 128 (2001), 498–518.

5 D. Fitzpatrick, 'The Logic of Collective Sacrifice: Ireland and the British Army, 1914–1918', *Historical Journal*, 38, 4 (1995), 1028–9; N. Perry, 'Nationality in the Irish Infantry Regiments in the First World War', *War and Society*, 12, 1 (1994), 68–76.

6 As Tim Bowman has shown, the number of more junior officers with UVF experience varied, with rural units like the 9th Irish Fusiliers having a relatively large proportion, and Belfast battalions such as the 10th Irish Rifles surprisingly few (Bowman, *The Irish Regiments in the Great War: Discipline and Morale* (Manchester 2003), 72).

7 C. Falls, 'Contact with Troops: Commanders and Staff in the First World War', *Army Quarterly* 88, 2 (1964), 178. Falls subsequently confirmed to Basil Liddell Hart that the 'divisional commander with a shocking temper was Oliver Nugent, and I believe it was largely due to a bullet remaining in his back since the Black Mountain expedition' [in fact Talana] (letter to Liddell Hart, 22 Aug. 1964, LHCMA, LH1/276/60).

8 Nugent's obituary in *The King's Royal Rifle Corps Chronicle* (1927).

9 F. P. Crozier, *The Men I Killed* (London 1937), 67; Spender to his wife, 3 April 1916 (SP, D/1633/1/1/205).

10 Lecture to Ulster Division Officers and NCOs, 1 Oct. 1915 (FC, D/3835/E/10/3A).

11 Cyril Falls recalled: 'One day, when I was commanding a platoon, I saw my then divisional commander [Nugent] on his way to the trenches and had to ask who he was. Yet when a little later I went to divisional headquarters as a staff "learner" I found that he went out five or six days a week, though often not beyond brigade headquarters. So far as I recall, he visited the trenches at least once a week, but, as I have suggested, the average platoon commander

might not encounter him for months on end.' ('Contact with Troops', 173–4).

12 Lt Col F. Macrory's account of the service of the 10th Royal Inniskilling Fusiliers (NA, WO95/2510).

13 Calculated from unit war diaries.

14 Spender wrote on 12 May 1916 '[Hickman] returns to the House of Commons fairly soon I expect. He will probably succeed in cooking N's chances, I expect, tho' he talks in the most friendly manner' (SP, D/1633/1/1/256).

15 Withycombe commanded 107 Bde from Oct. 1915 to April 1918, with a three-month absence from March to June 1917, when the brigade was commanded by Brig Gen F. J. M. Rowley (ex-Middx Regt; later commanded 56 and 138 Bdes). Griffith commanded 108 Bde from Dec. 1915 to May 1918. After Hickman's departure, 109 Bde was commanded successively by R. J. Shuter (ex-R. Irish Fus.), from May 1916 to Jan. 1917, who then left to instruct at the Senior Officers' School at Aldershot; A. St Q. Ricardo, from Jan. to Dec. 1917; and W. F. Hessey thereafter. For details of these officers, other than Rowley and Shuter, see Biographical Notes.

16 Macrory, op. cit., note 12.

17 API and DG [Samuels], *With the Ulster Division in France* (Belfast n.d. [1917?]); diary of 2nd Lt Young, 11th Inniskillings (PRONI, D/3045/6/11).

18 Spender to his wife, 13 Dec. 1915 (SP, D/1633/1/1/101); F. P. Crozier, *A Brass Hat in No Man's Land* (London 1930), 77.

19 Crozier, ibid.

20 After visiting 107 Bde in 4 Div. in Dec. 1915 Spender wrote 'They have done quite well. The men are anxious to come back to the Div. The Officers are not!' (SP, D/1633/1/1/114).

21 C. Falls, *The History of the 36th (Ulster) Division* (Belfast 1922) (hereafter cited as Falls), 23.

22 Bowman, *Irish Regiments*, 109–118, 124–7, 156–9.

23 Spender coached his wife on the answers she should give to inquirers; on 25 Nov. 1915 he wrote: 'You can always say that I think the GOC a strong man, and you can add if you like but I a little wish he were a more bigoted Ulsterman, and add a little laugh but of course my husband has very much stronger views still than many others' (SP, D/1633/1/1/80). Spender, in fairness, made no attempt to conceal his political contacts: on 14 Dec. he told his wife 'The GOC has once or twice cut short his conversation when I am there showing that our views in relation to Ulster ideals do not coincide and that he knows that I write freely to Sir Edward about them. I make no secret about this, as I should otherwise feel that I was going behind the back of my seniors' (SP, D/1633/1/1/103).

24 See note 10 above. The lecture is reproduced in part in Bowman, *Irish Regiments*, 110. Maj Perceval-Maxwell, 13th Rifles, wrote home that evening 'Our new General made all the officers and NCOs a very good address

today. Very straight and sensible and gave us some very useful hints about things in general. I feel that he will be a very good man for his job and I think we are lucky to have got him' (letter to his mother, 1 Oct. 1915: PRONI, Perceval-Maxwell papers, D/2480/6/4).

25 'Notes on the Attack of Entrenched Lines', 27 Jan. 1916 (FC, D/3835/E10/4).

26 A X Corps staff officer told the official historian after the war that 'a very great deal of extra work was thrown on div and bde staffs by the practice which was at its worst then of asking for plans and then trying to coordinate them at Corps HQ and Army HQ, with the result that they were often sent back to be done again. I think that the 36th Division's plan was made three times' (Col S. J. P. Scobell to Edmonds, 23 June 1930: NA, CAB45/191).

27 Place to Edmonds, 31 May 1930 (NA, CAB45/190).

28 The Ulster Div. was opposed initially by three battalions of the German 26th Reserve Div. The counter-attack forces amounted to a further four or five battalions in the course of the day (*OH*, 1916, i, 421–3). The five lines of trenches were the three in the German first position, the Hansa line (a continuation of the Mouquet switch line) running between the first and second German positions, and the first line of the German second position.

29 Maj Gen Perceval to Edmonds, 29 May 1930 (NA, CAB45/190).

30 *OH*, 1916, i, 410–16.

31 107 Bde war diary, 2 July 1916 (NA, WO95/2502).

32 The VC winners were Capt E. Bell (9th Inniskillings), Lt G. Cather (9th Irish Fusiliers), Pte W. McFadzean (14th Rifles) and Pte R. Quigg (12th Rifles). All except Quigg's award were posthumous.

Letters 4–87

1 Arthur was Lord Farnham. Pip was Lt John Aubrey Parke, Durham Light Infantry attached 9 Rifle Brigade, missing 25 Sept. 1915: Kitty's nephew, son of her sister Evie and Col Lawrence Parke (Ponto).

2 Capt R. Beamish, French interpreter with 14 and then 36 Divs.

3 The Bellewaarde assault was a two-division subsidiary attack at Ypres supporting the Loos offensive. No ground was gained. 3 and 14 Divs suffered nearly 4,000 casualties (*OH*, 1915, ii, 263–4).

4 Brig Gen Couchman. See Biographical Notes. The Division's staff were aware of impending changes: Spender told his wife on 10 Oct. 'Both Couch[man] and H[ackett] P[ain] may go and much tho' I like the former I'm afraid he has not been a success. He is too fussy at one moment and too kindly to his officers at the next. His COs can do no wrong' (SP, D1633/1/1/12).

5 Lt Col Meynell, KSLI, was AA&QMG from 7 Sept. to 29 Oct. 1915. He subsequently commanded 6 KOYLI and 1 KSLI, and ended the war commanding 171 Bde.

6 Lt Cols H. T. Lyle, 8th Rifles, and G. H. Ford-Hutchinson, 15th Rifles, had been removed by the end of the year (Bowman, *Irish Regiments*, 111). Hutchinson's cousin, Lt Stewart-Moore, serving in the 13th Rifles, believed that he had been 'sent home because he was not sufficiently robust. He had seen active service in the Sudan and in South Africa . . . and subsequently he had commanded the Connaught Rangers in India. It must have been a sad blow to him when he was adjudged too old at fifty' (Stewart-Moore papers, National Army Museum).

7 Canon King.

8 Capt Robin Henry, RA, Nugent's second ADC till late 1917.

9 Spender was also present: 'Just returned from a field day 108 and 109 brigades not very good I'm afraid, but the General's summing up was first rate' (SP, D/1633/1/1/18).

10 In late 1915 GHQ decided that one infantry brigade from each New Army division should be exchanged for a regular brigade. After a few months the experiment was discontinued. From Nov. 1915 to Feb. 1916 the Ulster Division exchanged 107 Bde for 12 Bde of 4 Div.

11 Westminster Cathedral is London's main Roman Catholic cathedral. Florence Elliott, Kitty's sister-in-law, had converted to Catholicism.

12 Spender told his wife on 1 Nov. 'The 107 Bde is still in hot water. The men are a hot lot and require careful handling whilst their present officers would many of them be the better for a change' (SP, D/1633/1/1/39).

13 Lt Col L.J. Comyn. See Biographical Notes.

14 Lt Col Russell was GSO1 from 14 Sept. 1915 to 5 April 1916; he had been military attaché in Berlin before the war.

15 Theffania, Nugent's eldest daughter.

16 Nugent and Allenby did not get on. On 24 Nov. 1915 Nugent wrote to Kitty: 'Did you call on Lady Allenby? Don't tell her that her husband is the most cordially hated man in the British Army' (FC, D/3835/E/2/6).

17 107 Bde's problems took time to iron out: on 12 Nov. Spender told his wife: 'The 107 Bde appears to have got rather a bad name for slackness in the trenches, not fear but lack of care in rebuilding and a general tendency to idleness. Consequently the others have to go back for another fortnight's instruction' (SP, D/1633/1/1/55).

18 John Redmond visited a number of Irish units at the front in Nov. 1915.

19 Thomas Pakenham (1864–1915), 5th Earl of Longford, killed at Gallipoli, 21 Aug. 1915, while commanding the Mounted Brigade.

20 A reference apparently to Redmond's call following his visit to France for 16 and 36 Divs to fight alongside one another: 'Let Irishmen come together in the trenches and risk their lives together and spill their blood together and I say there is no power on earth that when they come home can induce them

to turn as enemies one upon another' (quoted in J. Finnan, '"Let Irishmen come together in the Trenches": John Redmond and Irish Party policy in the Great War, 1914–1918', *Irish Sword* 22, 88 (Winter 2000), 183).

21 Spender believed that Hacket Pain 'has not been fit either physically (or mentally owing to physical causes) since he came out' (letter to his wife, 3 Dec. 1915: SP, D/1633/1/1/89). Hessey (11th Inniskillings) was promoted in June 1916.

22 Spender was attempting to retrieve a situation caused by his comments to his wife about the appointment of a number of Catholic officers to the Division, which he had clearly not expected to go further; he wrote to her on 3 Dec. 1915: 'I am writing . . . to Sir Edward Carson to let him know that Comyn Main and Ryan are all good chaps, in case your remark to Lady C may do them mischief' (SP, D/1611/1/1/89).

23 Brig Gen W. H. Greenly was BGGS of XIII Corps. He subsequently commanded 2 Cavalry Div. and, briefly, 14 Div., before breaking down during the March 1918 retreat.

24 Cavan (10th Earl) commanded 4th (Guards) Bde, 1914–15; Guards Div., 1915–16; XIV Corps 1916–18; and was CIGS 1922–6. Nugent thought highly of him. Spender wrote 'Lord Cavan our new Army Corps Commander came this morning to talk with our GOC. He did not get much chance of talking as the General did all the talking nearly and as soon as he had got one point settled jumped to another' (SP, D/1633/1/1/130).

25 To substantive Major-General.

26 The Church of Ireland Primate, Archbishop Crozier, visited the Division from 22 to 29 Jan. 1916, accompanied by Sir James Stronge, head of the Orange Order.

27 A note from Cavan praising the turnout of the 14th Rifles.

28 On 7 Feb. the Ulster Division took over its first sector of line, on the Somme, from the Mailly–Maillet/Serre road south to the Ancre; in early March this was extended south beyond Thiepval Wood. In the second half of March the 29 and 32 Divs took over the northern and southern parts of Nugent's line, as divisions 'squeezed up' in preparation for the offensive.

29 Nugent bought the projector and screen for £200 a short time earlier, recouping the cost from admission charges. It was also used for entertaining local civilians, not always with happy results: in Jan. 1917, in Belgium, Lt Herdman of Nugent's staff ran a Chaplin film for some nuns and schoolchildren but 'by bad luck it turned out rather a vulgar one for poor "Charles", and when he threw his leg across a girl's knee I went to the Sister and asked if she would like it stopped – she threw up her hands in dismay and said "yes please"' (PRONI, Herdman papers, T2510).

30 Three men of the attached tunnelling company were killed (Falls, 29).

31 Later Lord Birkenhead; Unionist MP whose ministerial posts included Attorney-General 1915–19 and Secretary for India 1924–28.

32 The shelling fell mostly on the 9th Rifles, which surprisingly suffered no casualties (Falls, 29).

33 This memorandum was written with the intention that it be forwarded to Lady Richardson, the driving force behind the dispute. Spender wrote to her, in some trepidation, the same day: 'I think what he [Nugent] feels is that your Association in Ireland did not begin taking up the question of helping prisoners of war until another Association had been started, and to recognise your Association in the present circumstances would be to give a distinct snub to the other Association which would certainly be regarded as based on his political predelictions.' Writing to his wife the same day, Spender commented: 'The Genl was very much put out by Lady R's letter and the evident attempt to scoop the nationalists by means of our COs. At the same time he did not want to play into the hands of the nationalists, perhaps partly with a view to his future in Ulster. What Lady R will say to my answer I really hardly dare think. Poor George [Sir George Richardson]!' (SP, D/1633/1/1/175,177).

34 Pte J. Crozier (18) of the 9th Rifles. This was a case of 'exemplary' justice: Nugent recommended against commuting the death sentence because 'there have been previous cases of desertion in the 107th Brigade' (NA, WO71/450). Frank Crozier gives an account of the execution in *A Brass Hat*, 97–100, using the fictitious name Crocker for the prisoner. Two other soldiers from 107 Bde, Ptes McCracken and Templeton of the 15th Rifles, were executed on 19 March 1916. In Templeton's case Nugent recommended confirmation of sentence because 'there have been recently 3 cases of desertion in the 15th Battalion Royal Irish Rifles for which the extreme penalty was not awarded', and hoped that it would act 'as a deterrent to other men in this unit' (NA, WO71/454); similarly with McCracken he recommended confirmation because of 'several recent cases of desertion in the 15th R.I.R' (NA, WO 71/453).

35 In early March the Division took over Thiepval wood, south of the Ancre.

36 See Biographical Notes. Place's assessment of the Division after a month, in conversation with Spender, was that 'our Infantry was as good as any in the Army now, but he holds a less good view of the officers and other branches' (Spender to his wife, 7 May 1916: SP, D/1633/1/1/247).

37 14th Rifles.

38 29 Div. was raided on the night of 6 April, lost 14 prisoners and suffered almost 100 other casualties (S. Gillon, *The Story of the 29th Division* (London 1925), 78). The 14th Rifles had six killed and six wounded.

39 Nugent had written to Carson on 13 April 'asking him to try and get universal service applied to Ireland. I told him this Division cannot exist unless we do and that it would be so bad for the future if there were 2 parties in the north of Ireland, those who gave their sons or husbands and the cowards who lurked at home, that if we must suffer, do let us all suffer together and so have a common band of union' (FC, D/3835/E/2/9).

40 The raid by the 9th Inniskillings was the Division's first. The 10th Inniskillings helped repel the simultaneous German raid on 32 Div. (Falls, 38–9).

41 Augustine Birrell (1850–1933), Liberal politician and Chief Secretary of Ireland from 1907 to 1916.

42 Reserve units from several Irish regiments, including the Royal Irish Rifles, were engaged in containing the initial stages of the Rising.

43 Two of Farnham's three sons, aged seven and three, died in April 1916.

44 Neills was the Nugents' steward. During the war Kitty and her daughters spent much of their time living in rented or borrowed accommodation in London or southern England, to be close at hand when Nugent came home on leave; St George was at Eton until 1918.

45 A reference to the emerging proposal that Cavan, Donegal and Monaghan should not be excluded from Home Rule.

46 Spender's soldier-servant.

47 Joseph Devlin (1872–1934), Belfast Nationalist MP.

48 Battle of Jutland.

49 On Railway Sap, north of the Ancre opposite Hamel (Falls, 41–2). Spender offered a less rosy assessment: 'One of our battalions 12 RIR made a raid last night a very fine performance but the enemy bolted into a tunnel and I'm afraid we suffered much more than he did. As I have said before I am very doubtful if these minor exploits do us much good, but there is a mad fashion for them, so I suppose we shall continue to advertise others gratuitously' (letter to his wife 6 June 1916: SP, D/1633/1/1/297).

50 Robertson had written similarly the previous month to John Redmond regarding 16 Div.: 'I had a look at your Division in France on Saturday last . . . it is, as you know, wanting more men' (NLI, Redmond papers, 9 May 1916). His and Macready's attempts to set up a joint meeting with Carson and Redmond on recruitment in May/June 1916 were unsuccessful.

51 HMS *Hampshire* was sunk by a mine off the Orkneys on 5 June.

52 Farnham, a Cavan representative on the UUC, argued unsuccessfully against the proposal. On 3 June Spender wrote 'N[ugent] said today he had never trusted the Belfast people who were now looking forward to their own little dung-heap' (SP, D/1633/1/1/293).

53 Maj Gen W. H. Rycroft commanded 32 Div. The officer with the Grand Fleet was Maj Claude Wallace, who left an account of Jutland in his memoir *From Jungle to Jutland* (London 1932). See also Andrew Gordon, *The Rules of the Game: Jutland and British Naval Command* (London 1996).

54 On William Redan, near Hamel, held by the 15th Rifles (Falls, 42).

55 Somerset Saunderson, son of Col Edward Saunderson, founder of the Ulster Party and a major Cavan landowner. He became Nugent's ADC in Aug. 1916 after Farnham's return to the North Irish Horse, and transferred to the Tank Corps in the autumn of 1917.

56 Two French artillery regiments equipped with 75mm guns were attached to Nugent for the opening of the Somme offensive.

57 Conservative and Unionist politician, Chief Secretary of Ireland 1905.

58 By the 13th Rifles on the trenches opposite Thiepval Wood. It was supported by gas, which was ineffective (Falls, 49).

59 9th Inniskillings, 11th Rifles and 9th Irish Fusiliers.

60 A shell hit a platoon and battalion headquarters of the 13th Rifles as they were leaving Martinsart for the front line (Falls, 50).

61 Nugent's order of the day before the attack.

62 The Division attacked with two brigades up: 109 on the right (9th and 10th Inniskillings in the first wave, 14th Rifles and 11th Inniskillings in the second); 108 on the left (south of the Ancre with 13th and 11th Rifles in the first wave, 15th Rifles (from 107 Bde) in support; north of the river with 12th Rifles and 9th Irish Fusiliers); 107 in reserve (8th, 9th, 10th Rifles). Detailed accounts of the attack are in Falls, 41–63, and P. Orr, *The Road to the Somme* (Belfast 1987), 140–202.

63 The final casualty figures were 5,104, including 79 officers and 1,777 other ranks killed and seven officers and 206 other ranks missing (*OH*, 1916, i, 421).

64 Spender wrote on 5 July: 'The Genl wrote an excellent order of the day, and made a very nice speech to all the Bdes nearly breaking down' (SP, D/1633/1/1/335).

65 Maj Burne, a gunner officer, observed the destruction of the 12th Rifles north of the Ancre: 'The tragedy began by their getting out of their trenches two minutes too early, and losing a big proportion as a result, while going through their own wire. The survivors had 600 yards of No man's land to cross, and they lost continuously all the way across. Eventually they took to rushes, and it became a sort of mathematical speculation whether the rate of wastage would defeat their rate of progress. Fifty yards from the wire there was still a party of fifteen still upon their feet, doubling forward up the hill, almost in single file. One after another they fell . . . There they lay, and eventually a Subaltern by my side exclaimed "Why do they stop there? Why don't they move?" "They will never move", I said' (letter to Edmonds, 23 July 1926: NA, CAB45/188).

66 Cyril Falls later attributed this delay at least in part to technical problems, writing to Liddell Hart on 28 Aug. 1964: 'As the two attacking brigades had got out deep on their own, Nugent wanted to stop the 107th in reserve from going through. The Corps Commander was in an O.P. in a tree. The telephone line to him got out of order for perhaps a quarter of an hour and Nugent felt he could not stop the brigade on his own responsibility. Permission came just too late and a great sacrifice resulted only in more loss' (LHCMA, LH1/276/60).

67 Crozier particularly resented this order and with Col Bernard of the 10th Irish Rifles, who was killed, went further forward than Nugent had directed.

Crozier told the official historian after the war: 'Nugent was "rigid" in so far as the obedience to his orders were concerned, although I see he asked Morland definitely if 107th Brigade should go forward as the situation had altered . . . [He] had laid down that no C.O. should go further forward than his battle H.Q. Had this been acted upon I do not think 9th or 10th Rifles would ever have deployed or got going . . . Yet Nugent, owing to Bernard's death, kicked up such a fuss about "disobedience" that I, for personal post-battle safety, drew a very heavy veil over events. I saw the original recommendation for a DSO for me, made out by Withycombe, scratched across in red ink by Nugent (a great friend of mine) "Rank disobedience of orders, should be court-martialled"!!!' (letter to Edmonds, 23 March 1930, NA, CAB45/188).

68 For example, the 14th Rifles in one four-week period practised attacking these dummy trenches on 15 occasions, including three brigade level exercises, while the officers and NCOs were taken forward in small groups to view their objectives from the front line (14th Rifles war diary: NA, WO95/2511).

69 Morland and Hunter-Weston. Morland was conscious of the vulnerability of his position, writing to his daughter on 10 July: 'Eddie Wortley [GOC 46 Div.] has been sent home – his Divn was engaged to the N of me. "Brief life is here our position." My turn may come next' (IWM, Morland Papers). Both men remained corps commanders till 1918, however.

70 See note 8 above.

2

Messines and Third Ypres, August 1916 to August 1917

Introduction

1 Fitzpatrick, 'Collective Sacrifice', 1017–18; idem, 'Militarism in Ireland, 1900–1922', in T. Bartlett and K. Jeffery (eds), *A Military History of Ireland* (Cambridge 1996), 388.

2 Fitzpatrick, 'Collective Sacrifice', 1017–30; K. Jeffery, *Ireland and the Great War* (Cambridge 2000), 5–8; P. Callan, 'Recruiting for the British Army in Ireland during the First World War', *Irish Sword*, 17 (1987), 42–56; Perry, 'Nationality in the Irish Regiments', 65–95.

3 Proportionately losses for the Irish infantry were as severe as for other British units: 2,200 soldiers in Irish infantry regiments were killed in 1914, 7,000 in 1915, 8,700 in 1916, 6,500 in 1917 and 6,300 in 1918 (Perry, 'Nationality in the Irish Regiments', 69–71).

4 Minutes of the 188th Meeting of the Army Council, 27 Sept. 1916 (NA, WO163/21).

5 190th Meeting of the Army Council, 19 Oct. 1916, Agenda Item 2 – Recruiting in Ireland and Wales. Precis No. 838 (27/Home/620). The same

paper noted similar problems facing Welsh units, particularly 38 Div. (NA WO163/21).

6 D. Gwynn, *Life of John Redmond* (London 1932), 530.

7 Perry, 'Nationality in the Irish Regiments', 79–87.

8 Nationalist demonstrators exploited Nugent's criticisms; he told Kitty on 3 March 1917: 'Fancy my letter being placarded in Dublin. I never heard that. I wonder by whom. Probably by the Sinn Feiners to show that the Ulstermen were not doing their share' (FC, D/3835/E/2/12).

9 Letter to Mrs Spender, 9 Jan. 1917 (SP, D/1633/1/1/554).

10 'All who served under [Nugent]', wrote Plumer in 1922, 'will always hold him in affectionate remembrance, and all Ulstermen should realize that they owe him a debt of gratitude' (Falls, x). The exhortation was more pointed than most readers would have realised.

11 Falls, 122–3.

12 F. P. Crozier, *Impressions and Recollections* (London 1930), 172.

13 Spender to his wife, 18 and 31 Jan. 1916 (SP, D/1633/1/1/137, 152).

14 See, for example, Bowman, *Irish Regiments*, 154–5. Perceval-Maxwell, 13th Rifles, wrote in May 1917: 'We are now side by side with the 16th Div. The men get on very well though of course now there is a very big English element in both.' In July his battalion took over billets from a 16 Div. unit and 'when they left our band played them out of camp and the men cheered them. They were Munsters. As Holt [Waring] and I watched it we couldn't help laughing as three years ago it would not have been safe to let the two Batts into the same Parish much less the same field' (letters to his parents, 12 May and 25 July 1917: PRONI, D/2480/6/4). An officer of the 14th Rifles recalled a less amicable trench handover before Messines: 'As the Dublins came in one of them remarked "Glory be to God will you look at the Carson Boys". "Get the hell out of that you bloody Fenians"' (IWM, Sir Percy McElwaine papers).

15 From Nugent's address at the opening of Lisburn war memorial, 28 April 1923 (FC, D/3835/E/10/8).

16 See, for example, T. Denman, *Ireland's Unknown Soldiers* (Dublin 1992), 149–51.

17 Had Nugent been aware of Gough's comments to Haig after the battle his dislike would have been even greater (Haig wrote in his diary that Gough 'was not pleased with the action of the Irish divisions . . . They seem to have gone forward, but failed to keep what they had won . . . The men are Irish and apparently did not like the enemy's shelling, so Gough said' (G. Sheffield and J. Bourne (eds), *Douglas Haig: War Diaries and Letters 1914–18* (London 2005), 317).

18 Spender to his wife, 19 Aug. 1917 (SP, D/1633/1/1/768). He was, of course, incorrect in both assertions (that 16 Div. had let 36 Div. down, and that bringing the two divisions together had been Nugent's idea). He visited 36 Div. the following month and heard that 'The 36th undoubtedly

were not given a fair chance this last time – chiefly the Corps, and this and the failure of the 16th were perhaps equally responsible, and of course optimism. They do not blame ON who is not well by the way.' Spender's brother, serving with 36 Div., told him that 'ON is not at all well, evidently nervy' (letters to his wife, 25 and 28 Sept. 1917: SP, D/1633/1/1/796,800).

Letters 88–167

1 See Biographical Notes.
2 Lt Col H. A. Pakenham, CO of the 11th Rifles, was invalided shortly afterwards. An Antrim landowner and leading Unionist, he was one of a group of officers (others being Ricardo and Lord Leitrim) with whom Nugent's relations were initially strained because of political differences. (Nugent told Kitty on 1 Nov. 1915, for example: 'I have met Leitrim and Pakenham of course. Pakenham is one of the COs and Leitrim is 2nd in command. Naturally I treat them [as] if such instances had never taken place, but I am slightly formal with them, just to let them see I have not forgotten' (FC, D/3835/E/2/6).) All were eventually reconciled. Pakenham's friend was Somerset Saunderson.
3 Romford was a pre-war acquaintance. The Divisional concert party was known as the 'Merry Mauves' (Falls, 137).
4 Nugent commanded V Corps from 11 to 17 Aug., in Lt Gen E. A. Fanshawe's absence. The Division moved to Hamilton Gordon's IX Corps shortly after; when later in the month Nugent had a second spell of temporary command he warned Kitty 'Dolly [his sister-in-law] need not write a 2nd letter of congratulation. It is only for a while' (letter of 25 Aug: FC, D/3835/E/2/10).
5 A former royal ADC, Nugent knew George V who, as Prince of Wales, became Colonel-in-Chief of the 60th Rifles in 1904, quite well. Stamfordham and Ingram were, respectively, the King's Private and Assistant Private Secretaries.
6 See Biographical Notes.
7 Nugent had sent a party of 13 officers and 40 men home on 8 Aug. on a recruiting drive.
8 By the 9th Rifles and 11th Inniskillings (Pratt's unit), in the Wytschaete sector. Two prisoners were taken, and an estimated 36 Germans killed (six confirmed), at a cost of 13 wounded and three missing (Falls, 74–5).
9 Nugent was in London on a 10-day leave from 25 Sept; on 21 Sept. he told Kitty 'I have to go and see the Adj General on the subject of reinforcements for the Division. We can't get Irishmen so we must have others and personally I don't care 2d who they are as long as they make us up' (FC, D/3835/E/2/11).

10 The raids by 107 and 109 Bdes each took prisoners; 108 Bde's raid against Petite Douve Farm failed (Falls, 75).

11 Congreve commanded 6th Div., 1915; XIII Corps, 1915–17; and VII Corps, 1918. A contemporary of Nugent's at Harrow, he served with him in Dublin before the war and relieved Nugent's brigade at Hooge in 1915. His son Billy was killed on the Somme in July, having, like his father, been awarded the VC.

12 61 Div's AA&QMG, Lt Col H. T. C. Singleton, had previously served on Nugent's staff.

13 H. E. Duke (1855–1939); Unionist MP 1900–18, Chief Secretary for Ireland 1916–18.

14 The raids were repulsed by 'showers of bombs from the stout-hearted Swabian peasants of the 26th (Wuertemberg) Division' (Falls, 75).

15 This was a growing concern for Nugent. On 13 Sept. he had written: 'Our Army has got too big for the number of trained officers available to fill such positions as Commanding Officers and even Brigadiers. Result I have to supervise and investigate and poke my nose into questions of detail which ought not to be necessary. It is no longer enough to issue an order, one has to see that it is carried out. This adds very materially to one's daily work I can assure you, also to one's anxieties and responsibilities. It is inevitable that we can't train officers as quickly as men' (FC, D/3835/E/2/11).

16 By the 11th Inniskillings against the Spanbroek salient. Twenty-three Saxons were confirmed killed and three prisoners taken. There were no British fatalities (Falls, 75–6).

17 The *Britannic*, sister ship of the *Titanic*, was torpedoed and sunk in the Aegean while serving as a hospital ship.

18 See note 16 above.

19 Godley shortly afterwards used very similar language about Redmond, following a dinner at his HQ at which Nugent, Redmond and Stephen Gwynn (another Nationalist MP) were present: 'we are all quite of the opinion that the Irish question will be settled in the trenches in Flanders, where the Ulster Division and the South Irish Division . . . are lying side by side. I had not met Redmond before, but now that I have, I quite understand why every Viceroy who goes to Dublin returns a Home Ruler. He was one of the most agreeable and pleasant people I have met, and most moderate and reasonable in his views' (Godley to his uncle Lord Kilbracken, 1 Jan. 1917, in *Letters of Arthur, Lord Kilbracken GCB and General Sir Alexander Godley, GCB, KCMG, 1898–1932* (privately published by the family, *c.* 1940), 82). Nugent would have been less than pleased to see himself described along with Somerset Saunderson as 'rabid Ulstermen and Unionists'.

20 Asquith resigned on 5 Dec., being replaced two days later by Lloyd George.

21 112 Bde, 37 Div. (comprising 11th Warwicks, 6th Bedfords, 8th East Lancashires, 10th North Lancashires). Ricardo (see Biographical Notes) returned to 36 Div. in Jan. 1917.

2 The boxing competition took place at the end of Jan. 1917. An Ulster Div. staff officer described the speeches made afterwards by Hickie and Nugent: 'They said the greatest compliment one could have was to fight beside, behind, or in front of each other, and neither wished for anything better and had perfect confidence in each other. It was grand to hear it and would have done all extreme "Sinn Feiners" and Orangemen quite a lot of good if they heard it. But I expect when they all get home into the "Unfortunate Country" it will be forgotten and they will be at each others' throats again' (Lt Herdman to his mother, 1 Feb. 1917: Herdman papers, T2510/1).

3 Mangin's counter-attack at Verdun began on 15 Dec.

4 It was not a visit Nugent had looked forward to, telling Kitty the previous day: 'The C in C comes here tomorrow and sees 2 of my battalions. I meet him and go along with him. I do hope I shan't come away with all my back hair standing up. He has that effect on me, I regret to say' (FC, D/3835/E/2/11).

5 Nugent had told Kitty on 19 Dec.: 'I am at the request of the Belfast News Letter sending a message to Ulster! Look out for it in the press cuttings. I am giving them beans and no mistake, laying it on with scorpions' (FC, D/3835/E/2/11).

6 Hessey, another Ulster Div. officer (see Biographical Notes), had also served as a brigade commander in 37 Div.

7 108 Bde's war diary reports the same incident, including the attempt to bring in the remaining German: 'At 5am we attempted to get in the other, but owing to the MG fire (the moon was full and night clear) the attempt was given up' (NA, WO95/2504).

8 The provisional government had been established in Petrograd a few days earlier: the Tsar abdicated on 15 March.

9 The German withdrawal to the Hindenburg Line began in late Feb.

0 America declared war on Germany on 6 April.

1 Nugent genuinely believed this. On 19 Feb. 1917 he told Kitty: 'The Englishmen coming to this Division seemed to be very happy. I read an extract from a letter of one to a pal at home in which he said "If these Ulstermen want my vote after the war for any old stunt, they can have it". They really do seem to appreciate coming to us' (FC, D/3835/E/2/12).

2 This followed a failed 36 Div. raid near the Bull Ring (Falls, 79–80).

3 By the 14th Rifles near Wytschaete. One prisoner was taken (Falls, 80).

4 Lt Col W. A. C. King RE.

5 Both these daylight raids were carried out by 108 Bde, the line-holding brigade in the forthcoming attack. On the afternoon of 3 June the 13th Rifles took 19 prisoners at Peckham; the following afternoon the 9th Irish Fusiliers captured 31 prisoners at a cost of two killed and six wounded (Falls, 89–90). Perceval-Maxwell (13th Rifles) told his wife: 'Our raid yesterday was a great success, only 3 officers and about 60 men in it. They

went over close behind a heavy artillery barrage, took 1 NCO and 15 private prisoner and came back with very slight casualties. Today I got a very nic letter from Oliver also an official one' (Perceval-Maxwell Papers D/1556/27/1/7).

36 The Ulster Division's two assault brigades each had two waves of tw battalions, with an attached mopping-up battalion of 108 Bde in betweer The configuration, from left to right, was: 109 Bde – 11th Inniskillings an 14th Rifles (first wave), and 9th and 10th Inniskillings (second wave), wit 11th Rifles as moppers-up; 107 Bde – 9th and 8th Rifles (first wave), 10t and 15th Rifles (second wave), 12th Rifles moppers-up. The defenders wer from the 3rd Bavarian Division's 23rd Regt. One of Nugent's staff officer wrote afterwards 'I understand . . . there was no quarter given to th machine gunners, they now have the satisfaction of knowing we have got ou own back on the brutes who got us on July 1st' (Lt Herdman to his mothe 9 June 1917, Herdman Papers, T/2510).

37 The after-action reports of Nugent's brigadiers were equally enthusiasti 107 Bde thought the 'complete success of the operations was undoubtedl due to the thoroughness of the barrage and to the way in which th Infantry kept close up to it . . . The new platoon organization was complete success.' 109 Bde attributed success 'chiefly to the platoo system of training, to thorough organisation and to the dissemination to a ranks of information they should know. Every man went over knowin what to do and how to do it . . . The lesson learnt from the Canadians a VIMY as regards dealing with enemy machine guns was acted upon wit excellent results, and it was confirmed in our operations that the platoo as now organised has at its disposal all the arms necessary to deal with an enemy Machine Gun which may come into action at close range.' Ther were still lessons to be learned, though: 108 Bde commented tha 'The whole subject of consolidation needs practice: the efforts of som parties merely resulted in a safe and inconspicuous shell hole bein converted into an insecure and very obvious target, with a few sandbags t give it a home-like appearance' (after-action report, 20 June 1917: NA WO95/2491).

38 The film footage survives in the Imperial War Museum's film archive (IWM 197 and 212). I am grateful to Roger Smither of the Museum for thi reference.

39 Lt Cols P. J. Woods (9th Rifles) and, possibly, F. L. Gordon (15th Rifles).

40 The infantry assault at Third Ypres began at 0350 on 31 Jul; the artiller bombardment had opened on 18 July. Gough's nine divisions achieve moderate success on the first day, before the weather broke.

41 107 Bde unexpectedly had to take over part of the front from 55 Div. o 2/3 Aug, at considerable cost; the other two brigades followed the followin day.

42 Anna Godley and Tom Burrowes were family friends from Co. Cavan.

3 The attack formation was: on the left 109 Bde, with 14th Rifles and 11th Inniskillings in the first wave, supported by 10th Inniskillings; and on the right 108 Bde, with 13th Rifles and 9th Irish Fusiliers leading and 12th Rifles in support. The German defenders were from the 5th Bavarian Division: their reserve regiment, reinforced by other troops, delivered a devastating counter-attack against the overextended attackers at about 9 a.m. The 36 Div. attack collapsed: the 11th Rifles, in 108 Bde reserve, found on moving up that 'stragglers from the two Assaulting Battalions and also from the Supporting Battalion were streaming back to and beyond the BLACK [start] Line' (War Diary: NA, WO95/2506). The Division's casualties from 16 to 18 August were 19 officers and 299 other ranks killed, 55 and 1,203 wounded, and 7 and 453 missing (in total, 81 officers and 1,955 other ranks): *OH*, 1917, ii, 198.

4 Pratt (11th Inniskillings) and Somerville (9th Irish Fusiliers) were killed, and Maxwell (13th Rifles) wounded; Macrory (10th Inniskillings) had been wounded some days earlier. Peacocke (9th Inniskillings) and Blair Oliphant (11th Rifles) were unhurt. The bitterness of the troops is reflected in an extract from the 14th Rifles' War Diary: 'The whole thing has been a miserable failure for reasons which are obvious to us all. Our men did all that was asked of them, but the peculiar attitude of the enemy and his methods were not properly appreciated by the powers that be. Our Divisional staff and Brigade staff did everything that was humanly possible . . . We went into this battle knowing that things were not right and that spirit is fatal, but all round us the signs were very clear and one could not blame either officers or men.' The battalion suffered over 330 casualties (NA, WO95/2511).

5 Maj C. R. Purdon-Coote, RASC (brother-in-law of Lord Farnham).

6 15 and 55 Divs on 31 July; 16 and 36 Divs on 16 Aug.; and 15 and 61 Divs on 22 Aug. The attacks cost these divisions over 14,000 casualties for minimal gains. The opinions that Nugent had heard of Lt Gen Sir Herbert Watts, the commander of XIX Corps ('He is said to be a very good Corps Comdr and a good fighting general' – letter to Kitty 14 July 1917: FC, D/3835/E/2/13) are scarcely borne out by these figures. Haig noted in his diary on 17 Aug.: 'At XIX Corps I saw General Watts who gave a bad account of the two Irish Divisions (36th and 16th). Nugent and Hickie are the respective GOCs. But I gather the attacking troops had a long march up the evening before the battle through Ypres to the front line and then had to fight from zero 4.45am until nightfall. The men could have had no sleep and must have been dead tired' (Sheffield and Bourne, *Haig Diaries*, 317–18).

3
Cambrai and St Quentin, September 1917 to June 1918
Introduction

1 Capt G. Whitfeld diary, 2 Feb. 1918 (IWM). Nugent visited the new arrival when he could and, as ever, spoke frankly to them, not always with entirel happy results. On 22 Jan. 1918 he inspected the 2nd Irish Rifles whose RC chaplain, Fr Gill, recorded: 'When the GOC did come, his speech was suc as to still further annoy the men . . . The CO spoke to the brigadie [Griffith] on the impression the address had made. The only consolation h got was to be told by that officer that he had never heard the general s complimentary before! As we learned later, his praise was always well salte with abuse' (J. W. Taylor, *The 2nd Royal Irish Rifles in the Great War* (Dubli 2005), 111).

2 Killed: Bernard (10th Rifles), 1 July 1916; Somerville (9th Irish Fusiliers and Pratt (11th Inniskillings) 16 Aug. 1917. (Blair Oliphant, formerly 11t Rifles, was fatally wounded with an entrenching battalion in March 1918. Wounded/shellshocked and evacuated: Macrory (10th Inniskillings) Perceval-Maxwell (13th Rifles), both Aug. 1917; Lucas-Clements (1st Iris Fusiliers), Dec. 1917; McCarthy-O'Leary (1st Irish Rifles), March 1918 Peacocke (9th Inniskillings), April 1918. Captured: Crawford (1s Inniskillings), Farnham (2nd Inniskillings), Cole-Hamilton (15th Rifles) Furnell (1st Irish Fusiliers), all March 1918. Promoted: Hesse (11th Inniskillings), Bull (12th Rifles), Crozier (9th Rifles), Ricard (9th Inniskillings), Cheape (14th Rifles) and Incledon-Webber (1st Iris Fusiliers); Hessey and Ricardo subsequently returned to the Divisior Crozier recalled that, on his promotion, Nugent advised him to 'Treat you four battalions like four big companies' (Crozier, *Impressions an Recollections*, 178); but according to Spender, whose wartime admiration fo Crozier changed as a result of the latter's post-war writings, Nugent had 'fel some hesitation in giving him promotion owing to his roughness and th ruthless way in which he handled his men' (letter to Edmonds, 3 May 193C NA, CAB45/191).

3 14th Rifles War Diary, 17 Jan. 1917 (NA, WO/95/2511).

4 IWM, Whitfeld Papers.

5 Nugent was ruthless in tackling incompetence, but could be sensitive i dealing with those he thought had done their bit. To Lt Col Macrory, fo example, who had recovered from wounds received at Langemarck bu whose brigadier did not want him back, Nugent wrote 'I cannot overrul the Brigadier in this matter and the best advice I can give you is that yo should now leave the Army and go home to Ulster to the retirement whic you have so well and honourably earned'. As Macrory's son later wrote, i was 'a very nice letter and he preserved it for the rest of his life, proudl

showing it to all and sundry at every opportunity, although when analysed it was nothing less than the sack' (Patrick Macrory, *Days That Are Gone* (Limavady 1983), 71).

6 For a full account of the battle see Falls, 143–80.

7 Sheffield and Bourne, *Haig Diaries*, 349.

8 Lt Gen Sir Charles Woollcombe, commanded IV Corps 1916–18.

9 Spender met Hessey in early Feb. 1918: 'He looks a bit older but is as nice as ever. He talks of Nugent being very much older, and feeling bitter that he was not made a K in these last honours, and of Place being tired out but on a month's leave which will probably set him up' (letter to his wife, 2 Feb. 1918, SP, D/1633/1/1/933).

10 Calculated from Maj A. F. Becke, *Order of Battle: Divisions* (Parts 1–4), (London 1934–45). The seven regular divisions, by contrast, were largely unaffected, the only change coming about because of de Lisle's promotion.

11 For accounts of the Division's operations see: Falls, 181–231; N. Perry, 'General Nugent and the Ulster Division in the March 1918 Retreat', *Imperial War Museum Review* 12 (1999). 4–17; idem, 'Journey's End: The Fight for the Ulster Division's Forward Zone, 21st March 1918', *Irish Sword* 95 (2004), 65–80.

12 Maj Gen Coffin (1888–1959), a RE officer, won his VC as a brigade commander at Third Ypres.

13 The other, Babington of 23 Div., had been in Italy since late 1917 (Becke, *Order of Battle*). The Ulster Division, under Coffin, went on to take part in Second Army's successful offensive in Flanders in Sept. and Oct. 1918.

Letters 168–228

1 Yorkshire Bank, a spoil heap beside the Canal du Nord near Havrincourt. Both the British and Germans had posts on it until 9 Div. expelled the Germans on 30 Aug. The Germans retook it that night, 108 Bde's first night in the line, but were driven out; took it again on the night of 1 Sept., but were ejected early on the 2nd; and tried again unsuccessfully three more times (Falls, 128–9).

2 See Biographical Notes.

3 Ronald (later Baron) McNeill, a prominent Ulster Unionist.

4 Battle of the Menin Road.

5 Nugent had written to Kitty on 23 Sept.: 'The feeling against serving in the 5th Army is very strong all through the Army out here. I can't understand why it has not been recognised that it is a great mistake to ask troops to fight under a commander in whom they have no confidence' (FC, D/3835/E/2/14).

6 Deneys Reitz, who fought at Talana as a 17-year-old, was second-in-command of 7th R. Irish Rifles which transferred briefly to the Ulster Div.

from 16 Div. in Sept. 1917 before being broken up (D. Reitz, *Trekking On* (London 1933),182).

7 By the 9th Irish Fusiliers, opposite Yorkshire Bank. (They had absorbed a large contingent from the North Irish Horse in Sept. 1917.) German losses were estimated to be 40 killed, British losses one killed, three missing, 15 wounded (Falls, 132).

8 Nugent's anger stemmed from anxiety that the British attack plans would be compromised. The Germans, however, appear to have discounted whatever information they obtained from the prisoners (*OH*, 1917, iii, 48). Nugent ordered the removal of Lucas-Clements, CO of the Fusiliers (also from Cavan), the same day, but his successor had not arrived by the time the battle began. Lucas-Clements commanded his battalion at Cambrai with distinction, refused (with considerable moral courage under the circumstances) to launch a hopeless attack some days into the battle, was wounded and awarded the DSO (Falls, 165).

9 10th Inniskillings broke into the Hindenburg Line at the Spoil Heap. The defenders belonged to 20 Landwehr Div.

10 62 Div. on Nugent's immediate right, 51 Div. beyond that.

11 On the 21st the 14th Rifles and 9th and 10th Inniskillings assaulted Moeuvres but were halted by heavy machine-gun fire: German reinforcements, from 214 Div., had by now reached the village. 109 Bde was relieved early on the 22nd.

12 Nugent's desire always to get as close as he could to the front line brought this comment from Cyril Falls, then his GSO3: 'In general, British commanders and staffs went forward much more often than the French, and indeed too often during a battle. It was absurd that the divisional commander and the GSO1 should be absent at the same time on such occasions, but this was too often the case. At Cambrai . . . [a]t one stage of the battle I was the only representative of the General Staff in the office and the divisional commander was out' ('Contacts with Troops', 174).

13 Nugent's sector here was narrow and overlooked from both flanks. On the morning of the 22nd 107 Bde attacked east of the canal, the 15th Rifles making some progress but the 10th Rifles, passing through, being stopped by machine guns. 108 Bde's 12th Rifles took most of Moeuvres, but were driven out by a strong counter-attack before supports could get forward. On the 23rd the same two brigades renewed the assault, 107 Bde this time with the support of 11 tanks, which arrived too late for proper coordination. The 15th and 8th Rifles made only small advances east of the canal, most of the tanks breaking down or being knocked out before making much progress (six were permanently lost). 108 Bde again captured most of Mouevres, using the 2nd and 12th Rifles and 9th Fusiliers, but that evening found themselves in an exposed salient and pulled back to the southern edge. Artillery support throughout these operations was weak, while two more German divisions (20 and 21 Reserve) had now arrived.

14 40 Div. was now on Nugent's right.

15 Maj Gen C. E. Pereira of 2 Div.

16 Lt-Gen Sir Charles Fergusson commanded XVII Corps 1916–18; he had commanded 5 Div. during the Curragh Incident. In the event 36 Div. did not move to his corps.

17 Kitty's nephews, both cavalry officers.

18 The German counter-stroke on the morning of 30 Nov. involved 20 divisions and demolished the eastern part of the British salient. From 4 Dec. 36 Div. came under command of III Corps (Lt Gen Sir William Pulteney). Pulteney did not enjoy a good reputation, one of his chiefs of staff describing him as 'the most completely ignorant general I served under during the war and that is saying a lot' (J. M. Bourne, *Who's Who in World War One* (London 2001), 239).

19 Although recces were carried out, 108 Bde did not go into the line on the 3rd.

20 On the night of 4/5 Dec. 108 Bde took over the Couillet valley sector, near Villers Plouich, from 29 Div.

21 GOC 29 Div.

22 Welsh Ridge, south-east of Ribecourt; 109 Bde relieved 61 Div. in this sector on the night of 5/6 Dec., in the midst of heavy fighting. 2nd Lt Emerson of the 9th Inniskillings won a posthumous VC for his role in halting the German advance. On the 7th the 11th Inniskillings retook the crest of the ridge.

23 Lt Col G. R. H. Cheape (1st DG) had commanded 7th Black Watch before taking over the 14th Rifles in March 1917. He left on promotion to command 86 Bde (29 Div.) in Aug. 1917.

24 The 14th Rifles had mixed fortunes during the Cambrai fighting: it was also, like other units, very tired by early Dec., with 118 men reporting sick on a single day (War Diary, NA, WO95/2511).

25 Bill Brown, Kitty's nephew and a cavalry officer serving with the Cavalry Corps at Cambrai.

26 The Division was relieved by 63 Div. on 14/15 Dec. It had suffered over 1,600 casualties during the battle, but only about 200 confirmed fatalities. Another 150 were missing (*OH*, 1917, iii, 382).

27 The Divisional concert party.

28 Maj Guy Campbell; he and Capt Freddie Drummond replaced Saunderson and Henry as Nugent's ADCs in late 1917.

29 The lack of promotion had been on Nugent's mind for some time. On 3 Nov. he had written to Kitty: 'I wonder how many of the present Generals will see the end of [the war]. We are most of us getting rather tired. There is no doubt in my mind that a lot of the Corps Commanders ought to be relieved. I expect many Divisional Commanders think the same. It is high time there was some promotion. Some of the promotions made to Corps startle us, but there have been none for nearly a year' (FC, D/3835/E/2/15). Spender had

speculated after Messines that Nugent might be promoted: 'Evidently ON is getting on happily and will I expect now become a Corps Comdr, where he may do well' (letter to his wife, 10 June 1917: SP, D/1633/1/1/682). Nugent's disappointment at being passed over for Corps command was doubtless intensified by his mixed experiences while serving under Morland on the Somme, Watts at Langemarck, and Woollcombe and Pulteney at Cambrai. Even Maxse, whom he admired, was to provide only limited support during the March retreat. He got on well with Hamilton Gordon (Messines), but the Corps commander he rated most highly, Cavan, did not command the Ulster Division in a major action. For a detailed study of Corps commanders in the Great War see Andy Simpson, *Directing Operations: British Corps Command on the Western Front 1914–18* (Stroud 2006).

30 The Division relieved the French 6 Div. south-east of St Quentin between 12 and 15 Jan.

31 Robertson was succeeded as CIGS by Wilson on 18 Feb. 1918, who was replaced on the Supreme War Council at Versailles by Rawlinson.

32 A detailed record of the conference is in the Maxse Papers (IWM).

33 The Mayor had argued that the 14th Rifles (Young Citizen Volunteers), which predated the formation of the UVF, having been raised as a volunteer rifle unit by Belfast Corporation in 1912, should be retained. Nugent's 'principles' involved some contortions to ensure he retained his best units, though he much regretted losing the 10th and 11th Inniskillings. (For the pre-war YCV, see I. D. H[ook], 'The Young Citizen Volunteers of Ireland', *Army Museum '87* (1988), 45–7.)

34 Probably a reference to Lukin (9 Div.), Hickie (16), Wanless O'Gowan (31) and Wilkinson (50), all of whom were replaced in Feb./March. Corps commanders who went between Jan. and March were Congreve, McCracken, Pulteney, Snow and Woollcombe (Becke, *Order of Battle*).

35 The thick fog which had descended overnight caused the Germans some problems but was a greater disadvantage to the defenders, obscuring pre-planned fields of fire and preventing effective artillery support. The defences were organised into three zones, each containing three battalions. The Forward Zone was intended to slow and disrupt the enemy attack and the Battle Zone to halt it; the Rear Zone battalions would then counter-attack and throw the enemy back. The scale of the German attack, however, coupled with manpower shortages and operational limitations on the British side, made those plans unworkable. (See, for example, Martin Middlebrook, *The Kaiser's Battle* (London 1978); Martin Samuels, *Command or Control? Command, Training and Tactics in the British and German Armies, 1888–1918* (London 1995), 198–269.)

36 Of the three battalions in the Forward Zone (2nd Inniskillings, 12th and 15th Rifles), only a handful escaped to the Battle Zone. Two forward redoubts and one or two other positions held out until the afternoon (2nd Lt

de Wind of the 15th Rifles winning a posthumous VC in one). Farnham, who had assumed command of the 2nd Inniskillings in Feb., was among the prisoners.

37 Nugent had to use two of his three reserve battalions (9th Irish Fusiliers and 9th Inniskillings) to prop up his right flank; as a result, his remaining reserve (2nd Rifles) was too weak to expel the Germans when they gained a lodgement in the centre of his Battle Zone in late afternoon. Nugent was attacked by four German divisions in the course of the day (238, 36, 1 Bavarian and 45 Reserve).

38 61 Bde, 20 Div. (12th Kings, 7th Somerset Light Infantry, 7th Duke of Cornwall's Light Infantry). Its commander, Cochrane, was afterwards critical of Nugent, telling the official historian: 'On the evening of the 21st I saw the 36th Division Commander at Ollezy. I never saw him again during these operations, nor did I ever see one of his Staff Officers, nor did I receive any assistance of any kind from Divisional Headquarters' (letter to Edmonds, 16 April?, NA, CAB45/192). It was not for want of trying (Perry, 'General Nugent and the Ulster Division', 15–16).

39 Apparently a detachment of 1st Irish Fusiliers. As the Division pivoted on its left flank back across the St Quentin canal and the Somme, which ran diagonally through its position, its engineers blew over 30 bridges to enable Nugent's rearguards to break clear. 2nd Lt Knox RE won the VC for destroying a bridge with an instantaneous fuse as the Germans rushed it.

40 The 1st Inniskillings were overrun by the Prussian 5 Guards Div. On the 22nd Nugent executed his second withdrawal across the Somme in 48 hours, which here curved north behind his position.

41 The section of this letter covering the 23rd was clearly updated at various times during the day. At dawn on the 23rd three German divisions (5 Guards, 231 and 10) forced the Somme on either side of the Ulster Division and caught it in a pincer movement. By mid-morning their converging attacks had been halted but at heavy cost. The attacks resumed in mid-afternoon and the situation once more became critical, but Nugent, at his HQ some miles to the rear trying to maintain contact with flanking formations and the French coming up in support, was unaware of this until Brig Gen Hessey briefed him that evening. When hastily organised counter-attacks failed to restore the situation overnight, on the morning of the 24th Nugent ordered a withdrawal from the Somme line (where the Division was now in a dangerous salient). All his units suffered heavy losses while doing so, but fortunately the French 62 Div. had now arrived in support. The Ulster Division pulled back through it that night.

42 On the morning of the 26th the Division hurriedly took up a blocking position west of Roye, 109 Bde on the right (resting on the River Avre), 108 Bde on the left with its left flank in the air. 61 Bde had returned to 20 Div., 107 Bde had virtually ceased to exist as an organised formation, and Nugent's artillery had been detached to support the French. This line was

held all day against attacks by the German 28 and 206 Divs, but that night the Germans penetrated the centre of Nugent's line and pushed strong parties into the Ulster Division's rear, one of which attacked Nugent's HQ. At dawn the following day, outflanked on both sides and with the enemy pouring through the centre, the Division conducted a desperate, scrambling withdrawal, with Nugent virtually powerless to influence events. Again, however, French reinforcements arrived and the Division was withdrawn that night. In the March retreat it lost over 6,000 men, perhaps 20 per cent of whom were killed.

43 With Place (who was wounded) were Col Furnell and Maj Brew, COs of the 1st and 9th Irish Fusiliers (Falls, 223).

44 Gough was replaced by Rawlinson on 28 March. Many have thought him unlucky; Nugent did not, either then or subsequently. After the war Gen Hutton wrote to him 'Most of the facts you tell me of the doings of your 36th Division in the German advance I know, and I had also heard of your too candid opinion of cavalry generals as leaders of infantry' (letter of 30 July 1921: FC, D3835/E/2/21).

45 Maj Gen (later Lt Gen) Sir John Fowler (1864–1939), RE, Director of Army Signals in the BEF and later Col Commandant of the Royal Signals. A neighbour of Nugent's, his family home being in Co. Meath.

46 Amongst the divisions reduced to training cadres in April/May 1918 were 14, 16, 34, 39, 40, 59 and 60 Divs, in many cases to be restored later in the year. Only 14 Div. fought alongside the Ulster Div. in March (Becke, *Order of Battle*).

47 During the fighting for the Somme crossings on 23 March (Falls, 210–11).

48 The battle of the Lys began on 9 April. 108 Bde was deployed in support of 19 Div.; the rest of the Division was not directly attacked, but took part in the British withdrawals around Ypres. The German attack was halted by the end of April, after heavy fighting.

49 For Repington's feud with Wilson, see A. J. A. Morris (ed.), *The Letters of Lieutenant-Colonel Charles a Court Repington CMG, Military Correspondent of* The Times, *1903–1918* (Stroud 1999), 7–10.

50 Lt Gen Sir Claud Jacob commanded II Corps 1916–18.

51 A reference to the British withdrawal from ground east of Ypres, which had cost so many casualties to take the previous year.

52 Sir Charles Monro was now CinC India.

Postscript: India and Ireland
Introduction

1 No material relating to these internal security operations survives in the Farren Connell collection, though there are some briefing papers on the Third Afghan War.

2 Letter, 25 Aug. 1920 (FC, D/3835/E/8).

3 Kitty's 'biography' of Nugent, covering just the post-war period, written in 1954 (FC, D/3835/E/4/5); Crozier (a controversial commander of Auxiliaries in Ireland until he resigned from his post) reported that Nugent had told him the Black and Tans 'should never have been let loose in this country; they are not gentlemen' (*Ireland for Ever* (London, 1932), 71).

4 Plumer to Nugent, 13 April 1924 (FC, D/3835/E/2/21).

5 Wilson to Hutton, 10 Jan. 1922 (FC, D/3835/E/13).

6 Hutchison Rai to Nugent, 2 Jan. 1922 (ibid.).

7 Address at Virginia, 26 Aug. 1923 (FC, D/3835/E/10/8).

8 Address at Ballymena, 11 Nov. 1924 (ibid.).

9 Crozier, always an admirer, wrote: 'I always thought General Nugent was one of the worst treated men in the war, and should have been a Corps commander, had the Gods been kind' (*Impressions and Recollections*, 179–80).

0 Maurice Crum to Nugent (with whom he served in the KRRC), 2 Jan. 1922 (FC, D/3835/E/2/21).

Letters 229–33

1 Gough's chief of staff at Third Ypres.

Bibliography

1 Manuscript Sources

Public Record Office of Northern Ireland

Carson Papers
Craigavon Papers
Farren Connell (Nugent) Papers (collection described in *Annual Report 1992–3 of the Public Record Office of Northern Ireland* (Belfast 1994), 51–6)
Herdman Papers
Montgomery Papers
Perceval-Maxwell Papers
Spender Papers

British Library

Hutton Papers

Imperial War Museum

Maxse Papers
Miller Papers
Morland Papers
Murray Papers
Whitfeld Papers

Liddell Hart Centre for Military Archives, King's College London

Liddell Hart Papers

National Army Museum

Stewart-Moore Papers

National Library of Ireland

Farnham Papers
Redmond Papers

National Archives, Kew

CAB45
NATS1

WO33
WO95
WO163

Royal Archives, Windsor
George V (correspondence with Generals Hutton and Nugent)

2 Official Publications and Works of Reference

Edmonds, Brigadier-General Sir James (editor in chief), *History of the Great War: Military Operations, France and Belgium* (London 1922–48) [particularly 1916 (i), 1917 (ii) and (iii), 1918 (i)]
General Annual Reports on the British Army for the Years ending 30th September 1913 to 1919 Cmd 1193 (1920)
Report on Recruiting in Ireland (1914–16) Cmd 8168 (1916)

3 Biographies, Autobiographies, Memoirs and Published Papers

Beckett, Ian (ed.), *The Army and the Curragh Incident 1914* (London 1986)
Bew, Paul, *John Redmond* (Dundalk 1996)
Crozier, F. P., *A Brass Hat in No Man's Land* (London 1930)
Crozier, F. P., *Impressions and Recollections* (London 1930)
Crozier, F. P., *The Men I Killed* (London 1937)
Falls, Cyril, 'Contact with Troops: Commanders and Staff in the First World War', *Army Quarterly* 88/2 (1964), 173–80
Farrar-Hockley, Anthony, *Goughie* (London 1975)
Godley, Alexander, *Life of an Irish Soldier* (London 1939)
Godley, Ann (ed.), *Letters of Arthur, Lord Kilbracken GCB and General Sir Alexander Godley, GCB, KCMG, 1898–1932* (privately published, *c*. 1940)
Gough, Hubert, *The Fifth Army* (London 1931)
Gough, Hubert, *Soldiering On* (London 1954)
Jackson, Alvin, *Sir Edward Carson* (Dublin 1993)
Jeffery, Keith, *Field Marshal Sir Henry Wilson: A Political Soldier* (Oxford 2006)
Jeffery, Keith (ed.), *The Military Correspondence of Field Marshal Sir Henry Wilson 1918–1922* (London 1985)
Lucy, John, *There's a Devil in the Drum* (London 1938)
Macready, Nevil, *Annals of an Active Life* (London 1924)
Reitz, Deneys, *Trekking On* (London 1933)
Sheffield, Gary and Bourne, John (eds), *Douglas Haig: War Diaries and Letters 1914–1918* (London 2005)

4 Unit and Formation Histories

Burrows, A. P., *The 1st Battalion the Faugh-a-Ballaghs in the Great War* (Aldershot n.d.)

Canning, William, *Ballyshannon, Belcoo, Bertincourt: The History of the 11th Battalion the Inniskilling Fusiliers (Donegal & Fermanagh Volunteers) in World War One* (Antrim 1996)

Cunliffe, Marcus, *The Royal Irish Fusiliers 1793–1950* (London 1952)

Falls, Cyril, *The History of the 36th (Ulster) Division* (Belfast 1922)

Falls, Cyril, *The History of the First Seven Battalions the Royal Irish Rifles in the Great War* (Aldershot 1925)

Fox, Frank, *The Royal Inniskilling Fusiliers in the World War* (London 1928)

Hare, Steuart, *The Annals of the King's Royal Rifle Corps* Vol 4 (London 1929)

Mitchell, Gardiner, *'Three Cheers for the Derrys!': A History of the 10th Royal Inniskilling Fusiliers in the 1914–18 War* (Londonderry 1991)

[Samuel], A. P. I. and D. G., *With the Ulster Division in France: A Story of the 11th Battalion Royal Irish Rifles (South Antrim Volunteers) from Bordon to Thiepval* (Belfast n.d. but *c.* 1917)

Taylor, James, *The 1st Royal Irish Rifles in the Great War* (Dublin 2002)

Taylor, James, *The 2nd Royal Irish Rifles in the Great War* (Dublin 2005)

White, Stuart, *The Terrors: 16th (Pioneer) Battalion Royal Irish Rifles* (Belfast 1996)

5 Secondary Works (Selected List)

Ashworth, Tony, *Trench Warfare 1914–18: The Live and Let Live System* (London 1980)

Bartlett, Tom and Jeffery, Keith (eds), *A Military History of Ireland* (Cambridge 1996)

Beckett, Ian, *The Great War 1914–1918* (Harlow 2001)

Bew, Paul, *Ideology and the Irish Question* (Oxford 1994)

Bourne, John, *Who's Who in World War One* (London 2001)

Bowman, Timothy, 'The Ulster Volunteer Force and the formation of the 36th (Ulster) Division', *Irish Historical Studies*, 32/128 (2001), 498–518

Bowman, Timothy, *Irish Regiments in the Great War: Discipline and Morale* (Manchester 2003)

Callan, Patrick, 'Recruiting for the British Army in Ireland during the First World War', *Irish Sword* 17/66 (1987), 42–56

Denman, Terence, *Ireland's Unknown Soldiers: The 16th (Irish) Division in the Great War 1914–18* (Dublin 1992)

Duffy, Christopher *Through German Eyes: The British on the Somme 1916* (London 2006)

Falls, Cyril, *The First World War* (London 1960)
Fitzpatrick, David, *Politics and Irish Life 1913–1921* (Dublin 1977)
Fitzpatrick, David (ed.), *Ireland and the First World War* (Dublin 1988)
Fitzpatrick, David, 'The Logic of Collective Sacrifice: Ireland and the British Army 1914–1918', *Historical Journal*, 38/4 (1995), 1017–30
Gregory, Adrian and Paseta, Senia (eds) *Ireland and the Great War: 'A War to Unite Us All'* (Manchester 2002)
Griffith, Paddy (ed.), *British Fighting Methods in the Great War* (London 1996)
Holmes, Richard, *Tommy: The British Soldier on the Western Front 1914–1918* (London 2004)
Jeffery, Keith, *Ireland and the Great War* (Cambridge 2000)
McCarthy, Chris, *The Somme: The Day-by-Day Account* (London 1993)
Mercer, Eric, 'For King, Country and a Shilling a Day: Belfast Recruiting Patterns in the Great War', *History Ireland*, 11/4 (2003), 29–33
O'Halpin, Eunan, *The Decline of the Union* (Dublin 1987)
Orr, Philip, *The Road to the Somme* (Belfast 1987)
Perry, Nicholas, 'Nationality in the Irish Infantry Regiments in the First World War', *War and Society*, 12/1 (1994), 65–95
Perry, Nicholas, 'Maintaining Regimental Identity in the Great War: The Case of the Irish Infantry Regiments', *Stand To*, 52 (1998)
Perry, Nicholas, 'General Nugent and the Ulster Division in the March 1918 Retreat', *Imperial War Museum Review*, 12 (1999), 4–17
Perry, Nicholas, 'Politics and Command: General Nugent, the Ulster Division and relations with Ulster Unionism 1915–17' in B. Bond (ed.), *'Look to your Front': Studies in the First World War* (Staplehurst 1999), 105–20
Perry, Nicholas, 'Journey's End: The Fight for the Ulster Division's Forward Zone, 21st March 1918', *Irish Sword*, 24/95 (2004)
Prior, Robin and Wilson, Trevor, *Command on the Western Front* (Oxford 1992)
Prior, Robin and Wilson, Trevor, *The Somme* (London 2005)
Rawling, Bill, *Surviving Trench Warfare: Technology and the Canadian Corps 1914–1918* (Toronto 1992)
Reilly, Eileen, 'Cavan in the Era of the Great War 1914–18' in R. Gillespie (ed.), *Cavan: Essays in the History of an Irish County* (Dublin 1995)
Robbins, Simon, *British Generalship on the Western Front, 1914–18* (London 2005)
Sheffield, Gary, *Forgotten Victory* (London 2001)
Sheffield, Gary, *The Somme* (London 2003)
Sheffield, Gary and Todman, Dan (eds), *Command and Control on the Western Front* (Staplehurst 2004)
Simkins, Peter, *Kitchener's Army* (Manchester 1988)
Simpson, Andy, *Directing Operations: British Corps Command on the Western Front 1914–18* (Stroud 2006)
Spiers, Edward, *The Army and Society 1815–1914* (London 1980)

Stewart, A. T. Q., *The Ulster Crisis* (London 1967)
Strachan, Hew, *The Politics of the British Army* (Oxford 1997)
Travers, Tim, *The Killing Ground* (London 1987)
Travers, Tim, *How the War Was Won* (London 1992)
Turner, John, *British Politics and the Great War* (London 1992)
Vaughan, W. E., *Landlords and Tenants in Mid-Victorian Ireland* (Oxford 1994)

Index

Note: for those officers holding senior positions in the Great War, ranks and titles are those held in 1919.

Abbeville, 220
Abercorn, Duchess of, 23, 51, 55
Acheux, 46, 53
Adair family, 2, 249 (n. 3)
Admiralty, the, 59
Alanbrooke, Field Marshal, 7
Albert, 178
Aldershot, 1, 17, 29
Alexander, Field Marshal, 7
Allenby, Gen Sir Edmund, 5, 35, 38–9, 90, 199, 242, 249 (n. 14), 254 (n. 16)
Allenby, Lady, 254 (n. 16)
Alsace, 227
American entry into the war, 137
Amiens, 17, 31, 219, 221, 224
Amritsar, 235
Ancre, River, 25–6, 123, 255 (n. 28), 256 (n. 35), 257 (n. 49), 258 (nn. 62 and 65)
Andechy, 229
Antrim, County, 2, 17, 207
Army Council, 97, 114
Arras, 146, 188
Asquith, Herbert (Squiffy), 39, 42, 56, 62–3, 70, 77, 122, 242, 262 (n. 20)
Auchinleck, Field Marshal, 7
Avre, River, 271–2 (n. 42)

Babington, Maj Gen J. M., 267 (n. 13)
Bailleul, 230
Balfour, Arthur, 42, 120
Ballymena, 237
Barrow, Maj Gen G. de S, 5
Beamish, Capt, 31, 253 (n. 2)
Beatty, Admiral of the Fleet Sir David, 7
Beaulieu, 217
Becquigny, 219
Belfast, 17–18, 21–3, 55, 64, 71, 73–4, 76, 104, 107, 129, 148, 160, 189, 207–8, 237, 257 (n. 52), 270 (n. 33)
Belfast Newsletter, 99, 126–9, 176, 263 (n. 25)
Bell, Capt E., 253 (n. 32)
Bellewaarde Ridge, 31, 253 (n. 3)
Berlin, 224
Bermuda, 6
Bernard, Col H. C., 258–9 (n. 67), 266 (n. 2)
Birrell, Augustine, 64, 113, 257 (n. 41)
Black and Tans, 236, 273 (n. 3)
Blacker, Lt Col S. W., 78, 171
Blackley, Mrs, 146
Boer War, 5–6
Bonar Law, Andrew, 42
Boulogne, 169, 222
Bourlon, 172, 182, 184–8, 190–2
Boyne, Battle of the, 83, 85
Braithwaite, Lt Gen Sir Walter, 5
Bramshott, 17
Brew, Maj, 272 (n. 43)
Britannic, SS, 120, 262 (n. 17)

BRITISH ARMY
Armies
Second, 15, 28, 87, 92, 99, 102, 105, 117, 132, 147, 153, 160, 178, 223, 227, 240, 267 (n. 13)
Third, 102, 175
Fourth, 24, 93
Fifth, 102, 164, 169, 178, 215, 219, 221–2, 227–8, 267 (n. 5)
Corps
II, 228, 272 (n. 50)
III, 269 (n. 18)
V, 12, 105, 261 (n. 4)
VI, 45
VII, 262 (n. 11)
IX, 100, 143, 178, 261 (n. 4)
X, 25–7, 253 (n. 26)
XIII, 42, 255 (n. 23), 262 (n. 11)
XIV, 41, 45, 255 (n. 24)
XVII, 188, 269 (n. 16)
XVIII, 229
XIX, 102, 265 (n. 46)
ANZAC, 154
Divisions
2nd, 269 (n. 15)
2nd Cavalry, 255 (n. 23)
3rd, 253 (n. 3)
4th, 21, 254 (n. 10)
5th, 269 (n. 16)
6th, 9, 15–16, 262 (n. 11)
9th (Scottish), 267 (n. 1), 270 (n. 34)
10th (Irish), 24, 97–8
14th (Light), 8, 9, 12, 16, 31, 45, 211–12, 232, 250 (n. 2), 251 (n. 1), 253 (nn. 2 and 3), 255 (n. 23), 272 (n. 46)
15th (Scottish), 265 (n. 46)
16th (Irish), 18, 40, 96–8, 100–3, 108–9, 111, 118–19, 125, 154, 169, 249 (n. 4), 254 (n. 20), 257 (n. 50), 260 (n. 14), 260–1 (n. 18), 265 (n. 46), 267–8 (n. 6), 270 (n. 34), 272 (n. 46)
19th, 272 (n. 48)
20th, 271 (n. 38), 271–2 (n. 42)
23rd, 267 (n. 13)
24th, 92
25th, 101
28th, 9
29th, 81, 84, 255 (n. 28), 256 (n. 38), 269 (nn. 20, 21 and 23)
30th, 229
31st, 270 (n. 34)
32nd, 25, 27, 81, 84, 255 (n. 28), 257 (n. 54)
34th, 272 (n. 46)
36th (Ulster), 5, 17–28, 29–30, 37, 72, 77–8, 80–95, 96–103, 106, 108–9, 111, 114–15, 118, 122–8, 130–1, 136, 139–40, 142, 146, 154–5, 160, 166–7, 170–4, 176, 181–3, 185, 195, 197–8, 207, 223, 225, 233, 253 (nn. 26 and 28; n. 2), 254 (nn. 10 and 20), 255 (n. 28), 260–1 (n. 18), 262 (n. 21), 263 (n. 22), 264 (n. 36), 265 (nn. 43 and 46), 267 (n. 13), 267–8 (n. 6), 269 (nn. 16 and 18), 269–70 (n. 29), 271 (n. 41), 271–2 (n. 42), 272 (nn. 44 and 46)
37th, 99, 122, 128, 262 (n. 21), 263 (n. 26)
38th (Welsh), 18
39th, 272 (n. 46)
40th, 269 (n. 14), 272 (n. 46)
46th, 259 (n. 69)
49th, 27–8, 82
50th, 270 (n. 34)
51st (Highland), 268 (n. 10)
55th, 264 (n. 41), 265 (n. 46)
59th, 272 (n. 46)
60th, 272 (n. 46)
61st, 229, 262 (n. 12), 265 (n. 46), 269 (n. 22)
62nd, 268 (n. 10)

63rd, 269 (n. 26)
Guards, 167, 188, 255 (n. 24)
Meerut, 235
Brigades
3rd Cavalry, 7
4th (Guards), 255
12th Infantry, 254 (n. 10)
41st Infantry, 8, 11, 15, 29, 55, 212, 251 (n. 1)
42nd Infantry, 16, 31
43rd Infantry, 14, 16, 31
61st Infantry, 271 (n. 38), 271–2 (n. 42)
86th Infantry, 269 (n. 23)
107th Infantry, 18, 21, 26–7, 35, 229, 252 (nn. 15 and 20), 254 (nn. 12 and 17), 256 (n. 34), 258 (n. 62), 262 (n. 10), 264 (nn. 36, 37 and 41), 268 (n. 13), 271–2 (n. 42)
108th Infantry, 18, 26, 37, 174, 228, 230–1, 252 (n. 15), 254 (n. 9), 258 (n. 62), 262 (n. 10), 263 (nn. 27 and 35), 264 (nn. 36 and 37), 265 (n. 43), 267 (n. 1), 268 (n. 13), 269 (nn. 19 and 20), 271–2 (n. 42), 272 (n. 48)
109th Infantry, 18, 21 26, 196, 252 (n. 15), 254 (n. 9), 258 (n. 62), 262 (n. 10), 264 (nn. 36 and 37), 265 (n. 43), 268 (n. 11), 269 (n. 22), 271–2 (n. 42)
112th, 262 (n. 21)
171st Infantry, 254 (n. 5)
15th Reserve, 118
Hampshire Infantry, 6
Mounted, 254 (n. 19)
Regiments
29th Regiment, 1
Bedfordshire Regt, 6th Battalion, 262 (n. 21)
Black Watch, 7th Battalion, 269 (n. 23)
Connaught Rangers, 254 (n. 6)
Dorset Regiment, 62
Duke of Cornwall's Light Infantry, 14
7th Battalion, 271 (n. 38)
Durham Light Infantry, 253 (n. 1)
East Lancashire Regiment, 8th Battalion, 262 (n. 21)
King's Regiment, 12th Battalion, 271 (n. 38)
King's Royal Rifle Corps (60th Rifles), 10, 261 (n. 5)
1st Battalion, 4–6
4th Battalion, 4, 6
7th Battalion, 9, 14
8th Battalion, 9
9th Battalion, 14, 16
King' Own Yorkshire Light Infantry, 1st Battalion 254 (n. 5)
King's Shropshire Light Infantry, 1st Battalion, 254 (n. 5)
North Irish Horse, 180, 257 (n. 55), 268 (n. 7)
North Lancashire Regiment, 10th Battalion, 262 (n. 21)
Rifle Brigade
7th Battalion, 9, 14
8th Battalion, 9, 16
9th Battalion, 253 (n. 1)
Royal Dublin Fusiliers, 260 (n. 14)
2nd Battalion, 6
Royal Inniskilling Fusiliers, 196, 207
1st Battalion, 213, 266 (n. 2)
2nd Battalion, 266 (n. 2), 270–1 (n. 36)
9th Battalion, 193, 253 (n. 32), 257 (n. 40), 258 (nn. 59 and 62), 264 (n. 36), 266 (n. 2), 268 (n. 11), 269 (n. 22), 271 (n. 37)

10th Battalion, 19–20, 171, 252 (n. 12), 257 (n. 40), 258 (n. 62), 264 (n. 36), 265 (nn. 43 and 44), 266 (n. 2), 268 (n. 9), 268 (n. 11), 270 (n. 33)
11th Battalion, 21, 255 (n. 21), 258 (n. 62), 261 (n. 8), 262 (n. 16), 264 (n. 36), 265 (nn. 43 and 44), 266 (n. 2), 269 (n. 22), 270 (n. 33)
Royal Irish Fusiliers
1st Battalion, 6, 180–1, 266 (n. 2), 268 (n. 8), 271 (n. 39), 272 (n. 43)
9th Battalion, 26–7, 251 (n. 6), 253 (n. 32), 258 (nn. 59 and 62), 263 (n. 35), 264 (n. 36), 265 (nn. 43 and 44), 266 (n. 2), 268 (n. 7), 268 (n. 13), 271 (n. 37), 272 (n. 43)
Royal Irish Rifles
1st Battalion, 170–1, 266 (n. 2)
2nd Battalion, 266 (n. 1), 268 (n. 13), 271 (n. 37)
7th Battalion, 267–8 (n. 6)
8th Battalion, 21, 254 (n. 6), 258 (n. 62), 264 (n. 36), 268 (n. 13)
9th Battalion, 21, 256 (nn. 32 and 34), 258 (n. 62), 258–9 (n. 67), 261 (n. 8), 264 (n. 36), 264 (n. 39), 266 (n. 2)
10th Battalion, 21, 207, 251 (n. 6), 258 (n. 62), 258–9 (n. 67), 264 (n. 36), 266 (n. 2), 268 (n. 13)
11th Battalion, 18, 258 (nn. 59 and 62), 261 (n. 2), 264 (n. 36), 265 (nn. 43 and 44), 266 (n. 2)
12th Battalion, 18, 21, 26–7, 71, 207, 253 (n. 32), 257 (n. 49), 258 (nn. 62 and 65), 264 (n. 36), 265 (n. 43), 266 (n. 2), 268 (n. 13), 270–1 (n. 36)
13th Battalion, 252 (n. 24), 254 (n. 6), 258 (nn. 58, 60 and 62), 260 (n. 14), 263–4 (n. 35), 265 (nn. 43 and 44), 266 (n. 2)
14th Battalion, 18, 20, 38, 94, 171, 196, 207–8, 253 (n. 32), 255 (n. 27), 256 (nn. 37 and 38), 258 (n. 62), 259 (n. 60), 260 (n. 14), 264 (n. 36), 265 (nn. 43 and 44), 266 (n. 2), 268 (n. 11), 269 (nn. 23 and 24), 270 (n. 33)
15th Battalion, 21, 207, 254 (n. 6), 256 (n. 34), 257 (n. 54), 258 (n. 62), 264 (n. 36), 264 (n. 39), 266 (n. 2), 268 (n. 13), 270–1 (n. 36)
16th (Pioneer) Battalion, 207
Royal Munster Fusiliers, 4
Royal Signals, 272 (n. 45)
Somerset Light Infantry, 7th Battalion, 271 (n. 38)
Tank Corps, 257 (n. 55)
Warwickshire Regiment, 11th Battalion, 262 (n. 21)

Brock, Brig Gen Henry, 20, 242
Brooke family, 2
Brouchy, 229
Brown, Bill, 189, 197, 269 (n. 25)
Brown, Jim, 189
Bruce, Maj George, 224–5
Bull, Brig Gen S., 266 (n. 2)
Bull Ring, 263 (n. 32)
Burne, Maj, 258 (n. 65)
Burrowes, Tom, 165, 264 (n. 42)
Byng, Gen Sir Julian, 102, 175–7, 242

Cambrai, 98, 102, 170–2, 181–95, 197–9, 211, 268–9 (nn. 8–26), 269–70 (n. 29)
Campbell, Maj Guy, 198, 219, 232, 269 (n. 28)

Canal du Nord, 171, 267 (n. 1)
Capper, Maj Gen Sir Thompson, 5
Carson, Lady, 37, 39–40, 51, 88, 138, 140, 189
Carson, Sir Edward, 7, 23–4, 30, 37–40, 42, 45, 57, 69, 71–2, 76–7, 85, 88, 97–8, 108–5, 170, 176–9, 202, 242, 252 (n. 23), 255 (n. 22), 256 (n. 39), 257 (n. 50)
Cassel, 230
Cather, Lt G., 253 (n. 32)
Cavan, County, 1, 3, 24, 47, 73–4, 88, 125, 146, 235–7, 257 (nn. 45, 52 and 55), 264 (n. 42)
Cavan, Lord, 42, 45, 255 (nn. 24 and 27), 269–70 (n. 29)
Cavan Volunteer Force (CVF), 6–7, 165
chaplains, 22, 32, 36, 68, 177
Chaplin, Lt Col, 16
Cheape, Lt Col G. R. H., 171, 196, 266 (n. 2)
Chitral, 4
Churchill, Winston, 48, 73, 120, 178
Clare, County, 2
Clements, Lt Col S. U., 266 (n. 2), 268 (n. 8)
Cochrane, Brig Gen, 271 (n. 38)
Cockburn, Brig Gen George, 16
Coffin, Maj Gen Clifford, 174, 267 (nn. 12 and 13)
Cole-Hamilton, Lt Col C. G., 266 (n. 2)
Coleraine, 1
Comyn, Lt Col Lewis, 20, 40, 70, 242, 254 (n. 13), 255 (n. 22)
Congreve, Maj Billy, 262 (n. 11)
Congreve, Lt Gen Sir Walter, 15–16, 42, 112, 121, 204, 262 (n. 11), 270 (n. 34)
Congreve, Mrs, 112
conscription, 22, 58, 63, 98, 110–11, 113–16
Cork, County, 235
Couchman, Brig Gen George, 18–19, 242–3, 253 (n. 4)
Couillet valley, 269 (n. 20)
Coullemelle, 219
Couper, Maj Gen Sir Victor, 12
Craig, Charles, 18, 30
Craig, James, 18, 23, 72–3, 92, 99, 136, 140, 202, 236, 243
Crawford, Lt Col E. W., 266 (n. 2)
Crozier, Archbishop, Church of Ireland Primate, 44–5, 243, 255 (n. 26)
Crozier, Brig Gen Frank, 19, 21, 100, 256 (n. 34), 258–9 (n. 67), 266 (n. 2), 273 (nn. 3 and 9)
Crozier, Pte J., 256 (n. 34)
Curragh, the, 7, 269 (n. 16)
Curran, Sgt, 209
Czar, the, 135

Daily Mail, 204, 222
De Lisle, Lt Gen Sir Beauvoir, 192, 267 (n. 11)
De Robeck, Admiral Sir John, 7
De Wind, 2nd Lt E., 270–1 (n. 36)
Debeney, Gen, 218
Defence, HMS, 74
Delvin, Lords, 1
Derby, Lord, 116
Devlin, Joseph, 70, 73, 257 (n. 47)
Dill, Field Marshal, 7
Donegal, County, 24, 73–4, 257 (n. 44)
Douglas, Pte, 70
Down, County, 17, 207
Drummond Capt Freddie, 214, 216, 232, 269 (n. 28)
Dublin, 23, 62, 64, 66–7, 101, 260 (n. 8), 262 (n. 11)
Duke, H. E., 113, 262 (n. 13)
Dundee (Natal), 5
Dyer, Brig Gen Reginald, 5, 249–50 (n. 14)

Easter Rising, 23, 257 (n. 42)
Edmonds, Brig Gen Sir James, 5, 249–50 (n. 14)
Elliott, Florence, 34, 254 (n. 11)
Emerson, 2nd Lt J. S., 269 (n. 22)
Erches, 173, 229
Eton, 257 (n. 44)
executions, military, 21, 52, 256 (n. 34)

Falls, Capt Cyril, 19, 236, 251 (n. 7), 251–2 (n. 11), 258 (n. 66), 268 (n. 12)
Fanshawe, Lt Gen Sir Edward, 261 (n. 4)
Farnham, Lady (Aileen), 194, 211–12, 220, 225
Farnham, Lord (Arthur), 6, 18, 24, 29, 33, 43, 47, 64, 68, 74–6, 91, 93, 162, 168, 171, 175, 181–2, 185, 194, 202–3, 210–12, 220, 224–5, 231, 243, 253 (n. 1), 257 (nn. 43, 52 and 55), 265 (n. 45), 266 (n. 2), 270–1 (n. 36)
Farren Connell, 1, 3–4, 6, 66, 237, 272 (n. 1)
Feetham, Maj Gen, 173
Fergusson, Lt Gen Sir Charles, 188, 269 (n. 16)
Fermanagh, County, 2–3
Fisher, Admiral of the Fleet Sir John, 120
Flers sur Noye, 219
Flesselles, 17, 31
Foch, Marshal, 238
Follies, The, 105, 120, 198
Ford-Hutchinson, Lt Col G. H., 254 (n. 6)
Fowler, Maj Gen Sir John, 5, 222, 249 (n. 4), 272 (n. 45)
French, Field Marshal Sir John, 4, 7
FRENCH ARMY
- 1st Army, 218
- 6th Division, 270 (n. 30)
- 62nd Division, 271 (n. 41)

Furnell, Lt Col M., 266 (n. 2), 272 (n. 43)
Furse, Lt Gen Sir William, 5

Gallipoli, 24, 254 (n. 19)
Gamaches, 220–1
GERMAN ARMY
- 1st Bavarian Division, 271 (n. 37)
- 1st Guard Division, 213
- 3rd Bavarian Division, 264 (n. 36)
- 5th Bavarian Division, 265 (n. 43)
- 5th Guards Division, 271 (nn. 40 and 41)
- 10th Division, 271 (n. 41)
- 20th Division, 268 (n. 13)
- 20th Landwehr Division, 268 (n. 9)
- 21st Reserve Division, 268 (n. 13)
- 26th Reserve Division, 253 (n. 28)
- 26th Wuertemberg Division, 262 (n. 14)
- 28th Division, 271–2 (n. 42)
- 36th Division, 271 (n. 37)
- 45th Reserve Division, 271 (n. 37)
- 206th Division, 271–2 (n. 42)
- 214th Division, 268 (n. 11)
- 231st Division, 271 (n. 41)
- 238th Division, 271 (n. 37)

German Spring 1918 offensives, 173–4, 209–32, 270–2 (nn. 35–48, 50–1)
Gill, Father, 266 (n. 1)
Ginchy, 96
Glasgow, 42
Godley, Anna, 165, 264 (n. 42)
Godley, Lt Gen Sir Alexander, 104, 143, 165, 183, 243, 262 (n. 19)
Gordon, Lt Col F. L., 264 (n. 39)
Gort, Field Marshal, 7
Gough family, 2
Gough, Gen Sir Hubert, 7, 90, 102, 128, 164, 168–9, 173, 219, 226, 228, 243, 260 (n. 17), 264 (n. 40), 272 (n. 44), 273 (n. 1)
Gouzeancourt, 192

Green, Lt Col, 14
Greenly, Maj Gen W. H., 40, 128, 255 (n. 23)
Griffith, Brig Gen Charles, 20, 174, 217–18, 244, 252 (n. 15), 266 (n. 1)
Guerbigny, 217–18, 229
Guillemont, 96
Gwynn, Stephen, 262 (n. 19)

Hacket Pain, Brig Gen William, 18–19, 37–8, 118, 244, 253 (n. 4), 255 (n. 21)
Haig, Field Marshal Sir Douglas, 5, 62–3, 99, 101, 125–6, 172–3, 202–3, 205, 216, 236–7, 244, 249 (n. 4), 260 (n. 17), 265 (n. 46)
Haking, Lt Gen Sir Richard, 5
Ham, 213–14, 217
Hamel, 257 (nn. 49 and 54)
Hamilton Gordon, Lt Gen Sir Alexander, 101, 106, 160, 200, 244, 261 (n. 4), 269–70 (n. 29)
Hampshire, HMS, 72, 257 (n. 51)
Hampshire Infantry Brigade, 6
Hargicourt, 219
Harington, Lt Gen Sir Charles (Tim), 7, 99–101, 132, 234, 240, 244
Harper, Lt Gen Sir George, 173
Harrow, 1, 262 (n. 11)
Havrincourt, 170, 183, 267 (n. 1)
Hazara expedition, 4
Hazebrouck, 230
Henry, Capt Robin, 33, 67, 91, 254 (n. 8), 269 (n. 28)
Herdman, Lt, 155 (n. 29)
Heriot-Maitland, Lt Col, 14
Hessey, Brig Gen William, 38, 128, 171, 198, 224–5, 231, 233–4, 244, 252 (n. 15), 255 (n. 21), 263 (n. 26), 266 (n. 2), 267 (n. 9), 271 (n. 41)
Hessey, Mrs, 225, 231
Hickie, Maj Gen Sir William, 100–1, 236, 240, 244–5, 249 (n. 4), 263 (n. 22), 265 (n. 46), 270 (n. 34)
Hickman, Brig Gen Thomas, 18–19, 37, 63, 245, 252 (nn. 14 and 15)
Hindenburg line, 171, 188, 192–5, 263 (n. 29), 268 (n. 9)
Home Rule, 3, 6, 22–3, 41, 69, 72, 74, 107, 115, 125, 138, 145
Hooge, 9, 11–12, 31, 49, 55, 100, 262 (n. 11)
Hull, 8
Hunter-Weston, Lt Gen Sir Aylmer, 5, 259 (n. 69)
Hutton, Lt Gen Sir Edward (Curley), 10, 12, 46–7, 94–5, 236, 250 (n. 2), 272 (n. 44)

Incledon-Webber, Lt Col, 266 (n. 2)
Ingram, Clive, 106, 261 (n. 5)
Irish Convention, 101, 170, 202
Irish Free State, 236
Irish gentry and the Army, 1–3, 7–8, 249 (nn. 4 and 7), 250 (n. 21)
Irish recruitment, 24, 30, 72, 96–9, 104, 107–16, 221, 256 (n. 39), 259 (n. 3), 261 (n. 9)
Irish Women's Association, 23, 50
Isazai expedition, 4

Jacob, Lt Gen Sir Claud, 228, 272 (n. 50)
Jerusalem, 199
Joffre, Marshal, 67
Johnston, James, 207–8
Jutland, 70, 74–5, 257 (n. 48)

Kaiser, the, 135
Kaiserschlacht, 98
Keir, Lt Gen Sir John, 9, 45, 100
Kemmel, 227–8, 230
Kerr-Smiley, Maj Peter, 18, 38, 141
Kerry, County, 7
Kiggell, Lt Gen Sir Launcelot, 7

Kilkenny, 44
King, Canon, 254 (n. 7)
King, Lt Col W. A. C., 149, 263 (n. 34)
King, Mrs, 151
King Edward VII, 44–5
King George V, 10, 17, 46, 82–4, 88, 105–6, 159–60, 261 (n. 5)
King James II, 48
King William III, 48
Kitchener, Lord, 7, 39, 58, 72–3, 251 (n. 1)
Knox, 2nd Lt C. L., 271 (n. 39)

La Vacquerie, 172
Ladysmith, 6, 250 (n. 18)
Langemarck, battle of, 98, 103, 166–9, 170–1, 265 (n. 43–4, 46), 266 (n. 5), 269–70 (n. 29)
Lawrence, Lt Gen Sir Herbert, 173, 208
Lees, Evan, 5
Leitrim, Lord, 18, 261 (n. 2)
Lenin, 194
Lens, 189
Liberal party, 18, 115
Liddell Hart, Basil, 251 (n. 7), 258 (n. 66)
Lisburn, 260 (n. 15)
Litton, Edward, 1
Litton family, 4
Lloyd George, David, 18, 23–4, 42, 67, 69, 73, 76, 122, 125, 203, 245, 262 (n. 20)
Lockhart, Gen Sir William, 4–5
London, 17, 23, 56, 97, 261 (n. 9)
Long, Walter, 76, 258 (n. 57)
Longford, County, 3
Longford, Lord, 37, 254 (n. 19)
Loos, 253 (n. 3)
Lorraine, 227
Low, Gen Sir Robert, 4
Lukin, Maj Gen Sir Henry, 270 (n. 34)
Lyle, Lt Col H. T., 254 (n. 6)
Lynden-Bell, Maj Gen Sir Arthur, 5
Lys, the, 174, 272 (n. 48)

McCalmont, Lt Col Hugh, 18
McCarthy-O'Leary, Lt Col H. W. D., 266 (n. 2)
McCracken, Lt Gen Sir Frederick, 270 (n. 34)
McCracken, Pte, 256 (n. 34)
MacDonnell, Lady, 23, 51, 53, 55, 68, 138, 146
McFadzean, Pte W. J., 94, 253 (n. 32)
Mackenzie, Maj Gen Sir Colin, 5, 113
McNeill, Ronald, 178, 267 (n. 3)
Macready, Gen Sir Nevil, 48, 97–8, 108–9, 245, 257 (n. 50)
Macrory, Lt Col Frank, 252 (n. 12), 265 (n. 44), 266 (n. 2), 266–7 (n. 5)
Mahon, Gen Sir Bryan, 4, 7, 236
Mailly-Maillet, 255 (n. 28)
Malakand Pass, 4–5
Malcolm, Maj Gen Neill, 239
Mangin, Gen, 263 (n. 23)
Maori, 104
Marcoing, 192
Margot, Gen, 215
Markham, Brig Gen C. J., 16
Marlborough, HMS, 74
Martinsart, 258 (n. 60)
Maude, Lt Gen Sir Frederick, 7
Maxse, Lt Gen Sir Ivor, 173–4, 202, 228–9, 245, 269–70 (n. 29)
Mayne, Maj, 40, 255 (n. 22)
Meath, County, 272 (n. 45)
Meerut, 238–9
Menin Road, 13–14, 267 (n. 4)
Merry Mauves, 261 (n. 4)
Messines, 98, 100–2, 153–8, 169, 171, 226, 230, 260 (n. 14), 264 (nn. 36–8), 269–70 (n. 29)
Meynell, Lt Col, 20, 32, 34
Milner, Lord, 73

Miranzai expedition, 4
Moeuvres, 171–2, 182, 184–8, 268 (nn. 11 and 13)
Monaghan, County, 3, 24, 73–4, 257 (n. 44)
Monro, Gen Sir Charles, 234, 272 (n. 51)
Montagu-Stuart-Wortley, Maj Gen E. J., 259 (n. 69)
Montdidier, 218–19
Montgomery, Field Marshal, 7
Morland, Lt Gen Sir Thomas, 27, 69, 94, 245, 259 (n. 69), 269–70 (n. 29)
Morning Post, 203
Mount Nugent, 209, 237
Munn, Capt, 37
Murray, Gen Sir Archibald, 5, 17, 49, 245, 249 (n. 4), 250 (n. 18), 251 (n. 1)

National Volunteers, 18, 97
Nationalist party, 115
Neills, Mr, 66, 209, 257 (n. 44)
Neuve Eglise, 227
Northern Ireland, 237
Nugent, Alison, 87, 235, 250 (n. 16)
Nugent, Catherine (Kitty) (née Lees), 5–6, 23, 53, 92, 235, 240, 253 (n. 1), 254 (nn. 11 and 16), 257 (n. 44), 260 (n. 8), 261 (nn. 4 and 9), 263 (nn. 24, 25 and 31), 265 (n. 46), 267 (n. 5), 269 (n. 17), 269 (n. 29)
Nugent, Emily (née Litton), 1
Nugent, Hugh de, 1
Nugent, Oliver Stewart Wood:
  early life and career, 1, 3–6
  involvement with UVF, 6–8, 46–7
  commanding 14th Brigade, 9–16
  assumes command of Ulster Division and initial impact, 17–22, 31–9
  Cambrai, 171–2, 181–95, 197–9
  conducts air reconnaissance, 64–7
  flamethrower attack at Hooge, 9–16
  German spring 1918 offensives, 173–4, 209–32, 271–2 (n. 37–42)
  Langemarck, 102–3, 162–9
  letters from
    Brig Gen Hessey, 233–4
    Brig Gen Ricardo, 122–4, 128–9, 239
    Sir Edward Carson, 30, 86, 111–12
    Sir Alexander Hamilton Gordon, 200
    Sir Charles Harington, 234, 240
    Sir William Hickie, 240
    Sir Ivor Maxse, 228–9
    Sir Herbert Plumer, 241
  letters to
    IX Corps, 143–4
    36th Division COs, 233
    Adj Gen GHQ, 130–1, 196
    Brig Gen Hacket Pain, 118
    Capt W. B. Spender, 50
    James Johnston, 207–8
    King George V, 82–4
    Kitty, 11, 29, 31–5, 36, 37, 38–9, 41–9, 51–3, 54–6, 57–69, 70–7, 78–82, 85–91, 92–4, 104–8, 110–11, 112–13, 115–17, 119–20, 121–2, 124–6, 129, 131–2, 134–69, 175–95, 197–206, 208–28, 230–2
    St George, 77–8, 120–1, 238–9
    Sir Edward Carson, 109–10, 113–15
    Sir Edward Hutton, 12–16, 94–5
    Sir Nevil Macready, 108–9
    Sir Herbert Plumer, 132–4
  manning the division, 98–9, 108–16, 118, 130–1, 170, 196, 198, 221–3, 256 (n. 39), 261 (n. 9)
  Messines, 100–1, 153–8

political views, 22–4, 42, 45, 48, 51, 55–8, 69–74, 76–7, 87–8, 90, 110, 113, 125, 136, 138, 145–6, 165–6, 202, 256 (n. 33)
reaction to Easter Rising, 62, 64, 66–7
receives knighthood, 236, 239–41
relations with 16th (Irish) Division, 100, 102–3, 119, 125, 157, 263 (n. 22)
replaced as GOC Ulster Division, 173–4, 205, 208, 210, 233
retention of Divisional title, 99, 139–45, 198
return to Ireland, 235–7
service in India, 4–6, 235, 238–9
tactical views, 24–6, 44, 95, 100, 123, 229, 264 (n. 37)
The Somme, 25–8, 78–95, 258 (nn. 64 and 66), 258–9 (n. 67)
views on
Allenby, 35, 38–9, 63, 254 (n. 16)
Asquith, 39, 56, 70
Carson, 76, 88
Cavan, 42, 45
Craig, 72, 136, 140
Gough, 164, 168–9, 219, 226, 228, 260 (n. 17), 267 (n. 5)
Haig, 125–6, 145, 147–8, 203, 205, 263 (n. 24)
Hamilton Gordon, 106
Kitchener, 39, 72–3
Lloyd George, 203
Maxse, 202
Murray, 49
Plumer, 158–9, 178, 227
Rawlinson, 89–90, 205–6
Redmond (Willie), 121–2, 262
Robertson, 58, 203–5
Wilson, 203–6
Nugent, St George (Oliver's father), 1
Nugent, St George (Oliver's son), 77–8, 108, 120–1, 235, 238–9, 250 (n. 16), 257 (n. 44)
Nugent, Theffania (Fania), 35, 250 (n. 16), 254 (n. 15)
Nugent family, 4, 166

Oliphant, Lt Col Blair, 166, 265 (n. 44), 266 (n. 2)
Ollezy, 271 (n. 38)
O'Neill, Maj Hugh, 18
Orange Order, 97, 255 (n. 26)
Orangemen, 104

Pakenham, Lt Col H. A., 78, 105
Pakenham family, 2
Paris, 67
Parke, Lt John (Pip), 29, 31, 253 (n. 1)
Parke, Col Lawrence (Ponto), 29, 253 (n. 1)
Parke, Mrs Evie (née Lees), 29, 253 (n. 1)
Passchendaele, 102
Peacocke, Lt Col John, 166, 171–2, 224, 235, 265 (n. 44), 266 (n. 2)
Peckham, 263 (n. 35)
Perceval, Maj Gen E. M., 27
Perceval-Maxwell, Lt Col Robert, 79, 143, 151, 166–7, 171–2, 209, 212, 225–6, 252–3 (n. 24), 260 (n. 14), 263–4 (n. 35), 265 (n. 44), 266 (n. 2)
Pereira, Maj Gen Sir Cecil, 269 (n. 15)
Petite Douve Farm, 262 (n. 10)
Petrograd, 263 (n. 28)
Place, Lt Col Charles, 20, 26, 56, 92, 217–18, 245, 256 (n. 36), 267 (n. 9), 272 (n. 43)
Plumer, Gen Sir Herbert, 28, 92, 99–101, 104, 132, 141–2, 160, 178, 223, 227, 234, 236–7, 241, 246, 260 (n. 8)
Pope, the, 43–5
Poperinghe, 11, 223
Powell, Maj Gen Sir Charles, 17, 91, 251 (n. 2)

Pratt, Lt Col Audley, 108, 119–20, 163, 166, 169, 175, 224, 261 (n. 8), 265 (n. 44), 266 (n. 2)
Pretoria, 6
Prince of Wales, 105
Pulteney, Lt Gen Sir William, 195, 269 (n. 18), 269–70 (n. 29), 270 (n. 34)
Purdon-Coote, Maj C. R., 168, 265 (n. 45)
Pyke, Mr, 222

Quigg, Private R., 253 (n. 32)

raids, trench, 24, 57, 59, 60–2, 64, 68, 70–1, 74–5, 77–8, 99, 108, 112, 117, 119, 120–1, 131–2, 141, 145, 147, 151–2, 175, 179–81, 209, 256 (n. 38), 257 (nn. 40, 49 and 55), 258 (n. 58), 261 (n. 8), 262 (nn. 10, 14 and 16), 263 (nn. 32 and 33), 263–4 (n. 35), 268 (nn. 7 and 8)
Railway Sap, 257 (n. 49)
Rawlinson, Gen Sir Henry, 89, 205–6, 246, 270 (nn. 31 and 44)
Redan, William, 257 (n. 54)
Redmond, John, 23, 36–7, 39–41, 62, 67, 71, 97–8, 100, 254 (nn. 18 and 20), 257 (n. 50)
Redmond, Mrs (John), 23
Redmond, Willie, 100–1, 121–2, 148–9, 176
Reitz, Deneys, 170, 179, 267–8 (n. 6)
Repington, Lt Col Charles, 228
Ribecourt, 269 (n. 22)
Ricardo, Brig Gen Ambrose, 60, 72–3, 78, 99, 122–4, 136, 171–2, 195, 198, 239, 246, 252 (n. 15), 262 (n. 21), 266 (n. 2)
Richardson, Lady, 23, 50, 53, 256 (n. 33)
Richardson, Sir F., 35
Richardson, Sir George, 88, 91, 256 (n. 33)
Richmond prison, 70
Roberts, Lord, 6
Robertson, Gen Sir William, 5, 58, 67, 72, 202–5, 257 (n. 50), 270 (n. 31)
Romford, Kennerley, 105, 261 (n. 3)
Rowley, Brig Gen F. J. M., 252 (n. 15)
Royal Irish Constabulary (RIC), 70
Roye, 271–2 (n. 42)
Russell, Lt Col, 20, 35, 43, 56, 254 (n. 14)
Russell, Mrs, 35, 52
Russian Revolution, 134–5
Ryan, Maj, 40, 255 (n. 22)
Rycroft, Maj Gen Sir Wiiliam, 74, 257 (n. 53)

St Anne's Cathedral, 237
St Jans Capelle, 230
St Julien, 102
St Omer, 105
St Quentin, 171, 173, 215, 269–70 (n. 30), 271 (n. 39)
St Vincent, HMS, 74–5
Sanctuary Wood, 9, 14
Sandhurst, 238
Saunderson, Col Edward, 257 (n. 5)
Saunderson, Maj Somerset, 75–6, 93, 105, 113, 115–16, 122, 124, 129, 257 (n. 55), 262 (n. 19), 269 (n. 28)
Schwaben Redoubt, 25–7
Serre, 255 (n. 28)
Shuter, Brig Gen R. J., 252 (n. 15)
Singleton, Lt Col H. T. C., 91, 113, 262 (n. 12)
Sinn Fein(ers), 45, 66, 70, 74, 77, 165, 209, 260 (n. 8)
Smith, F. E., 48, 255 (n. 31)
Snow, Lt Gen Sir Thomas, 270 (n. 34)
Sobraon (First Sikh War), 1

Somerville, Lt Col S. J., 166, 265 (n. 44), 266 (n. 2)
Somme, the, 25–8, 80–95, 100, 170–1, 173, 198, 214, 220, 258–9 (nn. 62–8), 262 (n. 11), 269–70 (n. 29), 271 (nn. 39–41), 272 (n. 47)
Sourdon, 219–20
Spender, Lt Col Wilfrid, 18–19, 21–2, 24, 93, 99, 100, 103, 236–7, 246, 252 (nn. 14, 20 and 23), 253 (n. 4), 254 (nn. 9, 12 and 17), 255 (nn. 21 and 22), 256 (nn. 33 and 36), 257 (nn. 46, 49 and 52), 258 (n. 64), 260–1 (n. 18), 266 (n. 2), 267 (n. 9)
  letters from
    James Craig, 30–1
    Oliver Nugent, 50
  letters to
    his wife 35–6, 38, 40–1, 53–4, 57, 69–70, 91–2
    Sir Edward Carson 37–8, 40
Spender, Mrs, 23
Spoil Heap, 268 (n. 9)
Staff College, Camberley, 5, 49
Stamfordham, Lord, 10, 106, 250 (n. 2), 261 (n. 5)
Stewart-Moore, Lt J. H., 254 (n. 6)
Strickland, Father, 43, 45
Stronge, Sir James, 255 (n. 26)
Supreme War Council, 270 (n. 31)
Symons, Brig Gen Penn, 5–6, 250 (n. 18)

Talana Hill, 6, 170, 179, 250 (n. 18), 267 (n. 6)
Templeton, Pte, 256 (n. 34)
Thiepval, 25, 28, 117, 177, 236
Thiepval Wood, 89, 255 (n. 28), 256 (n. 35), 258 (n. 58)
Third Afghan War, 235, 272 (n. 1)
Times, The, 189, 204, 228, 241
Titanic, SS, 120, 262 (n. 17)
Trafalgar, 2
Tyrone, County, 1

Ulster Division Fund, 236
Ulster Party, 257 (n. 55)
Ulster Tower, 236
Ulster Unionist Council (UUC), 18, 24, 71, 257 (n. 52)
Ulster Unionist Party, 71
Ulster Unionists, 76, 99
Ulster Women's Unionist Council Gift Fund, 23, 50–1, 53
Ulster Volunteer Force (UVF), 6–8, 17–18, 35, 46–7, 270 (n. 33)

Vandeleur family, 2
Vaughan, Brig Gen E., 231
Verdun, 52–3, 57, 68–9, 74, 263 (n. 23)
Versailles, 205–6, 270 (n. 31)
Victoria Cross, 28, 94, 174, 253 (n. 32), 262 (n. 11), 267 (n. 12), 269 (n. 22), 270–1 (n. 36), 271 (n. 39)
Victory, HMS, 2
Villers Plouich, 269 (n. 20)
Vimy Ridge, 146, 264 (n. 37)
Virginia (Cavan), 237

Walker, Resident Magistrate, 67
Wallace, Maj, 75, 257 (n. 53)
Wanless O'Gowan, Maj Gen Robert, 270 (n. 34)
War Cabinet, 98
War Office (WO), 29, 139, 141, 203–4, 206, 240
Waring, Maj Holt, 260 (n. 14)
Waterford, County, 2
Watts, Lt Gen Sir Herbert, 265 (n. 46), 269–70 (n. 29)
Welsh Ridge, 172, 269 (n. 22)
Westmeath, County, 2
Westmeath, Earls of, 1
Westminster Cathedral, 34, 254 (n. 11)

Whitfeld, Capt, 171
Wilkinson, Maj Gen, 270 (n. 34)
Wilson, Field Marshal Sir Henry, 4, 7, 203–6, 216, 228, 236, 270 (n. 31)
Wilson, President, 57
Withycombe, Brig Gen William, 20–1, 28, 174, 246, 252 (n. 15), 258–9 (n. 67)
Woods, Lt Col P. J., 264 (n. 39)
Woollcombe, Lt Gen Sir Charles, 172, 267 (n. 8), 269–70 (n. 29), 270 (n. 34)
Wyndham Act, 6
Wytschaete, 101, 154, 230, 261 (n. 8), 263 (n. 33)

Yorkshire Bank, 267 (n. 1), 268 (n. 7)
Ypres, 9, 13, 17, 45–6, 56, 74, 92, 100, 102, 163, 174, 195, 222, 225, 253 (n. 3), 264 (n. 40), 267 (n. 12), 272 (n. 48), 272 (n. 51), 273 (n. 1)
Ytres, 172

Zouave Wood, 9, 13–14

ARMY RECORDS SOCIETY
(FOUNDED 1984)

Members of the Society are entitled to purchase back volumes at reduced prices.
Orders should be sent to the Hon. Treasurer, Army Records Society,
c/o National Army Museum,
Royal Hospital Road,
London SW3 4HT

The Society has already issued:

Vol. I:
The Military Correspondence of Field Marshal Sir Henry Wilson 1918–1922
Edited by Dr Keith Jeffery

Vol. II:
The Army and the Curragh Incident, 1914
Edited by Dr Ian F.W. Beckett

Vol. III:
The Napoleonic War Journal of Captain Thomas Henry Browne, 1807–1816
Edited by Roger Norman Buckley

Vol. IV:
An Eighteenth-Century Secretary at War.
The Papers of William, Viscount Barrington
Edited by Dr Tony Hayter

Vol. V:
The Military Correspondence of Field Marshal Sir William Robertson 1915–1918
Edited by David R. Woodward

Vol. VI:
Colonel Samuel Bagshawe and the Army of George II, 1731–1762
Edited by Dr Alan J. Guy

Vol. VII:
Montgomery and the Eighth Army
Edited by Stephen Brooks

Vol. VIII:
The British Army and Signals Intelligence during the First World War
Edited by John Ferris

Vol. IX:
Roberts in India
The Military Papers of Field Marshal Lord Roberts 1876–1893
Edited by Brian Robson

Vol. X:
Lord Chelmsford's Zululand Campaign 1878–1879
Edited by John P.C. Laband

Vol. XI:
Letters of a Victorian Army Officer: Edward Wellesley 1840–1854
Edited by Michael Carver

Vol XII:
Military Miscellany I
Papers from the Seven Years War, the Second Sikh War and the First World War
Editors: Alan J. Guy, R.N.W. Thomas and Gerard J. De Groot

Vol. XIII:
John Peebles' American War 1776–1782
Edited by Ira J. Gruber

Vol. XIV:
The Maratha War Papers of Arthur Wellesley
Edited by Anthony S. Bennell

Vol. XV:
The Letters of Lieutenant-Colonel Charles à Court Repington 1903–1918
Edited by A.J.A. Morris

Vol. XVI:
Sir Hugh Rose and the Central India Campaign 1858
Edited by Brian Robson

Vol. XVII:
Lord Roberts and the War in South Africa 1899–1902
Edited by André Wessels

Vol. XVIII:
The Journal of Corporal Todd 1745–1762
Edited by Andrew Cormack and Alan Jones

Vol. XIX:
Rawlinson in India
Edited by Marc Jacobsen

Vol. XX:
Amherst and the Conquest of Canada
Edited by Richard Middleton

Vol. XXI:
At Wellington's Right Hand:
The Letters of Lieutenant-Colonel Sir Alexander Gordon, 1808–1815
Edited by Rory Muir

Vol. XXII:
Allenby in Palestine:
The Middle East Correspondence of Field Marshal Viscount Allenby,
June 1917–October 1919
Edited by Matthew Hughes

Vol. XXIII:
Military Miscellany II
Manuscripts from Marlborough's Wars, the American War of Independence and the Boer War
Edited by David G. Chandler in collaboration with Christopher L. Scott, Marianne M. Gilchrist and Robin Jenkins

Vol. XXIV:
Romaine's Crimean War:
The Letters and Journal of William Govett Romaine
Edited by Colin Robins

Vol. XXV:
Lord Kitchener:
and the War in South Africa 1899–1902
Edited by André Wessels